THE ILLUSTRATED
HANDBOOK OF
UPHOLSTERY

THE ILLUSTRATED HANDBOOK OF UPHOLSTERY

BY N. H. ROBERTS

TAB BOOKS Inc.

BLUE RIDGE SUMMIT, PA. 17214

FIRST EDITION

FIRST PRINTING

Library of Congress Cataloging in Publication Data

Roberts, Nadine H.
    The illustrated handbook of upholstery.

    Includes index.
    1. Upholstery. I. Title.
TT198.R6   684.1′2   81-18269
ISBN 0-8306-0054-X   AACR2
ISBN 0-8306-1328-5 (pbk.)

Contents

Introduction

Furniture upholstery is a fascinating decorative art that anyone can learn. Upholstery is both fun and profitable, either as a vocation or a hobby.

This art is unusual in several ways. It isn't nearly as difficult to practice as it might at first appear. On the other hand, there is a great deal of difference between superficially good and truly high quality work. If you want to complete an attractive, functional project, you cannot take the methods and techniques lightly. Upholstery requires patience and the willingness to do a particular job over and over if necessary in order to do it right.

Furniture upholstery attracts people for many reasons. Many times people simply need to have a sofa or chair reupholstered and want to do the work. Whatever the reason for beginning that first project, upholstery soon captivates the experimenter. It is one of the most satisfying do-it-yourself projects.

Upholsterers are people who love to make old and battered things beautiful and functional. Upholsterers are dedicated, patient people who take pride in their talents and in their work. They are not satisfied with slipshod products, but demand creativity and excellence of themselves. Upholsterers are imaginative men and women who have developed many skills to a fine touch and practice them daily. I hope you enjoy reading this guide to furniture upholstery.

Acknowledgments

Among those who shared their knowledge with me are Charlotte and Roscoe Kiefer, Debbie Leutert, Marilyn and Wayne Dowdy, and John Haley. Thanks also to Mary Ann Bliss for doing several of the book's illustrations.

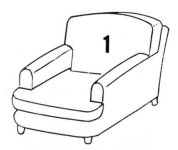

The History of Furniture Styles

This book is written to show you through text and illustration how you might restore usefulness and beauty to worn or damaged furniture. The stated purpose could be fairly well served with a less extensive text, but for many of you this would be inadequate. I direct this work to those of you who understand that any repair or restoration is more effectively accomplished when you have a thorough understanding of your subject.

REASONS FOR LEARNING FURNITURE RESTORATION

Furniture is strictly functional for many people. A chair must be comfortable and sturdy, a table must have a sufficiently broad surface, and a bed must be fine for sleeping. If these pieces meet such specifications and their color does not clash with that of the carpet, the furniture is suitable.

There is nothing particularly wrong with this view; it is more common than you might imagine. You take pleasure in widely differing things, and furniture style may not be one of them.

Those of you who hold another view of furniture recognize that much of your lives will be spent inside your homes. Furniture will thus hold more meaning for you. You feel that your furniture must be selected with great care, because you want it to provide comfort and pleasure for you and your family for a long time. You will know that the best buy for, say, a sofa might be a worn and damaged specimen going for five dollars at an auction.

You may find that the piece you especially want and need may not be available new anywhere in your area. The discerning shopper will not be wasteful; he will enjoy searching for the right piece that can be refinished or reupholstered.

Not the least of reasons for such an approach is the satisfaction to be gained by doing your own work. It is infinitely rewarding to use something, and have it used and admired by others, that you have either made or restored. You should not overlook an opportunity to do this kind of work, for the pleasure to be gained far exceeds the annoyances of occasional backaches and broken fingernails.

Many enterprising men and women shop for used furniture and refinish or reupholster it for their own use. Such an enterprise is also a fine income-producing sideline or hobby, if not a full vocation. Much money can be saved by restoring furniture, whatever its anticipated use may be.

It is my belief that upholstery work will proceed with more satisfaction and effectiveness if you know something about the background of furniture itself and the hows and whys of change and development in style and workmanship. This is true of any art or craft.

Furniture styles have developed in curious ways. Only one characteristic of furniture has remained relatively standard, and that is *strength*. This is not to say that neither beauty nor comfort were characteristics of furniture of the past. Beauty sometimes existed in the absence of comfort, or comfort existed without beauty. In some cases strength was lacking as well, but not often. The value of any chair that will not support your weight has surely always been questionable.

The style, form, materials, and workmanship of furniture are indicative of the lifestyle of the people of the period. Archaeological discoveries have in many cases included furniture, from which much has been learned about the daily life and social customs of the time and place. Because the present is always influenced by the past, in this book I briefly look at the types and uses of furniture from ancient days.

This should not be considered a complete explanation or description of furniture styles. I discuss some of the more well-known furniture styles. If you are a student of furniture restoration, you may gain a certain familiarity with the historical periods, providing the background for changing tastes and preferences. From this introduction to style, then, you should pursue the subject of furniture styles in other sources to gain a clearer perception of the way in which styles evolve into other forms, and sometimes reappear as they were previously.

PRE-RENAISSANCE FURNITURE

As in other areas of art history, students of the history of furniture tend to begin with the archaeological discoveries in Egypt. The *pharaohs* were buried in splendor. By providing the deceased with all the richness they had enjoyed in life, the Egyptians believed they were ensuring comfort and security during the afterlife. In many instances the great tombs were looted, and little remains for study and enjoyment.

The richly appointed tomb of King Tut, in the Valley of the Tombs of Kings south of Cairo, was so well concealed that it was almost intact and undisturbed when it was discovered in 1922. One of the most impressive pieces of furniture in this tomb is the golden throne. It is made of wood and overlaid with gold. The throne is lavishly decorated with silver, stones, and other decorative and precious materials.

Such an elaborate throne, or a chair of any sort, would have been used only by the nobility, and not only in Egypt. Today you are aware of the importance of the "chair" when you recognize the presiding officer at a business meeting as the chairman, chairperson, and so on.

Furniture was generally sparsely used prior to the *Renaissance.* Tables, stools, and chests of varying types and sizes might have been found. There might have been beds in the homes of the truly rich. Peasant classes had no beds. Ancient Greek vase paintings and some other sources depict couches, which were sufficiently wide for two to sleep on. It was the fashion for the wealthy to recline, rather than sit, while eating. Couches served both purposes.

Furniture of the *medieval* age, called *Gothic,* was massive. Most pieces were made of heavy timber, but they were often brightly painted or covered with cloth or leather. Much of the decorative work depended upon the type of wood used. For example, oak could be carved in intricate detail, while softer woods offered less opportunity for such work.

Medieval furniture in England tended to be more crude than that of France and Italy, but during the reign of the later Tudor monarchs, life became a little less nomadic. Furniture began to occupy a place and function in a household rather than being transported from court to court by wagons or on horseback. The formation of craftsmen's guilds in the cities contributed to a new development in furniture making—toward more refined construction principles and elegance in decoration.

Only the very rich enjoyed the beauty and comfort of pre-Renaissance furniture. Upon the advent of the Renaissance, more importance began to be attributed to furniture.

RENAISSANCE FURNITURE

The influence of Gothic furniture was gradually shed. Although early Renaissance furniture remained solid and heavy, new distinguishing characteristics began to appear. The rebirth or reawakening of interest in art and learning, particularly involving the *Classical* period, developed to different degrees and at different rates.

Henry VII ascended the English throne in 1485. Succeeding him were Henry VIII, Edward VI, Queen Mary I, and Queen Elizabeth. These were the reigning Tudors, though Queen Elizabeth's name appears to adorn a separate furniture style. Both the *Tudor* and the *Elizabethan* styles of furniture were in England during the Renaissance.

The *Jacobean* and *Restoration* furniture styles were also present in England during the Renaissance. *Jacobean* refers to the period of King James I, the first Stuart monarch, who followed Queen Elizabeth on England's throne. This period also includes the period of Oliver Cromwell and King Charles I.

The *Restoration* period includes the turbulent years following the execution of King Charles I, when his son King Charles II was "restored" to the English throne. English Restoration furniture is also called *English Baroque.*

Tudor and Elizabethan furniture remained heavy, with straight lines, mostly in oak but with some walnut and other woods. Beds became great four posters, with *canopies.* The appearance of higher chests on legs occurred. Chairs became lighter and cushions were used. One characteristic piece was the Elizabethan refectory table (Fig. 1-1) with melon-bulb legs.

The Jacobean and Restoration, or English Baroque, furniture involved more frequent use of upholstery. Chairs with cane seats appeared, with carved stretchers. Backs were high and paneled (Fig. 1-2) with turned or twisted legs.

The Renaissance period saw a great revival of interest in Classic forms (Greek and Roman) in architecture, which was also reflected in furniture styles. In Italy, Spain and France, the developments in style surpassed the English style. Furniture typically exhibited quite elaborate carvings, some velvet and leather upholstery, and Classical themes in design such as carved cupids and animals.

The periods of William and Mary and Queen Anne are often called the *Age of Walnut*. The *highboy* (Fig. 1-3) appeared during the reign of William and Mary, along with kneehole desks and drawer furniture. During these years some of the severity in design disappeared, and a more feminine influence was seen. Upholstery became very popular, curved lines appeared, and the Dutch influence appeared in chairs and chests with cabriole legs (Fig. 1-4).

The Queen Anne period (1702 to 1714) saw a distinctly feminine turn. For the first time, comfort became a strong consideration as the curved line was firmly introduced (Fig. 1-5). This period first produced the spoon back in chairs. The high-backed Queen Anne wing chair appeared, along with such items as decorative tables and grandfather clocks. There were also comfortably upholstered love seats. Chinese forms were commonly used.

GEORGIAN DESIGNERS

The *Georgian period* refers to the time marking the reigns of the first four Georges in Great Britain. This period saw the work of four famous English designers. In order of their productive years, the first was *Thomas Chippendale,* beginning in 1735.

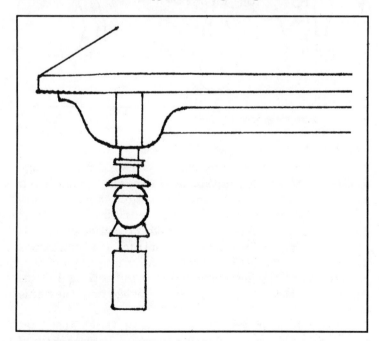

Fig. 1-1. Elizabethan refectory table.

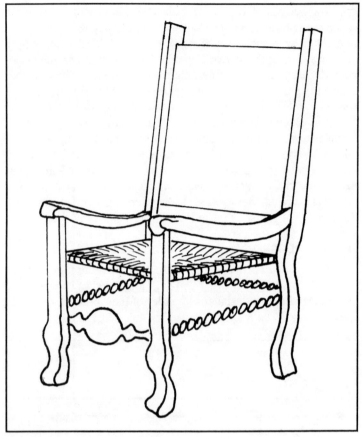

Fig. 1-2. English Baroque chair.

Chippendale

Mahogany (with lovely carvings) was the wood choice of Chippendale, but he was also responsible for some fine furniture in soft woods. His furniture was characterized by strength and fine workmanship. Chippendale's style was influenced during his more than 40 active years by developments from other countries and periods such as the Chinese, French, Gothic, and Dutch. His furniture was heavy, but it gradually became less massive than that of former periods. The cabriole leg with a claw foot or ball foot (Fig. 1-6) was still in vogue, but elaborately carved straight legs came later in his work.

Arched backs in sofas and settees along Queen Anne lines continued the Chippendale style, along with such pieces as chests of drawers with curved or bowed fronts, desks with slanted tops, and small tripod-based tables with raised, carved edges.

Even a very brief discussion of the work of Thomas Chippendale is incomplete without mention of *The Gentleman and Cabinet-maker's Director,* a famous catalog which he first published in 1754.

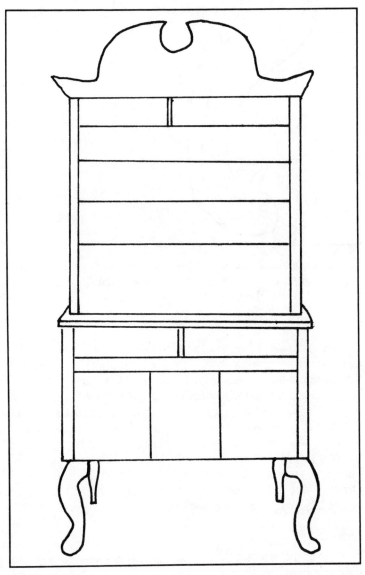

Fig. 1-3. Highboy.

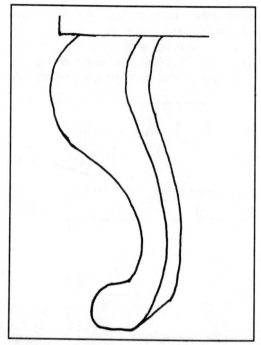

Fig. 1-4. Cabriole leg.

This was a publication of designs for furniture for the whole house. It is to a great extent responsible for Chippendale's great reputation, since it was the first publication of its kind.

Hepplewhite

George Hepplewhite was the second of the four Georgian designers, beginning work about 1760. He is particularly well-known for his shield-back chairs (Fig. 1-7), possibly because chairs and sofas indicate the tastes of a period more obviously than do other pieces. Hepplewhite's designs were simple and easy to reproduce, and they were not as magnificent as those of his predecessors. The furniture was lighter as well, continuing the trend toward less massive pieces. Hepplewhite's intent was to "unite elegance and utility," and this he did. One of his particular designs aside from seat furniture was a drop leaf table with one end oval and the other squared; two such tables end to end provide twice the surface area.

Adam

Robert Adam was a Scottish architect who spent four years in Italy absorbing the knowledge which would fit him as a classical architect. Adam did not "make" furniture, but he designed not only furniture but every facet of a room's decoration. He was remarkably adept at "classicizing" and bringing new life to difficult rooms, as he worked to produce a sense of harmony from floor to ceiling. Adam used a variety of woods: mahogany, sycamore, holly, and especially satinwood.

Sheraton

The fourth of the well-known Georgian designers was *Thomas Sheraton,* who began his most active career in 1790. Sheraton began as a cabinetmaker and created his own furniture early in his career. Later he concentrated on designing. Among other interesting accomplishments. Sheraton is known as the designer of the first twin beds. His long sofas are distinctive (Fig. 1-8) with the wood top rail and usually upholstered arms. Sheraton also designed some interesting kidney- and banana-shaped tables, along with table drop leaves supported by brackets.

These four famous designers take you into the early nineteenth century in furniture design. From this point I proceed with the more well-known English and French styles. Finally, American styles are examined.

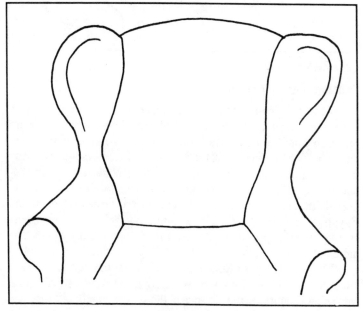

Fig. 1-5. Curved lines.

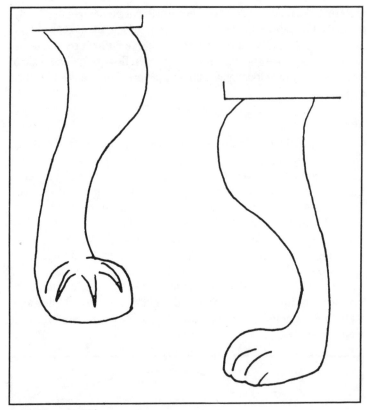

Fig. 1-6. Claw or ball foot.

ENGLISH REGENCY FURNITURE

At the beginning of the nineteenth century, tastes in furniture style and design once more turned toward the ancient. Designers began to copy from the vase paintings and bas-reliefs of antiquity, and they soon became dedicated followers of archaeology at least as far as furniture was concerned. Excavations of ancient tombs produced only whatever furnishings were actually used during the period. In designing pieces unknown to the Greek, Roman, and Egyptian past, furniture makers followed that period's materials and design principles to create furniture fitting to those things that did exist.

The title "English Regency" comes from the period of 1811-1820, when George, Prince of Wales, was England's regent (one who rules a country in the absence of the sovereign). In reference to furniture style, it was a brief period. One reason for the brevity of

Regency may be that the "archaeological" furniture was not really suitable to the households of the middle class or the general public. By this time beautiful and practical furniture was no longer reserved for the aristocracy, though their tastes did predominate to a great extent. Furniture did, however, assume more comfort than that of former periods.

Regency sofas had rolled ends, sloping backs and legs that curved outward (either *cornucopia* or saber legs), and sometimes paw feet of brass (Fig. 1-9). Upholstery may have been striped or otherwise patterned.

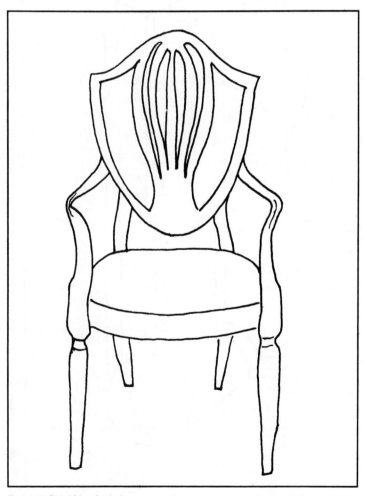

Fig. 1-7. Shield-back chair.

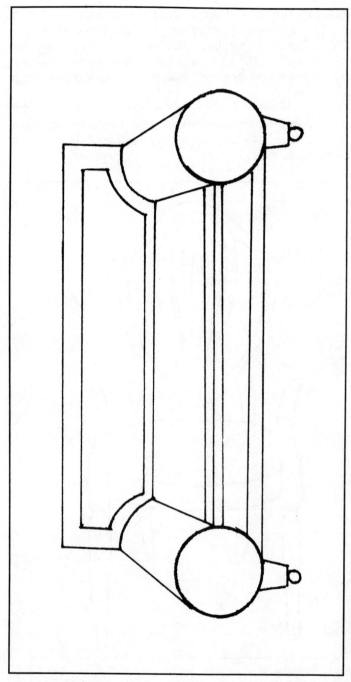

Fig. 1-8. Sheraton sofa.

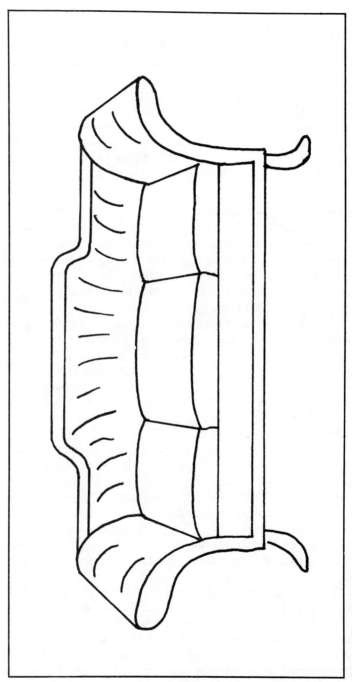

Fig. 1-9. Regency sofa.

Regency chairs were extremely varied. The straight line was not easily found. Backs were beautifully curved, or scrolled, often showing a distinct elongated S (Fig. 1-10). Armrests tended to be set high, often without arm posts, and both front and back legs were usually curved outward.

The best of Regency furniture was the less ornamental of the period, much of which was truly lovely and graceful. Furniture workmanship was not of as high quality as that of the preceding periods, particularly in joinery. Some specific characteristics of Regency furniture are cornucopias and animals, the use of brass in feet, and motifs in a variety of leaves especially, such as honeysuckle and ivy.

ENGLISH VICTORIAN FURNITURE

During the reign of *Queen Victoria,* styles in furniture fluctuated, usually in extremes. While it is a little difficult to separate attitudes of "Victorianism" from an objective appraisal of the products of the time, this period brought an end to consistency. This was due in particular to the *Industrial Revolution.* Furniture began to be produced by machines.

When a society, a way life, sees such stunning changes as the machine age produced, it cannot maintain consistency in furniture style or indeed in any area. Thus, you see a profusion of furniture types ranging from the picturesque to the grotesque. Frankly, it is easy to lump the works of Victorian furniture makers together in one pile and call them ugly. But before you condemn the Victorian period, consider the absolute novelty and excitement furniture makers must have experienced.

No longer was it necessary to labor for days on one elaborate chair rail. Since they could be machine-made at such a fantastic rate, apparently everyone took full advantage of the opportunity to experiment with style. If some less than gifted persons produced a sofa with a horrible mixture of motifs, this was the natural price of invention and experimentation. The intense pride they must have felt in their new ability to produce, imitate, and substitute resulted in much showy and exaggerated ornamentation and a noticeable lack of taste.

There were the heavy, ornamental horsehair sofas, and chairs of every size and description (Fig. 1-11). There were "whatnot" shelves and heavily carved and inlaid woods. There were "extra" chairs, love seats and tables. Characteristics of the Victorian furniture were heaviness, exaggerated curves and ornament, tufted upholstery, high backs and short legs, and a wide use of gilt metal.

The Victorian age of furniture design was the necessary prelude to the twentieth century return to consistency and fine workmanship. Without the vitality and pride in inventiveness of the Victorians, there would not be such a variety of furniture today.

BOURBON STYLES

Bourbon was the name of a French family from which came the rulers of France from 1589 to 1793 and from 1814 to 1830; of Spain

Fig. 1-10. Regency chair with an S-shaped back.

Fig. 1-11. Victorian chair.

from 1700 to 1808, from 1814 to 1868, and from 1875 to 1931; of Naples from 1735 to 1805; and of the two Sicilies from 1815 to 1860. This alone is a clear indication of their influence. I discuss Louis XIV, Louis XV, and Louis XVI, a period extending from 1643 to 1789. This period in history precedes the English styles and the furniture designed and built for royalty.

Louis XIV

Possibly at no other period in history has a monarch surrounded himself with so much sumptuous luxury in furniture. Louis

XIV maintained at least three royal homes, each lavishly furnished. Much of his furniture was of silver, and that of wood was magnificent. This is best expressed in the furniture of *Andre Charles Boulle,* in his stunning marquetry. Boulle used a variety of exotic and colored woods decorated with tortoise shell, ebony, and brass. His work is the best expression of Louis XIV furniture. Much of the upholstery of the period came from China, as did other furnishings and decorative objects.

In seat furniture, the lavish design was continued. Chairs and sofas were massive but well-proportioned. Stretchers were necessary because of the weight of the chairs, and these were often very beautiful in either the X or H shape (Fig. 1-12). Both sofas and chairs were often winged (Fig. 1-13), with fine moldings, though all furniture was much simpler in the homes of those without great wealth.

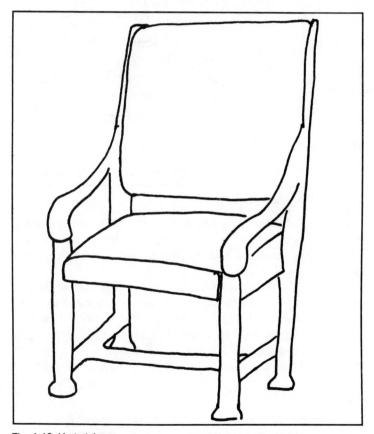

Fig. 1-12. H stretchers.

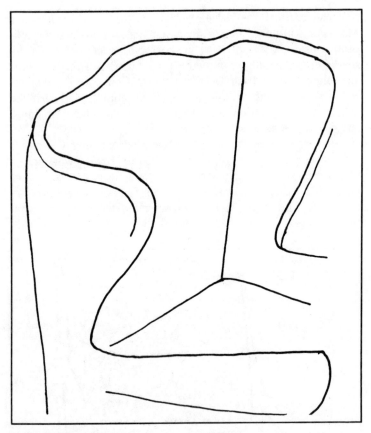

Fig. 1-13. Wing chair.

An example of simplicity used in both middle class and royal homes was the simple, lightweight chair with a straw seat and no arms. These chairs were so easily movable and convenient that they were popular everywhere.

Louis XIV beds were truly remarkable, and even in the less wealthy homes the people made their beds as sumptuous as possible. They were either recessed into alcoves or curtained with as rich a material as could be afforded. Aside from the grandeur of some of these draperies, there was a definite function—they interrupted cold drafts.

Louis XV

Furniture styles now move toward much lighter, more easily movable pieces to better fit the fashion of intimate, small rooms. At its height, Louis XV seat furniture features gracefully curving lines; nothing is rectilinear unless it must be so. The gracefully flowing curves come together as a unit, one part moving into another with no sense of interruption.

A chair really typical of the period would have either a rounded (medallion-shaped) back, or possibly a winged back. Seat cushions were loose. The arms, or sides, might be either upholstered (solid) or open. These chairs were very comfortable and might be upholstered in silk, velvet, or satin (Fig. 1-14).

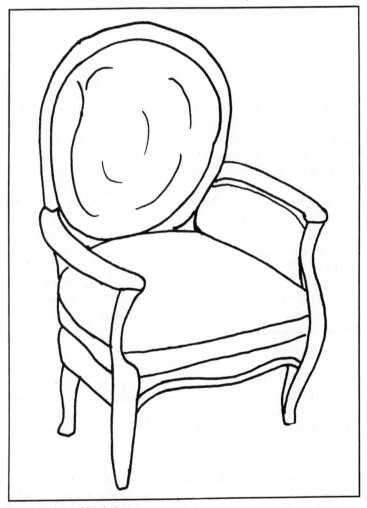

Fig. 1-14. Louis XV chair.

A variety of what I will call daybeds were in vogue during this period as well. They were a part of the feminine influence so noticeable in Louis XV furniture.

French Provincial

Local craftsmen began to copy court styles for the upper and lower middle class during the years, roughly, of 1700-1800 This furniture was much simpler, without elaboration and ornamentation, but it was basically Louis XV. This furniture was small and lightweight, but strong and well-proportioned. It has been and is a favorite furniture style in France. It features graceful curves, comfort, and utility. It is Louis XV without the elaborate marquetry and other decoration.

Louis XVI

Even before the accession of Louis XVI, a return to Classic themes had occurred. There was a dismissal of the gorgeous *rococo* of Louis XV and a return to simple, rectangular shapes with the pieces even smaller than those of the former period. Chair backs were square, with upholstered or cane backs and seats. All decoration, such as carving, was simple, in low relief. Marquetry or inlays were in Classic designs as were all motifs. Pastoral themes or Classic were most popular. All this came about primarily because of the archaeological excavations in Rome. These were widely written about, and the natural result was a revival of interest in Classicism. In a way it was a shame—the rococo, truly French, was beautiful and charming.

Chairs had straight lines and legs. The parts do not flow together as did the Louis XV chair lines. Backs were medallion-shaped or rectangular; some were square. Also, chairs were made without upholstered backs; one famous design displays the lyre motif (Fig. 1-15).

FRENCH DIRECTOIRE

Since there is some difference in opinion as to whether the *French Directoire* (Directory) is a style in its own right, I consider it only to identify the type. Directoire furniture continues the Classic style of Louis XVI, with even more severity in rectangular forms and austere simplicity. The furniture was small and light, well-proportioned, and emphasized such Classic motifs as swans, lyres, and mythological animals. In short, French Directoire furniture gives the overall impression of graceful restraint.

Fig. 1-15. Lyre motif.

EMPIRE

Louis XVI furniture was characterized by Classic themes, but not nearly to the point of strictness as that of the Empire. *Empire* furniture was formal, severe, and not as comfortable as that of former periods. Those designers who had more influence on style expressed contempt for most former French decorative arts; they disapproved of anything not truly and accurately representing antiquity.

Soon the intimacy and grace of the Bourbon styles disappeared. They were replaced by massiveness, austerity, straight lines, and sharp corners.

Seat furniture, chairs in particular, were heavy and more angular. Oddly, there was more variety in chairs than in other pieces of furniture during the *Napoleonic era*. Chairs did not all have straight lines as might be expected, though legs were always straight (Fig. 1-16).

Tables became especially interesting during this period. Greek and Roman tables were round; therefore, so were Empire

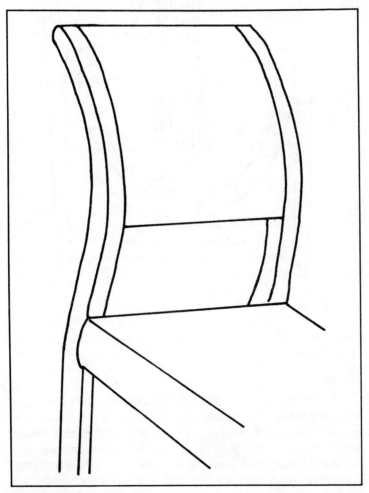

Fig. 1-16. Empire chair.

tables. They were supported either by columns or by legs terminating in fantastic animal shapes which supported the table top, which was often of marble.

Empire furniture was beautiful and generally very well executed. It was designed to suit the mood of the time. Classic motifs representing victory were very popular. Although the period was relatively brief and the style did not endure, Empire furniture was impressive. It was also the last of the Classical revivals in European furniture design.

AMERICAN STYLES

Furniture styles in early America were imported from or copied from those of England. This was to be expected, since the majority of early settlers were themselves English. They brought some furniture with them, but these pioneers had to make most of what they needed from native woods. These hardy folk were, for the first several years, primarily concerned with survival as they accustomed themselves to a new way of life. Furniture was important, since winters on the coast were long and difficult and many hours were necessarily spent indoors, but of necessity furniture was basically utilitarian at first.

When time and labor had taken the roughest edge off their new lifestyle, artisans began making more decorative furnishings for their own homes and for others. They copied English styles from memory or from a rather surprising number of publications from England. It is true that early American furniture was not as refined in workmanship or as elaborate in detail at first. As accumulation of both wealth and leisure occurred, furniture making took on more importance and more attention was given to detail and art.

There are various ways of defining early American styles. The simplest is to say there were two; *Colonial (pre-Revolution)* and Federal (after establishment of the American federal government). Historically, this is a helpful manner of perceiving styles. A more specific designation of styles follows, beginning with the approximate period of 1608 to 1720 known as *Early American.*

Early American

This style includes the earliest handmade furniture in this country. At first there was a strong Gothic theme—massive low chests with a hinged lid on top, the Gothic trestle—which gradually evolved into Tudor, Elizabethan, and Jacobean styles. Finishes on this early furniture were either natural, waxed or oiled, or painted.

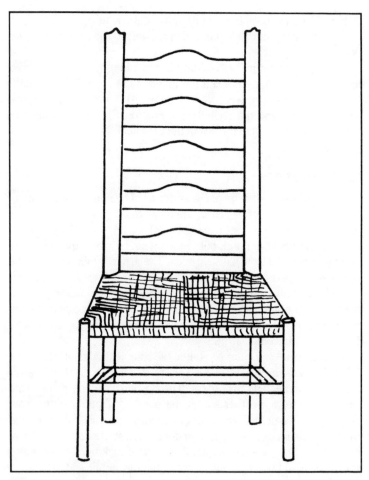

Fig. 1-17. Ladder-back chair.

Ladder-back chairs with rush seats were typical (Fig. 1-17). Up-holstery was scarce during this period, relying for the most part on cushions. At first there were heavy though somewhat crude Gothic carvings, which were replaced later by less elaborate carvings and painted motifs. Drop leaf tables were common such as the *butterfly* table in Fig. 1-18. Woods were the native oak, pine, walnut, cedar, cypress, ash, cherry, and so on.

American Georgian

This period is also approximate, lasting for about 60 years. At this time a strong local flavor was evident in furniture, though the

English Georgian influence was dominant for some time. There was an elevation of concern with comfort and beauty, as time and finances permitted.

The *Windsor chair* (Fig. 1-19) came into use and took the place of the ladder-back to a great extent. There was a high-backed wing chair (Fig. 1-20), along with Chippendale style wing and armchairs and settees. The highboy was popular, along with drop leaf tables and other distinctly Georgian seat and dining room furniture.

Queen Anne furniture also appeared during this period. This style brought new grace and comfort to American homes, with its lighter construction and attention to form. In the Queen Anne style in America, there were many types of chairs, settees, and tables for every occasion.

American Federal

The *American Federal* period saw the creation of much beautiful furniture particularly in the earlier years. Later the heavy French Empire influence became somewhat popular. Though this was excellent furniture in many respects, it was not as beautiful. The American Federal period was this country's neoclassical time, beginning with the Hepplewhite styles. In the Hepplewhite style there were upholstered chairs, wing and armchairs, settees, and the popular shield-back chairs.

Duncan Phyfe was a famous American cabinetmaker who made a lot of furniture in the Sheraton and Directoire styles. These styles became very popular in fashionable homes. The Classical influence

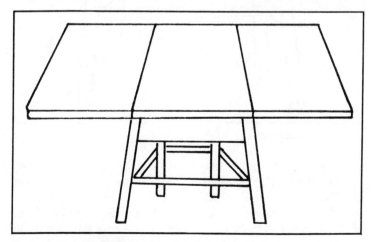

Fig. 1-18. Drop leaf table.

Fig. 1-19. Windsor chair.

was strong, with Duncan Phyfe's lyre one of the most remarkable. Another Duncan Phyfe design of the Federal period is illustrated in the *Grecian* couch in Fig. 1-21.

The Empire style was brief in America, ending with the advent of Victorian furniture. American furniture makers followed English patterns fairly closely until the Victorian period. Then a kind of deterioration occurred, with a seeming lack of interest in maintaining consistency in style. There were several years of ill-directed furniture production during the late nineteenth century, but by the turn of the century a noticeable preference was established once again. This was expressed in the severity, the straight simple lines, and the durable but stylistically plain leather upholstery of *Mission* furniture.

Fig. 1-20. High-backed wing chair.

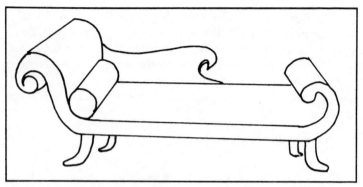

Fig. 1-21. Duncan Phyfe design.

MODERN TRENDS

When you shop for furniture today, you find a remarkable variety from which to choose. There are numerous styles in modern taste, a breathtaking array of fabrics, textures, and colors, and a suitable piece for any use or occasion. The richness and vitality of modern furniture design and manufacture is apparently not dictated by any specific sector. Nevertheless, some standard principles in design are followed, and home decorators seek many of the same features.

There is more emphasis on straight lines, simplicity of design, and use of color and texture to achieve the desired effects. Plain surfaces are common, curves are employed to prevent monotony and to enhance utility, and function is of greatest importance. This is not to suggest, however, that modern furniture sacrifices form and beauty. Comfort, a subdued beauty, and efficient utilization of space are all present in modern American furniture.

Guidelines to Successful Upholstery

Reupholstering furniture is an art that practically anyone can learn. Once you gain some familiarity with tools, materials, and techniques, it isn't particularly difficult. Nevertheless, if the project is to be a satisfactory and rewarding one, there are several ways in which you must be prepared. These requirements are practical and achievable, and they occur in areas and categories that are easy to understand.

PERSONAL ATTITUDE

No reupholstery project can be a complete success unless you have a real desire to learn the best methods and to do the very best possible job. The desire to do this kind of work may arise in any number of ways. In my own case, I had no particularly strong interest in furniture upholstery until I happened to visit a friend who was about to begin an upholstery project. When she showed me the chair that she was planning to reupholster, I could hardly believe what I was seeing and hearing. The chair was a piece of junk. My friend was amused and understanding of my incredulity. She simply suggested that I observe the reupholstering project from the beginning through its completion; she seemed to have no doubt that this would change my attitude.

My friend was entirely correct. As I watched her remove the ragged and dirty fabrics and padding from the chair, my doubts were even stronger than when I had first seen the chair. Little by little, as the work progressed, the doubts gave way to a reluctant admission that perhaps it really was possible to make a useful chair. As the day progressed, I again grew incredulous, but for a different reason. The chair was becoming beautiful before my eyes—not only beautiful, but strong, functional, and quite valuable. My friend had created a truly beautiful Queen Anne chair.

It is difficult to describe the excitement I felt as the project neared completion. My friend made something lovely in less than a day. I couldn't wait to try it. I obtained an old chair, did the reupholstery work, and now have an attractive and useful chair.

Economic necessity is a good impetus to such work. Perhaps a chair or sofa is sturdy, but it must be reupholstered in order to be useful. A do-it-yourself project like this often becomes a fascinating hobby or a profitable career.

There are problems in upholstery work. It is usually a dirty job and can become quite unpleasant at times. Ocassional difficulties will arise, and questions will come up about how a particular problem should be solved. On some occasions it will be difficult to find the necessary time and opportunity to do the kind of job you want.

EDUCATING YOURSELF

Any difficulties or disadvantages will have solutions if the desire to do upholstery work is strong enough. You must be not only willing but eager to learn and keep learning.

Visit Upholstery Shops

This learning is basically a task of self-education. Visit upholstery shops and observe the upholsterer at work. Some upholsterers may not be amenable to your request to visit and watch, but it doesn't hurt to ask. Eventually, you will find an upholsterer who will welcome you into his shop and demonstrate the techniques, materials, and tools that he has found most suitable. It is important to visit more than one shop. Each upholsterer has preferred tools and methods of approaching each phase of an upholstery project. Each one has likewise developed his own shortcuts and methods of problem solving. Try to keep an open and inquisitive mind when you visit a shop. Learn from the upholsterer all that you can and realize that there are always other ways to do any particular phase of upholstery work that may be more suitable for you.

Read Literature

Read books on upholstery. Go to your local library and examine do-it-yourself periodicals. Many magazines have regular or occasional articles concerning upholstery and related subjects that you will find useful.

Visit Dry Goods Shops

A third way to educate yourself in the subject is to visit *dry goods shops* where upholstery materials are stocked. Ask to see their catalogs to learn what other materials are being produced. Developments occur continually, as manufacturers of upholstery products strive to increase the variety and improve the quality of their products. Doing such shopping on a regular basis will help you keep abreast of recent developments and new and more convenient materials.

PATIENCE

You must develop patience. You must be willing, if necessary, to work with extreme and meticulous care. You must also have the patience to remove tacks, staples and stitches, and redo any phase that does not look and feel as it should. For many people, doing the same job over and over in order to get it right is a discouraging and irritating process. Be assured that even those who have been in the upholstery business for many years find it necessary at times to undo a *superficially* good job, and redo it so it is truly a good job.

WORK AREA

You can complete an upholstery project in your living room if you wish. While this is not the best choice, it is possible and has been done. The degree to which you organize and maintain a work area for your upholstery projects will depend largely upon the amount of work you expect to do. Obviously, if you plan to reupholster one chair or sofa, you will not find it practical to arrange for a sophisticated work area. You may complete your first project with such a high degree of success and personal satisfaction that you can't wait to get on to the second project. This work can soon become a consuming interest, and the living room is then definitely out for a work area.

Safety Precautions

Most of us are accustomed in our daily lives to taking precautions against easily recognized hazards to our health and well-being. Yet, when we change the order or our daily activities, we often neglect to take safety precautions that will eliminate any hazards connected with the new activity. The following precautions are essential for your safety as a single worker in your own home. They become increasingly important as other people enter the picture—members of your family, visitors, or your customers if you develop a small business.

There is the obvious matter of being careful as you work and paying attention to what you are doing. I suspect that there are few upholsterers who have not at one time or another driven a staple into a hand or thumb. Pay close attention to the way you handle a stapler, whether it is manually, electrically, or air-operated. The same applies to *any* tool.

You often need *extension cords* in upholstery work. It is wise to use heavy-duty extension cords. Put the cords back where they belong as soon as you are finished with them. It is all too easy for someone to trip over an extension cord lying in the floor and sustain an injury.

Keep cutting tools sharp; less damage will be done with them when they are sharp. Also, have a specific place for each and every tool. Keep your tools in their proper places when not in use.

Stop and clean your work area often. Trash on the floor can cause you to trip and fall. Clutter piled on your worktable is not only a detriment to the effectiveness of your work, but it can also cause you to hurt yourself.

Cleaning up after yourself often may reduce the danger of fire. Be careful where and how you discard trash and scraps. Some of the chemicals you might use are very flammable. Take care when you are working with them.

Often when you are reupholstering furniture, it is necessary either to strip completely and refinish the woodwork, or to at least touch it up in places. The materials that you will be using for such work are flammable. Keep all these materials, and any woodworking projects, away from the area where you do the actual upholstery. Always be sure to follow instructions on chemical containers. Store the containers properly. Do not set a can of lacquer thinner on a shelf above a space heater, for example.

Safety in a work area is assured primarily by cleanliness and organization. If you will observe these two practices wisely and without fail, chances of injury to yourself or others will be greatly reduced.

Convenience and Comfort

Convenience in your work area is not necessarily a matter of your own personal comfort. When your materials are conveniently and comfortably located, you will be able to work more rapidly and efficiently. Such comfort and convenience will make you feel better, be happier, and will help to assure that you will work at your best.

Make sure that your work area is properly lighted. Working in poor light can result in eyestrain, back and neck strain, and poor work. You can work faster and more efficiently with adequate lighting.

Prepare a specific place for each tool to be kept when it is not in use. Tools will thus not be lost, and time won't be wasted in fruitless searching. *Always* replace tools when you are finished with them.

You should build a table or tables as needed, so you do not have to bend and endure unnecessary strain. A worktable can be built quickly and easily. It will save your back, your patience, and your good nature. The first upholstery project may be done on the floor or in a similar manner. If you decide to do more, you should have a worktable so you can reach the piece of furniture you are working on conveniently and comfortably.

If you plan to reupholster a piece of furniture that has long been in your own home, you will know to some extent what to expect. When you buy a chair or sofa at an auction, or obtain one from some other unfamiliar source, it may be a good idea to remove the outer fabric and padding outside. If you find that the furniture needs to be sprayed with insecticide to eliminate bugs, you can do so with more freedom outside.

You may obtain furniture that exudes some pretty offensive odors. This is another situation where it may be wise to dismantle the piece outside.

It is a good idea to have an undisturbed work area. Do not let your children or perhaps company roam freely, possibly disturbing or damaging work in progress. In the home shop this is not always possible, but it should be attempted. When someone spills soda pop or coffee on your upholstery fabric, you will see why an undisturbed work area is a good idea.

Protect upholstery fabrics and materials, and any finished upholstery work with plastic or some other kind of cover. An upholstery shop will be dusty much of the time.

UPHOLSTERY AS A BUSINESS

When you have reupholstered a few pieces of furniture for yourself with success, it is so easy to suddenly find yourself doing the same for friends. Your friend may show your work to his friend, and you can be in the upholstery business before you realize what has happened.

You may deliberately engage yourself in upholstery as a business, or the business may develop incidentally. When you begin accepting pay for your work, you must also begin behaving like a business person. You must observe the practices you will be required to follow locally, such as licensing. You must keep records. Develop a system of record keeping that will clearly show all your expenditures and income. Be meticulous and consistent. You will need these records in order to know whether you are actually making a profit; you will also need them for tax purposes. Keep your records neat and orderly. Always put them in the same place and maintain them in the same manner. The method you follow is not as important as being consistent.

How will you know how much to charge? This will depend upon what other upholsterers in your area charge. Don't undercut their prices. You should respect their experience and match your prices accordingly until you have become absolutely certain that a change is necessary.

If you set a low price for your work, you may not be flooded with customers. It has been my experience that you must be wary of the customer who is attracted to a very low price for labor. This customer is almost invariably impossible to please.

Some upholsterers charge a deposit on work they take in. It is a good idea to charge a deposit. You may need the money to pay for the materials needed for that particular job. There is another, more important reason. Some customer may bring a sofa to you to be reupholstered. If he has not paid a deposit, and if the sofa isn't terribly important to him for some reason, it is possible that he may never return to claim it and pay you for your labor. On the other hand, if he has already invested money in the project, he will have a strong interest in claiming the finished work. People who are serious about having the work done do not object to paying a deposit.

When you accept the job tell your customer when you expect to complete it. Give yourself plenty of time. When it is finished, do not just load the furniture onto your truck and deliver it. Call ahead, announce that the work is finished, and remind the customer of the balance due. If he is not prepared to pay the amount owed when you deliver, simply arrange to deliver at a later date when he is able to pay.

I strongly suggest that any person contemplating going into upholstery business take a course in small business operation at a nearby college. Many colleges offer such courses in their continuing education programs. Such a course will give you basic information that will be important. The course won't take long and will not require much of a cash investment.

Finding an Employee

After you have been in business for awhile, you may find it necessary to find someone to help you. The sort of person you hire will make a difference regarding the degree of success of your business. Many beginning businesspersons hire a friend or relative.

I think the single most important personal attribute of an employee is *enthusiasm*. A person who demonstrates enthusiasm for the work will be truly interested in learning and in doing a satisfactory job at whatever task you assign him. You will find that the enthusiastic prospective employee will almost always be someone who has a high regard for his own abilities. This attitude is to your benefit. Such a person will not be satisfied with careless work.

The employee should also be neat and personable. Sex of the employee is unimportant.

A high school student may be a good employee choice. You might find it worth while to call the principal of your local high school and inquire about any work-study programs the school has. He will also be able to direct you to students who possess the qualities you are looking for. Given a choice between a well-to-do and a needy student, and assuming that both possess the qualities you need, you will probably prefer to hire the economically disadvantaged student.

The job of finding the right person to help in your upholstery shop is an interesting and sometimes tricky one. I have concentrated on the positive aspects; one word about the negative side is necessary.

If you hire someone with whom you find you cannot work comfortably for some reason, you should first do some careful, thinking about the reasons for your incompatibility. If you determine that the situation cannot be remedied, do not continue trying to work with this person. This will only lead to unpleasantness and tension. It will eventually affect your work and the manner in which you operate your business. It isn't fair to you or to the employee to attempt to continue such a relationship.

Dealing with Customers

The way that you handle customers in your shop is important. You must be friendly and helpful. The customer is always right; you must never argue. You must help the customer select the fabrics most suitable for the furniture and eventual surroundings. In the final analysis, however, if the customer wants his sofa covered in burlap, do it.

Keep your shop, particularly any display area, clean and attractive. Potential customers do not always realize what a sometimes messy business yours is. A cluttered, poorly organized shop may create the impression that you work is the same.

It is a good idea to take before and after photographs of your work. Post them in some highly visible place. As time passes, discard some photos and add others. If your work is good, such a display will be an asset to your business. Use a 35 mm camera if you can, because this will produce a more accurate representation of your work. In the absence of a 35 mm camera, use whatever is available and learn to take the most complimentary pictures.

If you have finished work on hand, keep it where potential customers can see it. Don't put finished work where visitors can accidentally damage it. Use common sense and display work when you can. It is a positive reinforcement to the potential customer.

Advertising Your Business

You might choose to employ commercial advertising such as radio, television, or newspapers. Commercial advertising is expensive, but it may be wise.

There are other things you can do to advertise your business in a more subtle but effective manner. Begin by seeing to it that the outside of your shop is neat and attractive. Keep the windows washed, thus creating a favorable impression for the arriving customer.

You will probably want a sign announcing your place of business. The business sign should be large enough to be seen and understood by passersby. This is best determined by a simple experiment. Create a mock sign and place it in what you feel is a good location. Get into your automobile and drive past your sign. You can easily determine if the sign is the right size and advantageously located.

Keep your sign very simple. The more words that appear on a sign, the more distracting it is. The name of your business is usually sufficient. Avoid "cute" signs, misspelled words and sloppy lettering. Your sign, like the work you do, is representative of you as a businessperson. Make it clear, clean, simple, visible, and positive.

You may find opportunities to do public demonstrations of your work. Take advantage of these opportunities.

Where do you do such public demonstrations of your work? Most high schools have or are instituting career education programs. Instructors of career education classes are always looking for people to talk to the students and demonstrate some aspect of their occupations. Some of the students may go home and tell their parents about the exciting demonstration they saw. When those parents need some reupholstery work done, they will think of you first. You took a positive part in the education of their children, and you did it without pay.

There is a second valuable aspect to doing a free public demonstration. Have someone take a few good black and white pictures of you at work, surrounded by eager and interested students. A brief account describing the occasion, along with a good photograph, will make a fantastic public service article for your newspaper. This will be a positive public relations project, not only for you and your business, but for the school as well. There is nothing sneaky about this kind of advertising. People should know about such activities in their community.

The principal of the school should see the proposed photograph and article before you submit it to the newspaper editor. The principal shouldn't object, but he should have the opportunity. To avoid such a complication, talk to the teacher in charge of providing school news to the media before you appear for the demonstration. Mention that such an article would be a fine project for a student and for the school.

The best advertisement your business will ever get is that of word of mouth. When a person has a piece of furniture reupholstered and is proud of it, he is going to show it to others and tell them who did the work. This is the kind of advertising that will prove most effective in the long run.

3

Tools and Materials

The tools and materials required for an upholstery project can either be simple and inexpensive or quite elaborate. If you are planning a single job for your home, you can do the work with relatively few tools. Other materials for a single job can be obtained in a department store with an upholstery department.

Even when planning a professional shop, it is wise to begin simply and acquire additional equipment as the need arises. Some tools are quite expensive. It is possible to spend a lot of money and then learn by experience that the investment was an unproductive one.

Buying padding and similar materials in a department store is more expensive than obtaining them from a wholesale supplier. If it appears that you will do quite a bit of upholstery work, you should contact several suppliers to learn what materials are available and their quantities and prices. Some suppliers of upholstery materials are listed in Appendix A.

The degree to which you prepare for upholstery work is a matter of choice. Tools and other supplies are shown and discussed here. Study these and learn from upholsterers and other sources. Soon you will become familiar enough to make practical selections suitable for the upholstery projects you have planned.

HARDWARE

A very basic selection of home upholstery hardware is shown in Fig. 3-1. The back row shows ½-inch staples and a manual stapler. Often the ½-inch size is too large, and ¼ or ⅝ inch are more suitable. The size required depends upon the kind of wood frame you have, as well as the thickness of fabric and padding.

A *tack* and *staple puller* is a real necessity. Although you can get by with diagonal pliers and other tools, anyone planning even one upholstery project should buy a tack and staple puller.

Hog ringers, the pliers used to put rings in hogs' noses, are one of the handiest gadgets in any upholstery task. The rings are used to connect springs, and no other tool will do this job quite as well and quickly.

Most upholsterers keep a variety of hammers on hand. Although few tacks are used in upholstery nowadays, there will often be occasions when they are necessary. A small tack hammer is essential.

You can always use a really good pair of shears. Upholstery fabrics are sometimes difficult to cut with small household scissors, and some of these materials will quickly ruin scissors that aren't made for this purpose. Suitable shears are another necessity, even for a single upholstery project.

Practically any department store will have a needle kit similar to the one in Fig. 3-2. Curved needles are needed in close places, such as when you must sew springs to webbing. Obtain a package of these needles before you begin; you will be sure to need them.

Fig. 3-1. Basic tools.

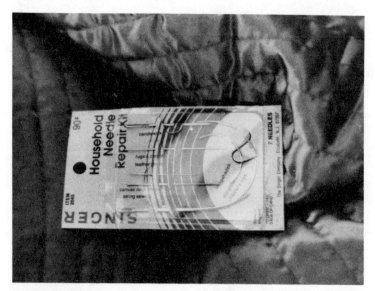

Fig. 3-2. Needle kit.

Figure 3-3 shows the best kind of stapler, if one will be practical for you. This stapler is air-operated, so you must have some kind of air supply. The only sensible solution is to obtain a good compressor of sufficient capacity to power the stapler. When you buy a compressor, keep other possible uses in mind. Make the initial investment one that will serve you well.

The hand stapler shown previously will be suitable for a single project. It does require some strength to use and will tire you if you must use it much at one work period. Electric staplers are also available, and many upholsterers use them. They are convenient and easy to use.

The sewing machine in Fig. 3-4 is one made for upholstery fabrics. Such a machine is expensive and is not a wise investment unless the need for one is definite. This machine will handle heavy fabrics easily, and the sewing is immensely faster than with a standard sewing machine.

Most upholstery fabrics can be sewn with a standard sewing machine if the proper needle and threads are used, but do not plan on doing very much heavy-duty sewing on your regular machine. It was not built for such heavy work, and you should subject it to very little. If you plan a single project and feel that your machine will not serve the purpose, someone at a professional shop may be willing to do the sewing for you.

Fig. 3-3. Air-operated stapler.

Fig. 3-4. Industrial sewing machine.

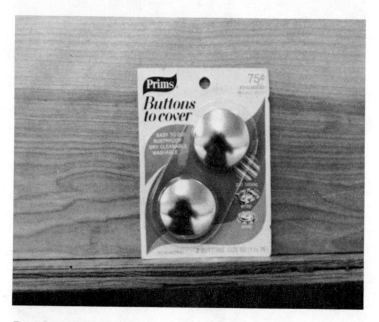

Fig. 3-5. Uncovered buttons.

Buttons are available from most department stores in several types and sizes. These buttons can be covered by your upholstery fabric with no special tools, or you can even pad and cover regular buttons for some uses. If much button work is done however, this will be time consuming and difficult (Fig. 3-5).

Professional upholstery shops usually have a button press like the one illustrated in Fig. 3-6. With this machine, buttons can be covered in a matter of seconds. Again, it may be possible for you to take some of your upholstery fabric to a professional shop and have the buttons covered.

Fig. 3-6. Button press.

Fig. 3-7. Clamps.

Figures 3-7 and 3-8 show a variety of clamps. You may need some kind of clamps even on your first upholstery task. When you strip old finish from wood, this often loosens glued joints. These joints must be reglued and clamped.

When you visit upholstery shops and examine catalogs of upholstery supplies from wholesale dealers, consider the variety of tools that are used and offered. Be sure that you will actually use a

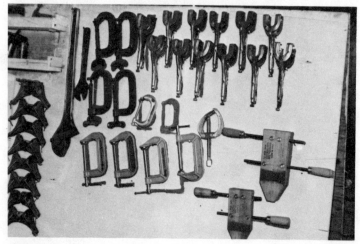

Fig. 3-8. Clamps.

Fig. 3-9. Upholstery webbing.

Fig. 3-10. Welting cord.

Fig. 3-11. Decorative trim.

Fig. 3-12. Sisal padding.

tool before you buy it. The *webbing stretcher* used by many up-holsterers is very convenient, but it is not used as often as you might expect. Most people find that they are able to stretch webbing sufficiently tight by hand, and after awhile they stop using the stretcher altogether. This is *not* a recommendation, just an observation.

SOFTWARE

One of the first things you are likely to need is a good quality of webbing (Fig. 3-9). You will need to experiment with different kinds and weights to determine which kind will be most suitable for the work you plan. Use strong webbing for seats. The webbing often supports most of the stress in furniture, so you should never skimp on this material.

Welting cord (Fig. 3-10) is available in several sizes. Since welting is such a popular and attractive touch in much furniture, you will soon become familiar with its use and the different kinds and sizes that can be bought from wholesale suppliers or in department stores.

Decorative trims not only add to the appearance of an up-holstered sofa or chair; they also cover staples and tacks. Sometimes you will be able to find a good variety in department stores (Fig. 3-11), but you cannot always find what you need there. Almost anything you could want will be available from suppliers of up-holstery materials.

Figure 3-12 is a close-up of a scrap of padding. Such padding is made from a variety of materials, all of which are good and will last for years. It comes in large rolls from suppliers and can usually be bought in small amounts from professional shops if you need only enough for a single job.

Fig. 3-13. Quilt batting.

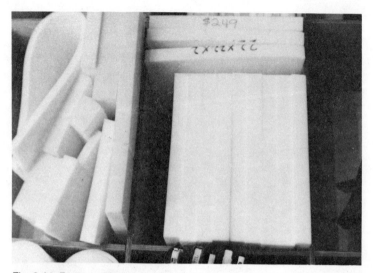

Fig. 3-14. Foam padding.

Seldom can any reupholstery project be done without using some new cotton padding. Again, this can be bought in very large rolls from suppliers. If you aren't involved enough to deal with suppliers yet, you can buy *quilt batting* in cotton or synthetic fabrics in small packages at your department store (Fig. 3-13). This would be too expensive for much work, but it will be fine for your beginning projects.

Fig. 3-15. Foam padding.

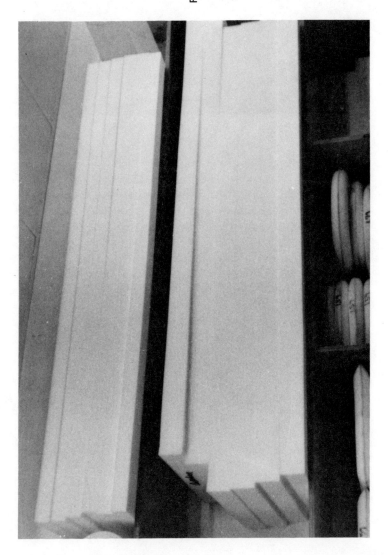

Fig. 3-16. Foam padding.

Fig. 3-17. Fabric chart.

Foam padding saves time, works well, and lasts quite a long time. You may be surprised at the many thicknesses and densities stocked in even a small department store. Figures 3-14 through 3-16 show some of the kinds available in many stores.

You will soon learn to estimate the yardage in covering fabrics needed for a particular project. At first, until you have actually dismantled a piece of furniture for reupholstery, you will probably

Fig. 3-18. Upholstery fabrics.

Fig. 3-19. Upholstery fabrics.

53

be a little distrustful of your own inexperienced measurements. In the upholstery department of most stores, you will find a chart similar to the one shown in Fig. 3-17. This chart indicates the yardage needed for a variety of seat furniture styles. The chart may recommend even more yardage than you will probably need, but this may not be too bad an idea for your first project.

Figures 3-18 and 3-19 show upholstery fabrics. It is fine to buy your fabrics in a store if you find what you need, but do observe some cautionary tactics. Sometimes you will find runs or other flaws. Examine the fabrics carefully before you take them home. The second thing you must be particularly careful about is whether you are buying some closeout style. You may need a little extra fabric before you're finished. If you've already bought all there was of that kind, you may be in trouble. You may cut a piece improperly and then need additional fabric to do the job again.

So many things are available for upholstery that at times it is difficult to know just what is the best choice. The best way to be sure that you are choosing a material wisely is to educate yourself in the subject thoroughly before you begin buying.

Frame, Spring, and Upholstery Repair

Some knowledge of how to make repairs to furniture, whether in the upholstery or the structural parts, is important for you. Many pieces of essentially sound furniture have been discarded when they could have been saved with a few basic repairs.

Aside from the possibility of actually discarding damaged furniture, there are times when even a reupholstery project can be reasonably avoided. Some repairs are actually reupholstery, but only of a part of the piece rather than the whole thing.

Finally, it is sometimes possible to postpone an upholstery project until a more convenient time. To look at this task in another way, simple things can be done to prevent wear or damage, or to temporarily conceal such things until proper repairs can be made.

It is sometimes necessary to make repairs to the frame or springs of a piece of furniture before the reupholstery process is begun. Although a piece of furniture may look so bad that it cannot ever be made useful, you soon learn what kind of repairs are most commonly needed. Any piece of furniture may appear to be in a great deal worse condition than it actually is. The repairs most likely needed are regluing joints and possibly reinforcing them, fixing or making new legs, arms, or rails, and possibly stripping and refinishing the woodwork.

Springs often need some form of repair. The sofa in Fig. 4-1 is an excellent example. In the beginning there was no damage to the frame, in spite of the awful appearance of the piece. The legs had to be removed, stripped, and refinished, and the springs had to be repaired to some extent.

Frame and spring repairs need not frighten you, for they are usually less difficult than they may at first appear. There are some standard practices to observe in frame and spring repair. Once these techniques are mastered, most repairs can be made easily.

REINFORCEMENT

Look at the chair in Fig. 4-2. This is a simple wood chair with a drop-in upholstered seat. This chair has a broken dowel which must be repaired (Fig. 4-3). None of the parts except the legs are strong enough to support much weight (Fig. 4-4), and a new stretcher must be made to connect the two on each side at the center in an H shape.

Since this chair has such a simple seat which rests on the corner glue blocks, some changes can be made to strengthen the frame. A plywood insert could be made and installed over the corner blocks. The glue blocks themselves could be replaced with blocks having a better fit, and thus a broader gluing surface (Fig. 4-5).

The chair frame could also be strengthened by adding a second set of seat rails, gluing them inside the original rails. If the top edge of the new set were dropped a bit below the level of the original rails, this would not interfere with the replacing of the padded seat. If you add a second set of rails, know that unless they are fitted well and glued over the maximum available surface, they do not do much to really strengthen the chair.

If the chair has a spring seat, the springs might need to be shortened in order to make up for the space used with a plywood insert or a second set of seat rails. An alternative to this might be to discard the springs entirely. Pad the seat with two layers of foam or some other kind of stuffing and a top layer of medium density foam. This kind of seat would be less thick; thus, the original height of the chair seat would be maintained.

Any time a foam pad is installed over a plywood slab, air holes must be drilled in the slab. This allows the easy escape of air when weight is imposed on the foam. Furthermore, if the seat is covered in vinyl or anything other than cloth, the compression of air resulting when there are no escape vents will weaken the seams, possibly causing them to rip when weight is imposed.

BROKEN DOWELS

A good, well-fitting dowel joint is almost always preferable to the use of nails or screws. When you are repairing an antique, you will want to redo the broken joint in precisely the way it was originally done. The dowel joint is simply a wooden peg that is introduced with glue into a dowel socket.

Fig. 4-1. A sofa to be reupholstered.

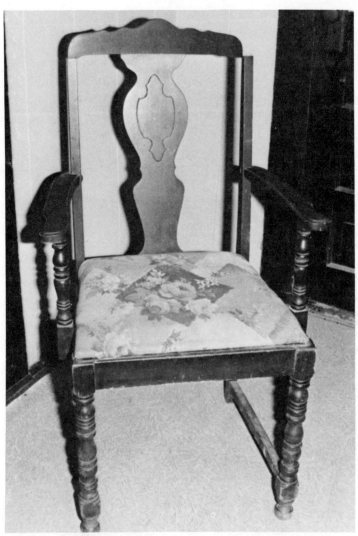

Fig. 4-2. Antique chair.

The first thing to do in removing a dowel joint is to twist the dowel loose with your fingers or with pliers. Be very careful as too much force might twist the broken dowel off inside. If enough of the broken piece protrudes, you can sometimes tap the rod gently next to the wood member and loosen it in this way.

When you use any tool in attempting to loosen or remove dowels, be very careful. You can easily damage the wood member.

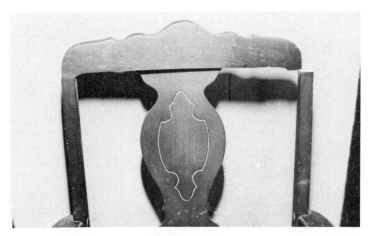

Fig. 4-3. Broken dowel joint.

If you cannot remove the dowel by twisting or tapping it, then it must be drilled. In order to properly remove a dowel by drilling, you must use a bit of the same diameter as the dowel. You must drill in a straight line. This is sometimes difficult to do without a drill press, but with care it can be done.

Determine the depth you will need to drill in order to reach the end of the joint. Wrap a piece of masking tape around the bit at this point, so you will not go too far (Fig. 4-6). Be very cautious in this

Fig. 4-4. Slender rails.

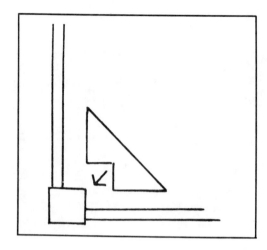

Fig. 4-5. Make glue blocks fit the corner.

process; when the broken pieces are removed, prepare to install the new one.

Dowel rods can be obtained in building supplies or hardware stores. These ordinarily are in 3-foot lengths and a variety of diameters. When you go to buy a new dowel rod, take a piece of the original one with you, if possible. You will be sure to get a new dowel of the right size. Before buying a new dowel, however, check to see whether you might have enlarged the socket when you drilled earlier. If so, you might need to get the next largest size dowel.

A dowel that fits properly is one that you can slide into the hole without much difficulty. On the other hand, it must not be really loose.

Remove any dried glue that may remain in the dowel socket or on the dowel itself if you are regluing instead of replacing a dowel. Dried glue will prevent fresh glue from being absorbed into the wood to form a tight joint. Scrape the old glue off carefully or use sandpaper. Again, take care that you don't damage the wood itself.

The most commonly used glue in furniture repair is probably the white *polyvinyl glue* that can be bought in plastic squeeze bottles or in large jugs in building supply or hardware stores. This glue will set up in approximately 30 minutes when the weather is agreeable. You should always allow more time for a freshly glued joint to be completely dry, though, before you continue work on the project.

Cut your new dowel to a length slightly less than the combined depths of the dowel sockets in each of the two pieces to be joined. This bit of extra space permits a good fit.

White polyvinyl glues are water soluble. This is to your advantage. Before you apply glue, be sure you have some damp cloths handy to wipe off the excess. You must always apply plenty of glue to insure a strong joint. Apply glue on both the dowel and the inside of the socket. Cover both parts generously. Insert the dowel in the sockets and prepare to clamp them. Wipe off the excess glue immediately before it dries. If there isn't any excess, you should remove the clamp and dowel. Apply more glue.

When you apply clamps to any piece of furniture, be sure to put some kind of pad between the wood and the grip of the clamp, so it will not damage the wood (Fig. 4-7). Tighten the clamp with your fingers only. Do not exert any kind of extreme pressure; it is not at all necessary. The clamp is only there to create a moderate pressure and keep the surfaces in contact while the glue sets up. If possible, always let clamped pieces set up at least overnight before you return to the work.

There might be occasions when you feel that a joint will not be sufficiently strong without the addition of a metal screw. Always drill a pilot hole before inserting a screw. This will help keep the wood from splitting. Generally, avoid the use of screws, nails, and other metal fasteners when you are repairing furniture.

Fig. 4-6. Tape indicates drilling depth.

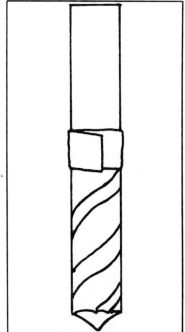

Fig. 4-7. Cushion the grips of clamps.

BROKEN LEGS AND RAILS

If a piece of furniture has a broken leg, but all of the parts of the broken piece are there, it is often possible to repair the break. The best method of repairing a broken leg is to reinforce the leg with a dowel insert.

First, determine whether the broken edges can be fitted together attractively. It is possible to fit splintered pieces together, glue and clamp them, and make an attractive leg again. Sometimes, however, it will be necessary to cut out an area on either side of the break, including splintered parts (Fig. 4-8), and insert new piece of wood to replace this part.

In either case, drill a dowel socket into both broken pieces, or both pieces and the new insert. Be sure to drill in a straight line. Apply glue liberally. Insert the dowel, clamp, and remove excess glue.

There will be times when a leg cannot be repaired. It will be necessary to make a new leg to replace the former one. If it is a simple style, it will not be difficult to make one. Simply take a pattern from the matching leg on the piece. An elaborately turned leg may require that you remove the matching good leg and have someone make a new one like it. A third alternative would be to remove both legs and make two new ones, not necessarily like the original but like each other.

When rails or rungs are broken, you may find it necessary to disassemble several joints in order to install a new piece. Sometimes it is possible to do this without taking apart good joints, particularly if the broken piece has a *mortise and tenon joint.*

Before you decide whether to disassemble the piece or repair it by the method which follows, check the piece of furniture over carefully. It could be that there are other loose joints. It might be better to disassemble and reglue the other joints. If other joints are firm, and you have a straight mortise and tenon joint to work with on the broken rail, it can be repaired as follows.

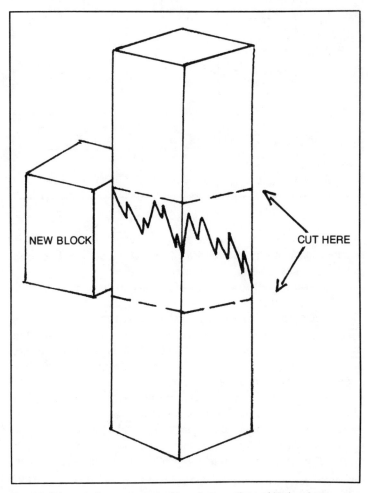

Fig. 4-8. It is sometimes necessary to replace sections of broken legs.

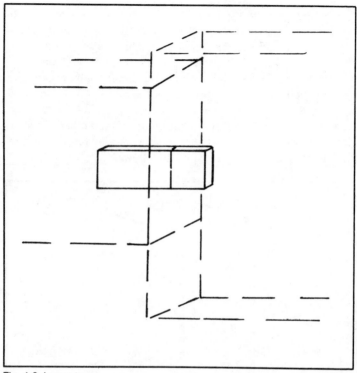

Fig. 4-9. Loose tenon.

Remove the broken piece, taking the tenons loose carefully in much the same manner as you would remove old dowels. Clean the mortises of any dried glue that may be in them.

Cut two loose tenons (Fig. 4-9). Loose tenons are much like dowels, except that they are squared rather than rounded.

Make a new rail to fit. Cut a mortise in each end as illustrated in Fig. 4-10. The loose tenons should fit in this mortise, and the mortise should fit in the furniture piece. The fit should not be loose, but you should be able to slip the tenon into the mortise fairly evenly. If the fit is good, remove the pieces and apply glue liberally to the tenons and mortises. Insert them into the furniture piece. Add glue to the mortises on the new piece you just cut and onto the extended part of the tenons, and fit the rail mortises over the tenons. If the fit is as good as it should be, you will have to fit both ends at the same time. Clamp the piece, wipe off the excess glue, and allow plenty of time for drying before continuing with other work on the piece.

SPRING REPAIR

Sometimes a set of springs will have to be replaced entirely. In most cases you will only have to retie them or install new spring clamps, or make similar minor repairs.

Figure 4-11 illustrates a very dilapidated set of pocket springs. Should you come across a set of these springs in such a deplorable condition, know that they are not necessarily ready to be discarded. In fact, these are perfectly good. They only need new pockets made for them.

Pocket springs are small individual coil springs inserted into muslin pockets. These pockets are then sewn together along the edges. You can create a set of pocket springs in any size or shape you desire. They are often found in seat cushions in old furniture, or perhaps in the backs. New pocket springs can be bought from upholstery supply sources in all kinds of sizes and shapes, or you can buy the springs and make your own pockets.

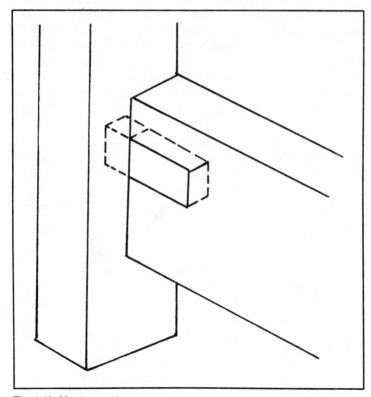

Fig. 4-10. Mortise and loose tenon.

Fig. 4-11. Pocket springs.

The springs in Fig. 4-11 are in good shape. In order to restore this set, it would be necessary to remove all the springs first. These springs are 3½ inches tall. Measure yours and make fitting adjustments.

In order to make new pockets, cut a strip of muslin 15 inches wide (for 3½-inch springs) and fold it along the length in the center. Sew one end closed. Move 10 inches from this first seam and make a second seam (Fig. 4-12). Take one of the springs, compress it, and slide it into the pocket sideways (Fig. 4-13). Baste the opening shut, work this spring into an upright position,and check to see whether it fits properly. You may need to widen or narrow the pocket a bit. When you have determined any necessary adjustments, remove the basting and the spring. Continue seaming the additional pockets, making as many as you need to create a set in the right width. Make as many rows of pockets as you need in order to create a cushion of the desired size.

Insert the springs, as you did previously to determine fit, by compressing them and putting them into the pockets sideways. Then sew the open end of the pockets closed, and turn the springs upright by hand. When you have finished, simply sew the rows of pockets together along the edges, along the bottom and top. You have a new set of pocket springs.

A more familiar kind of spring repair is where coil springs need to be retired or clamped. In Fig. 4-14 a new clamp is required to connect the springs. After this is done, the old tying cord is removed. The springs are retied from the back of the sofa toward the front (Fig. 4-15).

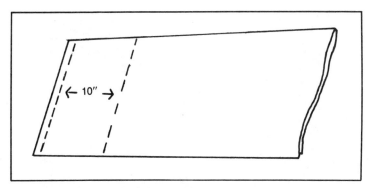

Fig. 4-12. The pocket is 10 inches long.

Nylon strips are wrapped around springs at each clamp and stapled to the seat rail of this sofa (Fig. 4-16). This reestablishes the original position and shape of the spring seat. Note the convenient position of the sofa in Fig. 4-17. It doesn't make sense to bend and strain yourself for this work. Position the piece where you can get to it easily.

Webbing is another important facet of furniture repair. It most often happens in reupholstery that new webbing is not necessary. It is often advisable to reinforce the old webbing by applying new strips as the upholsterer is doing in Fig. 4-18. He is not using a webbing stretcher. These stretchers are very convenient at times, but be careful that you do not stretch the webbing too tight. It is possible to exert too much pressure on fragile rails, causing them to break. The upholsterer in Fig. 4-18 finds that he can comfortably

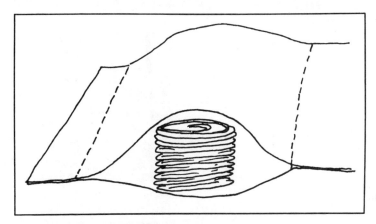

Fig. 4-13. Put the compressed spring in sideways.

Fig. 4-14. Spring clamp.

exert just the right amount of pressure on the webbing by hand, thus avoiding stretching it too tightly.

If new webbing needs to be installed, turn the piece of furniture upside down. Remove the dust cover and all the old webbing. Tack and staple the new webbing securely to the frame. Fold the end of the webbing over as shown in Fig. 4-19. If you use tacks, stagger them so you will not split the seat rail (Fig. 4-20).

Stretch the webbing firmly into the right position on the opposite side of the frame, and tack or staple it three or four times. Fold the end over and tack or staple again, and then cut it loose.

Continue installing webbing strips in this manner, spacing the strips evenly and applying equal pressure in stretching each strip. Interweave the webbing if there is sufficient room to work (Fig. 4-21). When all the necessary webbing is installed, turn the chair

Fig. 4-15. Tie from back to front.

Fig. 4-16. Straps hold the spring edge straight.

Fig. 4-17. Work at a comfortable height.

right side up and continue with the upholstery. Individual springs must be sewn to the webbing (Fig. 4-22).

REPLACING INDIVIDUAL PARTS

Before discussing specifically how to replace single pieces of the upholstery pattern, some comment must be given regarding fabrics. Should you wish to do any of the partial upholstery projects to be considered here, it will be most helpful if you can obtain fabric like that already on the piece of furniture. This is quite possible, though not certain.

Assuming that you will be working on a chair, you might turn the chair upside down and find a small scrap of upholstery fabric that can be safely cut off to take when you shop. If you cannot find an area to snip off for matching, remove the damaged piece according to directions soon to follow.

Visit any shops in your area that stock upholstery fabrics to see whether the fabric can be matched this simply. Actually the odds aren't too much in your favor, but since this is the simplest approach, it's a logical first step.

Should you fail to find an exact match in fabric shops, your next stop should be an upholstery shop. Most shops have a very wide sample selection. You may be able to find and order exactly what you need.

You might never find the exact match to repair your chair. The next approach will be to find the same kind of fabric in a color that

Fig. 4-18. Reinforced webbing.

matches or contrasts with your original fabric. The objective is for the chair, once repaired, to look natural—as though it has been made that way. It is usually not as difficult to match vinyl as to match other woven fabrics, but even with vinyl the contrast can be employed well. You simply must select what best fits on the chair itself and with surrounding furnishings.

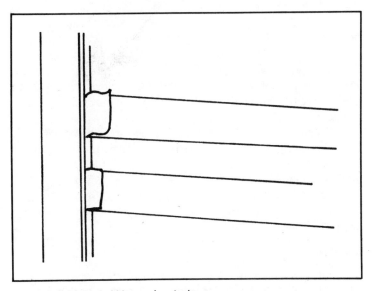

Fig. 4-19. Fold the webbing and restaple.

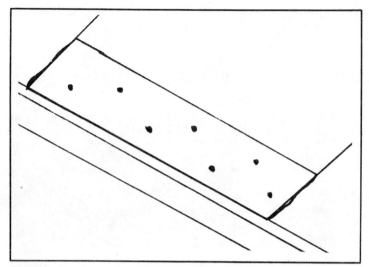

Fig. 4-20. Stagger tacks.

Cushions

If the damaged area on your chair or sofa is a cushion, you will need to refer to Chapter 7. Either make completely new covers for the cushion(s) or replace one part, as is needed and fabric is available.

If only one side of the cushion is to be replaced, do so as follows, after reading Chapter 7 to obtain a clear overall concept of how cushions are put together. Remove the cover fabric from the cushion. Examine it to learn how to best remove the damaged part. In a conventional rectangular cushion with a zipper in the boxing, you can simply use a seam ripper or a sharp knife to rip the seams and remove the damaged part. Turn the cover wrong side out and rip the seams.

Use the piece you removed as a pattern for the new piece. If the new fabric is right side up, be sure to place the pattern right side up as well. Determine the direction of the grain in the original piece, and place the pattern on the same grain on the new fabric.

Once your new piece is cut, simply sew it back into the cover as it was. Turn the cover right side out again, insert the cushion, and you're finished.

Arm Covers

There are many different styles in chair arms, but not as much difference as you might expect when it comes to removing a part of

Fig. 4-21. Interweave webbing strips.

73

Fig. 4-22. Sew the springs to the webbing.

the cover. This does not apply to every single style; yet there are more similarities than differences.

Consider the two arm styles in Fig. 4-23. They are quite different; yet the cover fabric is installed in approximately the same manner on both. Your chair may be different in some ways, but the basic steps of dismantling and reassembly will be the same as those which follow. By following these steps, you will be able to perceive any differences that might exist and make adjustments in the work as you proceed.

Feel carefully each seam that must be taken apart to determine how it is secured—whether with tacks, staples, or stitches. Determine before you remove any piece how you will replace it. If there is sufficient solid material beneath the seams, you will be able to use either staples or tacks. There will nearly always be wood beneath the seams; rarely will an arm piece need to be sewn.

The outer arm cover (A in Fig. 4-24) will have been attached after the inner cover. Pull the tacks or staples to pull part A away as in Fig. 4-25.

Go to the back of the chair. Pull the tacks or staples along line B in Fig. 4-26. It will not be necessary to remove this back panel completely. Even if you are replacing both inner arm covers, you'll usually only need to remove the back far enough to get under it to work.

The only place remaining where you might have to remove a good piece of the cover is on the front panel of the chair arm. This will depend upon which piece was installed last—probably the front panel. If so, you'll need to undo it as well.

Before continuing, you should consider the possibility of a front panel like Fig. 4-27. The wood (or cloth) trim was installed last. If wood trim, it may have plugs in it that conceal screws. These plugs can be removed, but if they are glued, take care not to damage the wood. If anything must be damaged, let it be the plug. You can

Fig. 4-23. Different arm styles are similarly upholstered.

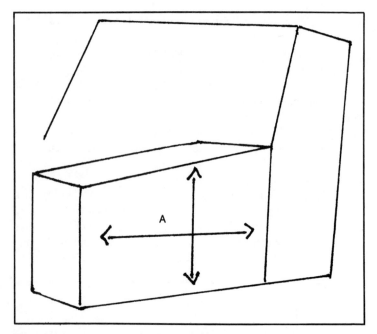

Fig. 4-24. The outer arm cover is attached last.

get new plugs and stain them to match. such trim can be removed. It can be replaced just as it was, after you've installed the new arm cover.

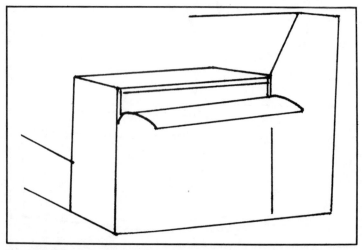

Fig. 4-25. Take the outer arm cover off.

76

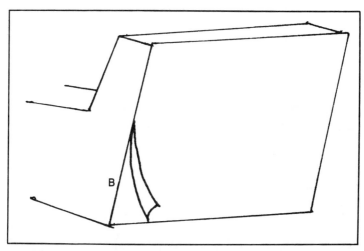

Fig. 4-26. Pull staples from the back panel.

Now you are ready to remove the damaged cover. It will have been stapled or tacked at the points indicated by arrows in Fig. 4-28. Work carefully and deliberately to remove all staples or tacks. Then take the cover off, being careful to leave all stuffing material in place.

Straighten the damaged fabric, and use it as a pattern to cut a new piece. Remember to cut it on the same grain, and with the right sides of both the pattern and the new fabric up.

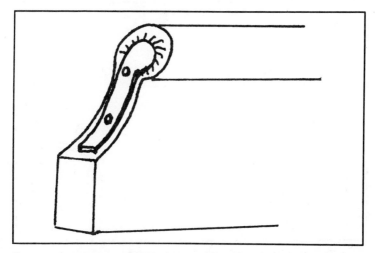

Fig. 4-27. The trim must be removed on this style.

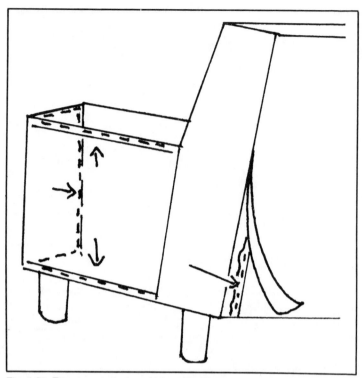

Fig. 4-28. The cover is fastened at arrow points.

SLASH
TO FIT AROUND POST

Fig. 4-29. Don't slash the fabric until you are fitting it.

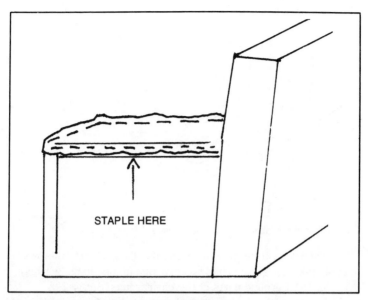

Fig. 4-30. Staple along the top of the outer arm.

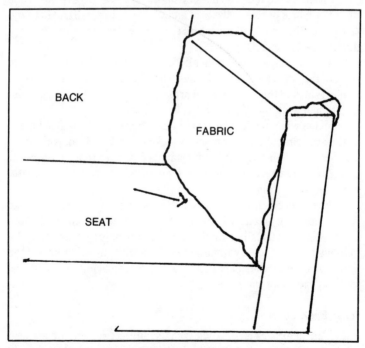

Fig. 4-31. Push the fabric between the arm and seat.

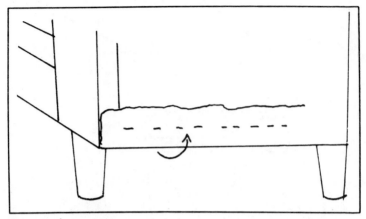

Fig. 4-32. Pull the fabric through and staple it.

When you cut the new piece, cut only the *shape*. In other words, do not make any slashes like you may find in the old piece where it was cut to fit around parts of the chair frame (Fig. 4-29).

When the new piece is cut, place it on the chair arm as the old piece was. Staple it on the outside of the arm first (Fig. 4-30). Then stuff the fabric between the arm and the seat (Fig. 4-31). Go to the outside of the arm, pull the fabric through and over the bottom rail, and staple it there (Fig. 4-32).

You may have some difficulty in fitting the fabric on the inside back of the arm (Fig. 4-33). This is where you will probably have to make a slash in the fabric to fit it around the back leg or post. It must be stapled at points A, B, and C in Fig. 4-34.

When you have it secured at these points, go to the front panel of the arm. Staple the new piece as in A or B in Fig. 4-35, whichever applies with your chair. All that remains now is to replace the outer arm cover, reattach the chair back cover where you took it loose, and finish the front arm panel attractively.

In the preceding instructions, it is clear how you would go about replacing an outer back cover or an outer arm cover. In both cases these are usually simple rectangular panels that can easily be removed and replaced without interfering with any other part of the chair. The only other part that might need replacing in the typical chair is the inner back cover.

Inner Back Cover

The inner back chair cover isn't usually as tricky to replace as it appears. The back cover, though it may be in several pieces, is

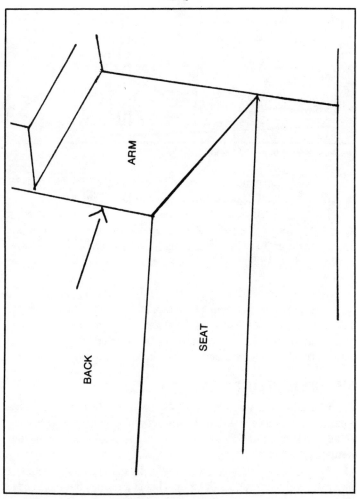

Fig. 4-33. The fabric must be cut to fit around the back post.

BACK

ARM

SEAT

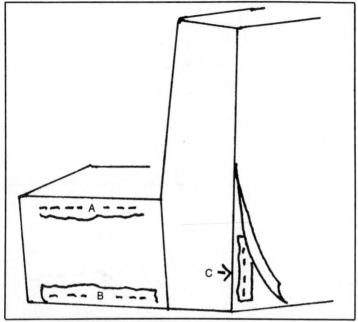

Fig. 4-34. Staple at the points indicated.

basically a wraparound as indicated by the broken line in Fig. 4-36. It will be attached at points A, B, C, and D in Fig. 4-37.

Begin by feeling carefully all seams and determining whether any specialized problems exist. On the chair in Fig. 4-38, you would find it necessary to remove the gimp (decorative trim that conceals staples) at line A. Then pull the staples or tacks holding the cover fabric.

Remove the back panel as previously described. You will find the inner back cover attached as either A or B in Fig. 4-39. Simply pull tacks or staples and take the damaged cover off. Use it as a pattern to cut a new piece, install it as the original was, replace the back cover and the trim, and you're finished.

GIMP AND DECORATIVE TACKS

If you find that some of the new seams in the furniture you have repaired are not as attractive as they should be, you have two ways to solve the dilemma. First, you can do the seams again, making them stronger and more pleasing to see.

Another possibility exists. Any shop that stocks upholstery materials will have spools of gimp. This is a pretty, but not gaudy,

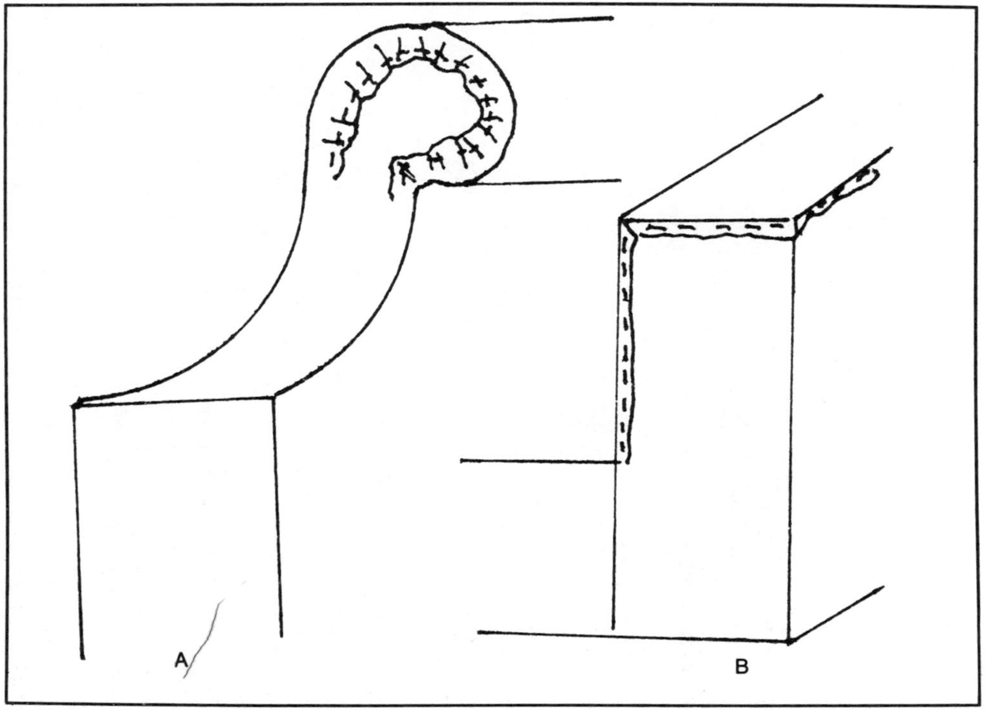

Fig. 4-35. Staple neatly along the front panel.

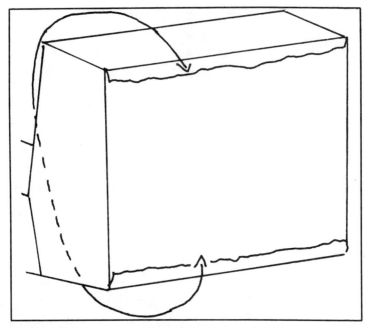

Fig. 4-36. The back cover is a wraparound.

narrow woven trim. It is available in several colors. Gimp is used to highlight the upholstery and to conceal the seams.

Gimp can be glued over the seams with white glue or hot glue. In addition, you can buy decorative upholstery tacks. Space these evenly along the gimp if you choose to use them. They are attractive if used tastefully, and they will also strengthen the seam and secure the gimp.

PREVENTING OR CONCEALING WEAR

The time to begin thinking of ways to protect new furniture from undue wear is when you buy it. It is certainly difficult to put covers over a brand new chair. You want to be able to see and enjoy the new chair.

You can expect the arms, the inner back, and the forepart of the seat to begin showing the effects of soil and wear before too long. There is a way to cover these parts rather unobtrusively. Then the covers can be removed for a time on appropriate occasions.

These covers are also used to conceal wear or damage and to prevent further damage. By using covers, I have been able to postpone upholstery until it was more convenient to do it.

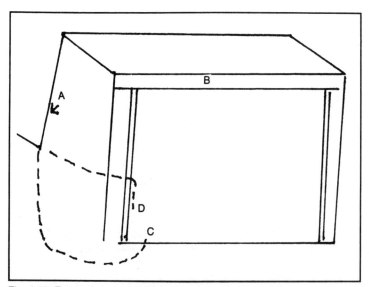

Fig. 4-37. The back cover is attached at the points indicated.

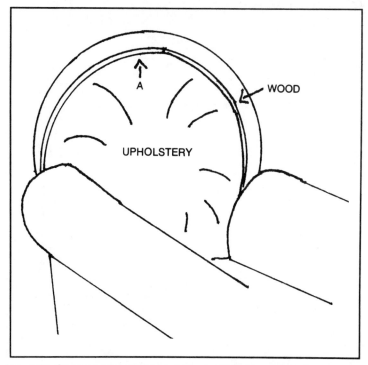

Fig. 4-38. On chairs with wood trim, gimp must often be removed.

85

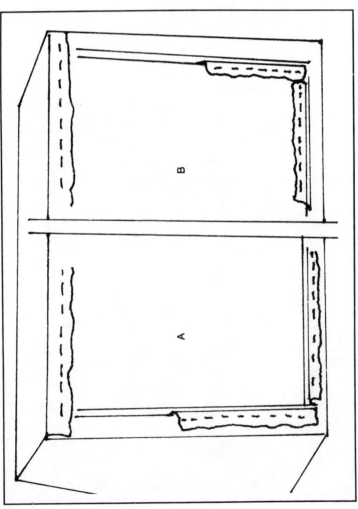

Fig. 4-39. The back cover will be attached in one of these ways.

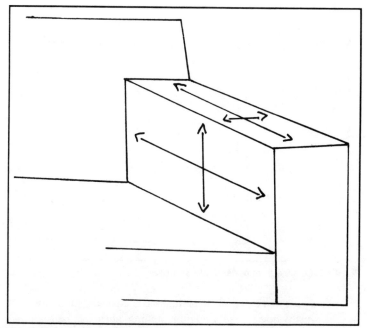

Fig. 4-40. Measure the chair arm.

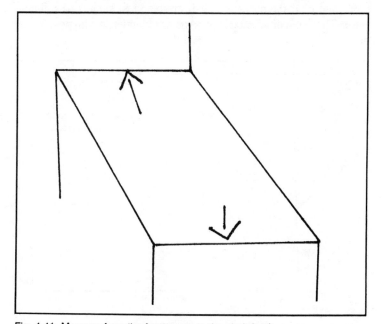

Fig. 4-41. Measure from the front seam to the chair back.

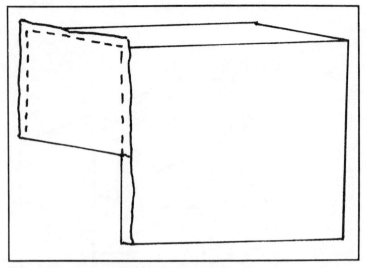

Fig. 4-42. Sew the front panel to the arm cover.

You will need extra fabric of the kind used on the furniture. It is always worthwhile to see if some matching fabric can be obtained before buying the furniture. You can make neat fitting covers of the same fabric for the parts of a chair or sofa most subject to soil and wear. These covers can be slipped off and laundered with no trouble at all.

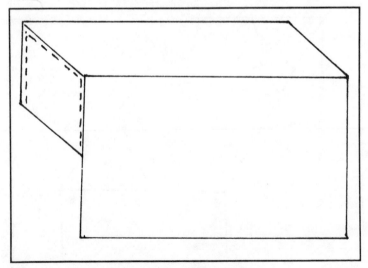

Fig. 4-43. Topstitching keeps the cover trim looking.

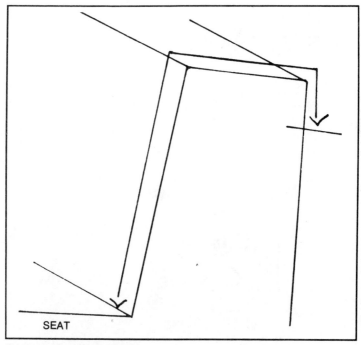

Fig. 4-44. Measure the back.

Begin by measuring the chair arm as indicated in Fig. 4-40. Then measure the front panel of the arm as well. When you measure along the top of the arm, measure from the front seam to the chair back (Fig . 4-41). Add 1 inch for a hem at the back and ¾ inch for a

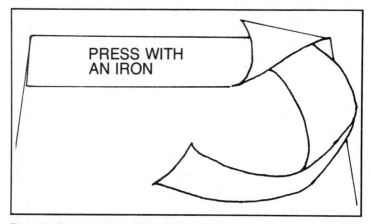

Fig. 4-45. Stitch witchery makes a neat, smooth hem.

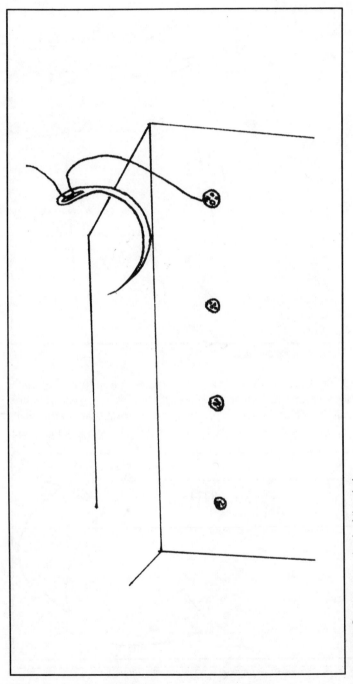

Fig. 4-46. Sew snaps on back of the chair.

seam allowance at the front. Now add 2 inches more, so you will be able to tuck the cover snugly between the arm and the back. Add ¾ inch all the way around the front panel.

It has been my experience to receive arm covers with a new chair. They were only about 12 inches long and fell off every time someone sat in the chair. With a cover long enough to tuck in, the cover will stay in place and hardly be noticed.

Sew the front panel to the arm cover as in Fig. 4-42. Clip the corners to prevent bunching and topstitch if you like (Fig. 4-43). Hem the raw edges all the way around. Put the cover over the arm. Tuck the excess length between the arm and seat, and the covers will remain neatly in place.

A temporary cover for the inner back of a chair is usually very simple. Measure the back as indicated in Fig. 4-44. Then add 6 inches for a tuck-in between the seat and back. Cut the fabric by these measurements, allowing ¾ inch all the way around for a hem.

If the chair will ordinarily be placed near a wall, the simplest way to attach the cover is with snaps.Hem the cover on all sides.To avoid bulkiness, it is a good idea to hem with a hot iron and a hem

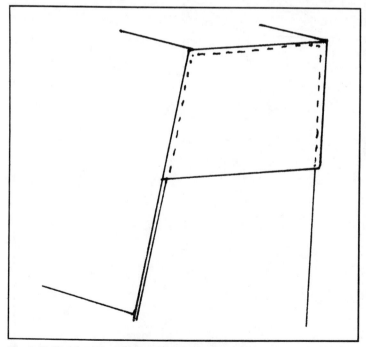

Fig. 4-47. Sew boxing at each side of the back cover.

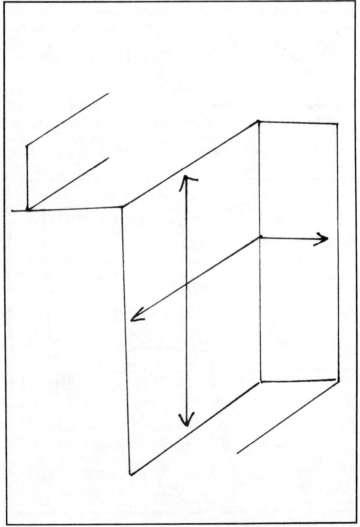

Fig. 4-48. Measure the seat.

tape called *stitch witchery* (Fig. 4-45). This iron-on material is available at most fabric shops.

Use a curved needle to sew four snaps on the chair back (Fig. 4-46). Sew matching snaps along the inner end of the cover.

Simply snap the cover at the back of the chair, smooth it over the inner back, and tuck the excess length between the back and seat. Replace the chair cushion, and the cover is complete and pleasing.

If for some reason you do not want to sew snaps on the chair, the cover can easily be made in another way. The long part of the

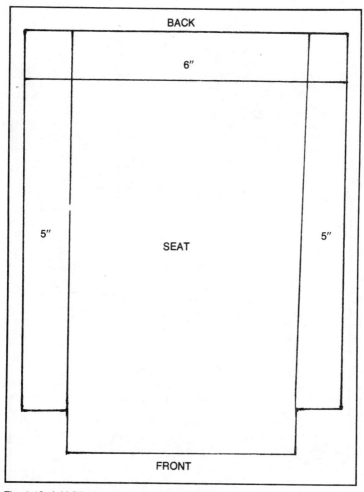

Fig. 4-49. Add 6 inches to the length and 5 inches to each side.

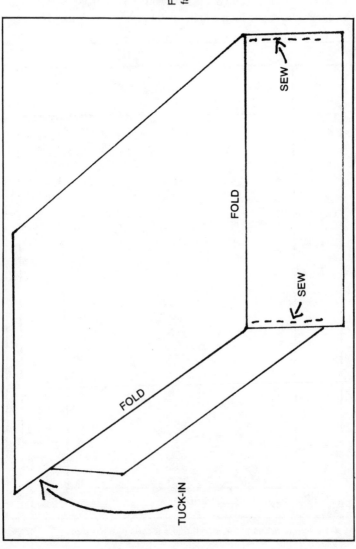

Fig. 4-50. Fold and sew the fabric to fit.

94

cover is made just as previously discussed, but a small piece of boxing is sewn at either side as shown in Fig. 4-47. Hem all raw edges, and fit the cover over the chair back.

For a seat cover on a chair without a removable cushion, measure the seat as in Fig. 4-48. Add 6 inches to the length for a tuck-in between seat and back, and add 5 inches to each side (Fig. 4-49).

Carefully cut the pattern. When cut, it will look like Fig. 4-49. At the front, fold and sew the fabric as in Fig. 4-50. Simply hem all raw edges. Fit the cover over the front part of the seat. Then tuck the excess length and width between the seat and arms, and the seat and back. You have a very neat seat cover that will stay where you put it.

REPAIRING VINYL

There are several upholstery materials which I will refer to in general as *vinyl*. When vinyl tears or is cut or burned, it would seem to be irreparable. Usually it can be repaired quite neatly. The only serious qualification here is that sometimes when vinyl is quite old or has become brittle, the repair does not work as well.

At fabric shops you can buy a gluelike material in a small tube. Directions for use appear on the package. The material itself is a neutral color. Any color of vinyl can be repaired with it.

If a tear, cut, or burn is reasonably small, the repair will work very well and look nice. Some reinforcement is necessary on more extensive damage. Before considering a total reupholstery project on your damaged vinyl furniture, try this easy repair.

Padding Furniture

Which step in furniture upholstery is most important? As in any such endeavor, the success of one phase rests upon the excellence of another; therefore, each step should be accomplished with equal care. If necessary frame repairs aren't done, the upholstery is so much useless work, for a chair that will not support any weight is not functional even though it may look fantastic. If springs aren't tied, sewed to webbing, or stapled to wood and appropriately padded, the seat will be uncomfortable and unattractive.

Padding or stuffing a piece is a critical step, though not a difficult one. Padding must be sufficiently deep and of suitable materials to make comfortable furniture. Padding must be evenly and smoothly distributed if the final cover is to fit attractively and maintain its shape. You must not expect to complete a project within too rigid a time schedule. If you hurry, you may not do a good job. The first few attempts should actually be approached in a leisurely fashion.

The first step is to evaluate the piece of furniture. Look it over carefully, end to end and side to side. Determine whether any frame repairs are necessary. Are there loose joints to be reglued, and will you be able to retain the old finish on the wood? Is the webbing good enough, or must it be replaced or reinforced? Think the project through carefully.

REMOVING THE OLD UPHOLSTERY

When you have the time, place, and opportunity to begin, check to see whether you have all the things you are likely to need. You'll want a tack and staple puller, and perhaps a pair of diagonal pliers to remove tacks without heads. Chalk is necessary to identify the pieces of the cover, and you will also want a marking pen.

The cover fabrics will be removed first. Resist the temptation to rip them off and discard them. Remove all tacks and staples. Don't leave any of these; they will only get in your way later. Be careful about pulling tacks and staples, and don't damage the wood. If you have to pry some of these loose, put something between your tool and the wood so you won't gouge or dent it. Discard all the staples and tacks.

Remove each piece of cover fabric carefully, and identify it with the chalk or marking pen such as "right inner arm," "outer back," and so forth. Smooth these pieces out, fold them, and put them away for future use.

While you are removing the fabric, pay particular attention to the way each piece was cut and installed. Note in particular how the pieces were fitted around difficult places like legs, wings, and other potential problem areas. If you are removing original upholstery, it is likely that it was a careful, professional job. You can learn much in this process of disassembly about ways to solve problems. Make notes or draw rough sketches as you work. You will seldom see two pieces that have been handled in just the same way, so it is good to be a thoughtful observer throughout this step.

Return briefly to Fig. 4-1. I use this particular sofa through most of the steps in reupholstery. The cover has been partially removed, so you can readily see that the back and arms are in very good shape. This is a Victorian sofa. Since the padding on the back and arms has remained firm and nicely shaped for 100 years or longer, there is no reason to think it will not remain so for awhile.

There is simply no point in moving good padding if you don't have to. The padding has attained a good shape, and it is not likely that you could improve upon it by starting from scratch. Use the padding as it is when you can do so.

If it is necessary to remove padding, do so carefully. Even though parts may need to be replaced, you can often use a lot of the old padding. This is not advice for the beginner only; professional upholsterers reuse any material that is still good. It's practical.

Beneath the outer cover fabric, you will often find a cover of muslin. If the muslin is still good, you may be able to reuse it as well, but it may have to be discarded after new pieces have been cut. Remove and label any such muslin covers just as you did the cover fabric.

Fig. 5-1. Victorian sofa with burlap covering the springs.

Seats are the parts usually needing most repair. You may have to remove everything down to the springs and do spring repairs. The burlap covering the springs may be pretty rotten; discard it. You won't usually need a pattern.

VICTORIAN SOFA

Spring repairs have been completed on the sofa in Fig. 5-1. The legs have been removed for refinishing. The next step is also done. Springs must be covered with a sheet of burlap or some similar material. This prevents parts of the stuffing from falling into the springs.

The burlap is spread over the springs, and pushed between the seat and back, to be stapled along the back rail as shown in Fig. 5-2. Place staples or tacks sufficiently close together to hold the burlap well when it is pulled tight to be stapled along the front rail. Notice that the burlap has been turned at the edge and stapled to prevent raveling.

At the ends of the sofa, the burlap is pushed through between seat and arm and is tacked or stapled to the rail. The material should be stretched taut, but not so tight that it is in danger of ripping loose when someone sits upon the sofa (Fig. 5-3).

The next step in the upholstery of this sofa is the installation of an *edge roll*. The edge roll is sewn along the edge of the springs (Fig. 5-4).

Edge rolls serve several purposes. Where upholstery fabrics must be stretched over an angular area, they wear out at that point very quickly. The edge roll makes a padded corner instead, thus preventing the fabric from wearing badly.

This sofa will have three cushions in the seat. The edge roll raises the edge of the seat slightly, enough to keep the cushions from sliding onto the floor at a little provocation. Edge rolls add to the comfort of the persons using the furniture by eliminating hard corners.

Edge rolls are not exactly difficult to make, but some practice is required to make them of uniform density and dimension. They may be made of rolled burlap, rolled paper, or loose fillings such as *excelsior* stuffed in a casing strip. It is simple and convenient to buy commercially made edge rolls. They can be bought in different thicknesses, are uniformly shaped, and are very neat and easy to work with.

The edge roll is most quickly and effectively stitched to the sofa or chair (Fig. 5-5). The stitch is simple and holds the roll in place well. Use a curved needle and heavy, dependable thread to sew the edge roll in place.

When the edge roll is stitched all along the sofa spring edge, it should be prevented from rolling forward or backward. This is accomplished with another stitch, sewing through the flange to the burlap as the upholsterer is doing in Fig. 5-6. Thus, the edge roll is held securely from turning or rolling.

The next step involves work with the final upholstery fabric to some extent. It must be done before further padding of the seat can be accomplished. Look carefully at Fig. 5-7. This shows quite clearly how the upholstery fabric was cut and sewn to some less expensive material, and how the corner was formed to fit. I return to this later, but it is necessary to understand what this part of the

Fig. 5-2. Staple the burlap to the rail.

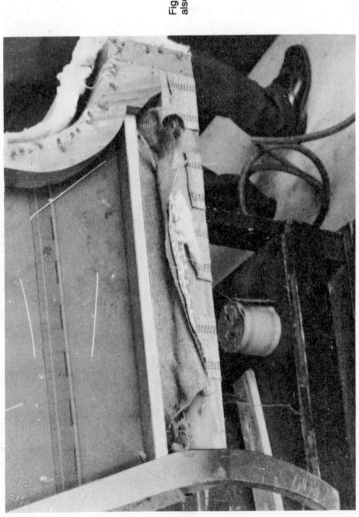

Fig. 5-3. At the ends, the burlap is also stapled to the rail.

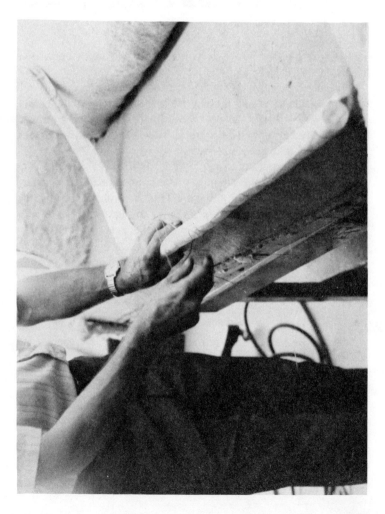

Fig. 5-4. Sew the edge roll over the spring edge.

101

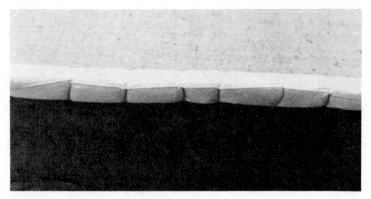

Fig. 5-5. Sew around the edge roll.

cover looks like and how it is constructed if the next step is to be clear.

Figure 5-8 shows the upholsterer fitting this cover in place. It will not remain there at this point. He is trying it for fit only. Notice that the dark fabric is sewn to the upholstery fabric in a straight seam. The reason is to save material. The dark area will be covered by cushions, so it need not be done in cover fabric.

With the corners of this new piece still in place, fold this dark material (known as *pull strips, stretchers,* or *extensions*) backward until the seam is revealed. Align this seam neatly, and sew it to the burlap cover as the upholsterer is doing in Fig. 5-9.

This step is necessary to help hold the padding of the seat in place and to maintain a neat and attractive spring edge. This will be more evident as you study the following information and photographs. The stretcher and cover seam are sewn to the burlap all the way across (Fig. 5-10).

Measure the seat. Cut a piece of springy padding and lay it over the burlap, tucking it under the back upholstery (Fig. 5-11). This padding can be sisal, rubberized hair, or other kinds. It is easiest and most suitable to use a kind of slab padding when padding a seat or other straight place. When you are padding a curved surface, however, you may find it more desirable to use some of the loose fiber stuffing materials such as hair, moss, sisal, or excelsior. These loose materials can be built up to whatever shape the piece requires. Many professional upholsterers now use more foam and cotton stuffing or padding than any other kind, but even these are more comfortable if they are installed over a layer of resilient, springy padding.

Fig. 5-6. The flange of the edge roll is sewn to the burlap.

When the slab resilient padding is in place, the upholsterer in Fig. 5-12 places a thick layer of felted cotton padding over it. He fits the cotton over the seat, with the front edge butting against the edge roll installed earlier. Instead of cutting the cotton with scissors, it is better to tear it apart by hand (Fig. 5-13). This makes a thinner, softer edge.

Once the felted cotton is torn to fit, tuck it neatly in at both ends and under the back upholstery (Fig. 5-14). See that the cotton lays smoothly, and that there are no lumps or thin spots.

Fig. 5-7. The cover fabric is sewn to fit corners.

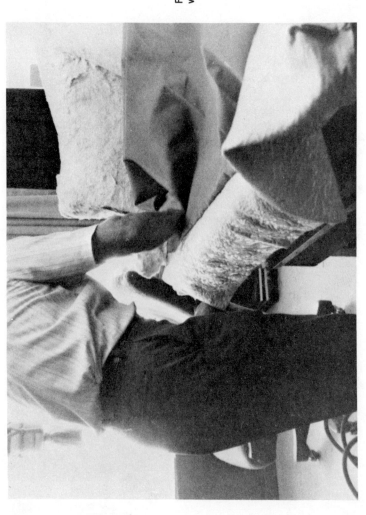

Fig. 5-8. Check to see that the cover will fit.

With all the padding in place, neat and smooth, raise the stretcher (dark fabric here) that has been hanging in front of the sofa (Fig. 5-15). Place this material neatly over the cotton padding, tucking it beneath the back and arm upholstery.

Fig. 5-9. Sew the seam allowance to the burlap.

Pull this stretcher through. Staple it to the rails as was shown with the burlap in Fig. 5-2. With the stretcher firmly stretched and stapled, place a layer of cotton over the edge roll. Pull the upholstery fabric back over it (Fig. 5-16), preparing to staple it in place. This will be further illustrated in Chapter 6.

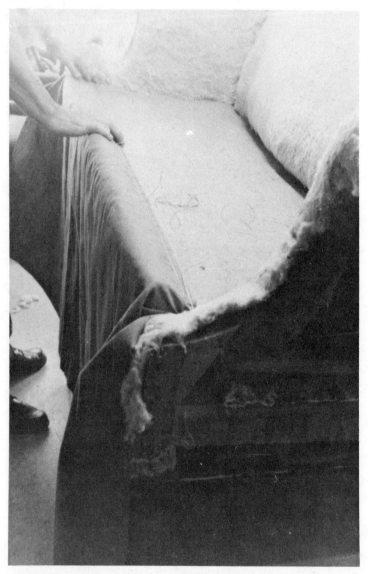

Fig. 5-10. The stretcher and cover seam are finished.

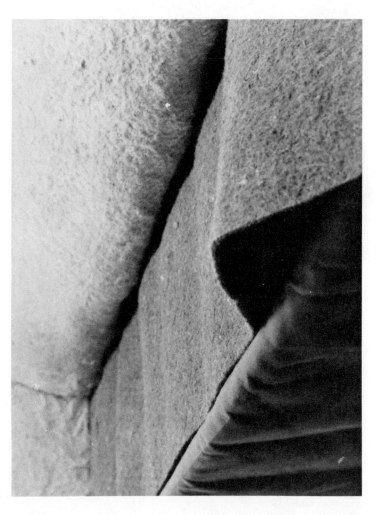

Fig. 5-11. Resilient padding over burlap.

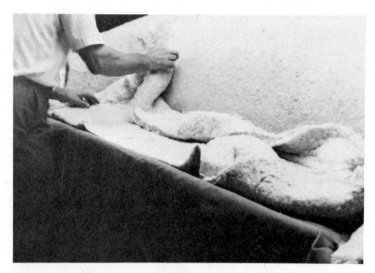

Fig. 5-12. Cotton felt over resilient padding.

ARMCHAIR

With the old upholstery fabric removed, the chair in Fig. 5-17 looks pretty bad, but it isn't bad at all. Most of the padding is still in pretty good shape. The springs are setting loose on a plywood

Fig. 5-13. Tear the cotton by hand.

Fig. 5-14. Tuck the cotton under the arm and back upholstery.

Fig. 5-15. Cover the cotton with the extension.

Fig. 5-16. A layer of cotton further softens the edge.

insert that was used to add strength to the chair frame. This upholsterer, working at home, eventually decided to pad the seat with layers of high density and medium density foam, and then with a layer of soft cotton batting. The springs were not replaced at all, and the completed chair is quite comfortable.

The padding on the chair back is in good shape. The upholsterer in Fig. 5-18 puts a few staples through a part of the padding and into the frame to help secure it as the work progresses.

The padding on the arms is also better secured with staples where it seems a bit loose (Fig. 5-19). The chair back is then covered. This process is further illustrated in Chapter 6. It is not really essential to cover the back before the arms and other padding are done.

With the original resilient fiber stuffing stapled in place, a layer of soft cotton batting is spread over the arm (Fig. 5-20). Again, this upholsterer tears the cotton rather than cutting it to create a soft edge (Fig. 5-21).

This final layer of padding is covered with a piece of muslin (Fig. 5-22). The muslin not only helps to hold the padding in place, but it also makes the fitting of the cover fabric more convenient and attractive.

The muslin is stapled under the curve of the armrest and is then smoothed in place. It is pushed between the arm and back upholstery. Then it is stretched over the arm and under to be temporarily stapled to the frame (Fig. 5-23). After the final cover fabric is installed and stapled to the bottom rail, the muslin will be stapled to the rail. The temporary stapling holds everything in place while other steps are completed.

In Fig. 5-24 a layer of cotton is placed over the other arm. The muslin cover is stapled under the curve of the arm and stretched over the padding (Fig. 5-25). It is stapled to the frame as was done on the first arm (Fig. 5-26).

Parts still requiring padding are the seat, the back, and the outside of both arms, beneath the curve. The back of this chair is webbed. The webbing is in good condition, requiring only a couple of staples. Some padding is needed between the webbing and the final cover. Cut a piece of ordinary cardboard to fit the opening in the frame, and staple it in place. (Fig. 5-27). Spread a sheet of soft cotton over the cardboard, and cut it to the same size (Figs. 5-28 and 5-29). With the cotton batting cut to fit over the cardboard, spray adhesive is used to hold the cotton to the cardboard. The back of the

Fig. 5-17. Armchair with the old upholstery fabric removed.

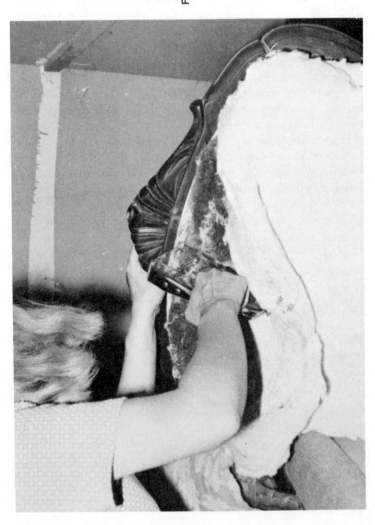

Fig. 5-18. Reinforce the padding.

chair is ready for the final cover. The resulting job is very neat and attractive.

The area under the curve of each arm is padded in the same way, with a sheet of cardboard cut and stapled in place. A sheet of cotton batting is glued to it, and then the final cover is installed.

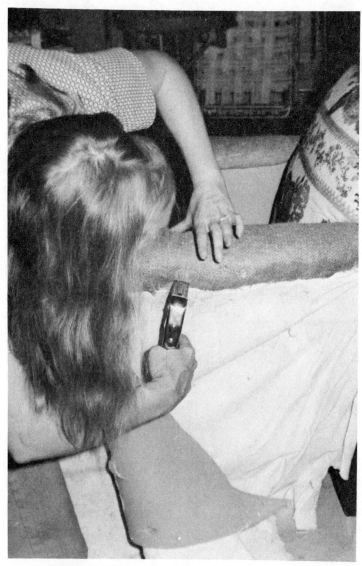

Fig. 5-19. Secure loose places with staples.

Fig. 5-20. Soft cotton covers the arm padding.

The seat in this chair originally had springs. The upholsterer, after talking with automobile upholsterers about the success of their solid foam seats, decided to discard the springs. The seat was padded as follows.

First, the upholsterer places a thick layer of high density foam directly over the plywood insert, after four holes are drilled in it for an air escape. The foam is attached to the plywood insert with spray

Fig. 5-21. Tear the cotton.

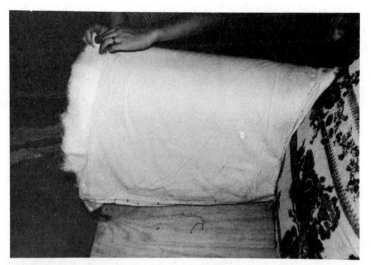

Fig. 5-22. The padding is covered with muslin.

adhesive. A second layer of medium density foam is then secured on top of the first layer, and then comes a thin layer of very soft foam. Finally, a narrow, wedge-shaped edge roll of foam is secured to the top edge. The seat is ready to be covered. The seat, before covering, looked like Fig. 5-30.

This chair has a cushion. The cushion will be discussed along with final covers in Chapter 6.

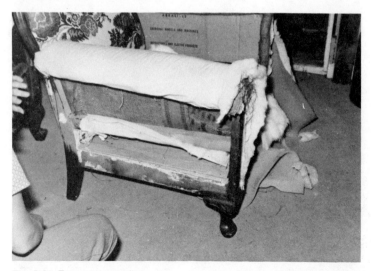

Fig. 5-23. Temporary stapling.

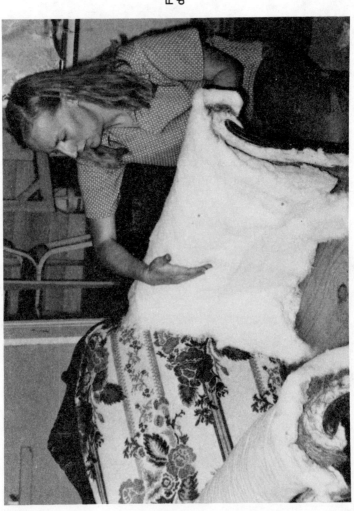

Fig. 5-24. Cotton over springy padding.

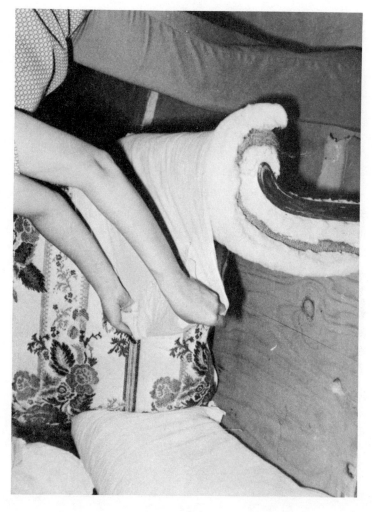

Fig. 5-25. Muslin cover.

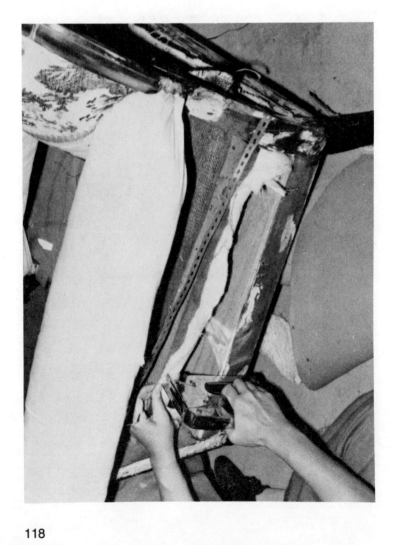

Fig. 5-26. Temporary staples.

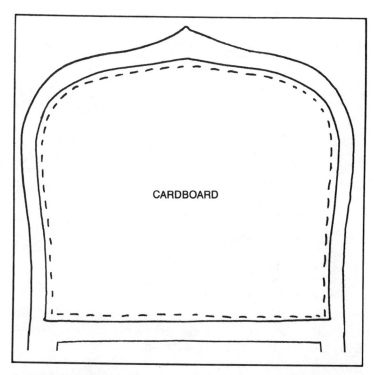

CARDBOARD

Fig. 5-27. Cardboard insert.

Fig. 5-28. Cotton glued to cardboard insert.

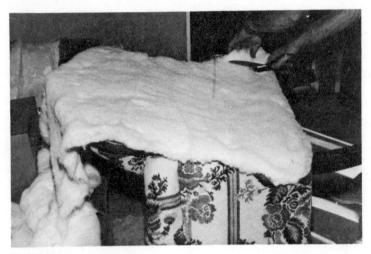

Fig. 5-29. Trim the cotton.

SPRING CHAIR SEAT

Some of the nicest small chairs, whether recent or antique, are those with spring seats and a back panel with some kind of padding and upholstery. The one that is shown and discussed here is completed through the final cover stage in the following chapter.

Begin by removing the dust cover to check on the condition of the webbing. Remove it by releasing the tension on the springs, if necessary.

On a chair such as this you should find, beneath the cover fabric, a sheet of muslin, some padding, a sheet of burlap, an edge roll, and the springs and webbing. Remove all these, being very careful not to damage the wood as you pull tacks or staples. Pay close attention to the manner in which all these parts were originally installed. Keep whatever padding that may be good enough to use again. The springs should be good, but if they aren't, obtain new ones.

Begin by putting new webbing on as discussed in Chapter 4, and tie the springs in place. In this example the webbing and springs are left in place, being solid. Two new strips are added, however, for reinforcement (Fig. 5-31).

Lay a piece of burlap over the top of the tied springs, and tack or staple it in the center of one rail. Pull it snugly across. Staple it in the center of the opposite rail. Do the same with the other two rails. Then add more staples until the burlap is evenly stretched over the springs (Fig. 5-32).

Fold the edges of the burlap over toward the center and staple again. Then trim away any excess burlap. The tension on the springs should be evenly distributed if you have done this work properly.

Stitch the burlap to each of the springs. You will need to use a curved needle.

In order to retain a desirable shape in a spring seat like this, an edge roll is necessary. It is sewn around the spring edge to the burlap, or in some cases it is tacked to the seat rails. The edge roll reduces strain and wear where the cover fabric passes over spring edges and other angular areas. It adds to the overall appearance and comfort of the seat. The completed edge roll will look like that in Fig. 5-33.

You must put some kind of padding inside the edge roll. This can be the slab stuffing shown earlier in the sofa seat or some other kind. If the slab stuffing is used, stitch it to the edge roll all the way around (Fig. 5-34).

All that remains is to pad the rough spots with some soft material. Tear scraps of cotton batting to fill any low or rough spots. Place a couple of layers of soft cotton over the whole seat. Tear the cotton to shape by hand for a soft edge.

Finally, a muslin cover is put over the padding. Cut a piece of muslin a little bigger all the way around than you will actually need, and spread it over the seat. Tack or staple it in the center of the front rail, and then in the center of the back rail. Place tacks in the center of the side rails, applying equal tension in all directions. Don't stretch the muslin so tightly that it actually compresses the springs; pull it until it makes a neat, snug fit.

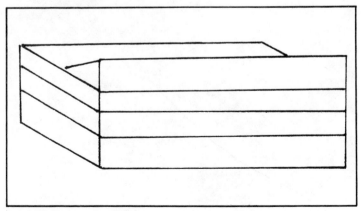

Fig. 5-30. Foam seat padding.

Fig. 5-31. Reinforced webbing.

Fig. 5-32. Staple burlap over the springs.

Begin at the center of the front rail, pulling the muslin and stapling. Work toward each side from the center. When you come to the corners, fold the muslin into a neat pleat (Fig. 5-35) and staple it.

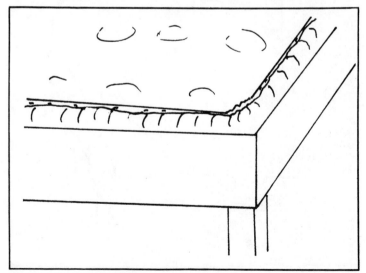

Fig. 5-33. Completed edge roll.

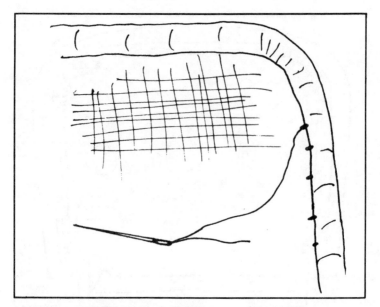

Fig. 5-34. Sew stuffing to the edge roll.

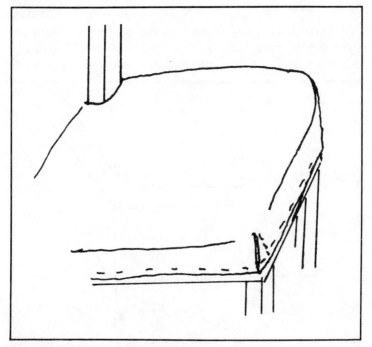

Fig. 5-35. Pleat muslin at the corners.

124

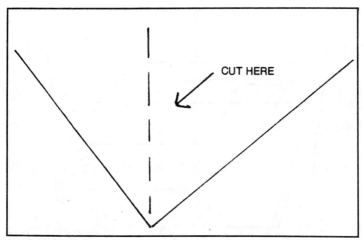

Fig. 5-36. Bias cut.

Staple the sides or the back next. Instead of corners, you will have to cut the muslin so it will slip between the padding and the chair back (leg). Don't cut this until you are ready to staple it. Cut deeply enough to fit the muslin neatly, but not so deeply that the cut will show. This is a single bias cut (Fig. 5-36). Fold the muslin under, and tack it close to the leg (Fig. 5-37).

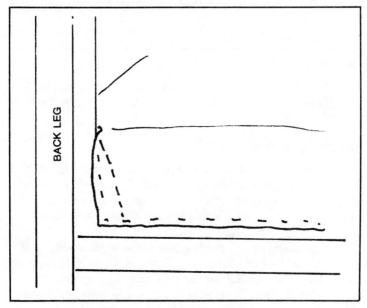

Fig. 5-37. Fold and staple muslin around the leg.

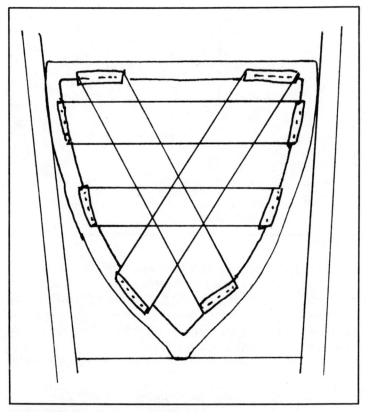

Fig. 5-38. Center opening is webbed.

This muslin cover completes the padding on the spring chair seat. If the seat is smooth and well shaped, it is ready for the final cover fabric to be discussed in the next chapter.

PADDED CHAIR BACKS

Sometimes a chair will have a wood panel back with a padded and upholstered area in the center. Usually this requires simply applying a neat layer of cotton over the area and covering it. The padded back is a wood frame that is actually open on the back when the padding is all removed.

In the center of this padding, staple the webbing (Fig. 5-38). Cover the webbing on both sides with burlap, stapling it inside the frame. Over the webbing on the back side, tear a thick layer of cotton felt to fit (Fig. 5-39). Smooth it to a nice, appropriate shape (Fig. 5-40). A sheet of muslin is stapled over this cotton.

126

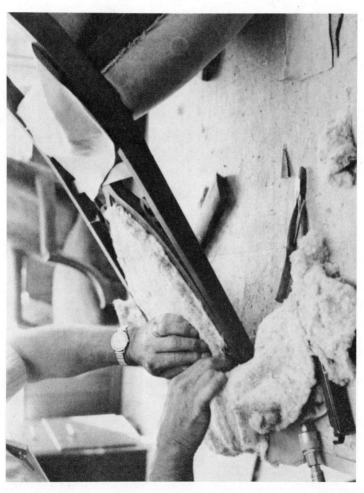

Fig. 5-39. Cotton felt over burlap.

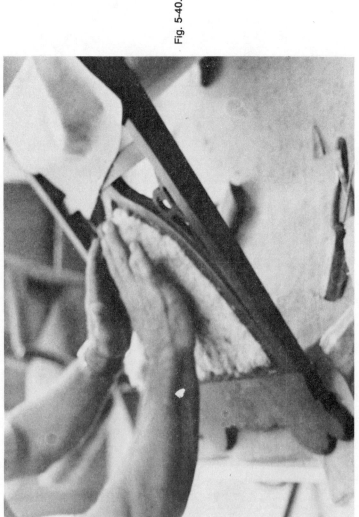

Fig. 5-40. Shape the cotton neatly.

Fig. 5-41. Wood is protected with foam scraps.

Turn the chair over and apply another layer of felted cotton and another muslin cover. Note in Fig. 5-41 that a scrap piece of foam padding is placed under the wood to protect the finish from scratches as the upholstery is completed.

DROP-IN PADDED SEAT

The padded seat in Fig. 5-42 has been removed from the chair shown in Fig. 4-2. The cover fabric shown in that photo has been

Fig. 5-42. Drop-in seat.

Fig. 5-43. Original fabric cover.

removed to reveal the original cover fabric, just about worn out (Fig. 5-43).

It was decided that this chair seat would remain as nearly original as possible. When the ragged cover was removed, the rest of the seat consisted of cotton padding lying on three very thin wood sheets (Fig. 5-44). Since these were still in good shape, everything was simply put back together and a new cover was added.

Fig. 5-44. Parts of the drop-in seat.

If the padding had been discarded, a sheet of resilient slab padding (hair, sisal) covered with a layer of felted cotton would have been a logical choice. A sheet of medium density foam over the slab padding would work equally well.

6

Covering Furniture

After the frame has any necessary repairs done and the finish is redone or touched up, the sofa, chair, or whatever is ready for the final cover to be installed over the padding. This is one of the most exciting moments in furniture upholstery, because at this point you can begin to see the results of your hours of labor.

The application of the final cover fabric can possibly be a little scary. It needn't be so, because at this point most of the steps should be fairly clear. You will already have done most of these things in the "dry run" of putting the muslin undercover on the piece.

The final cover must be applied with great care if the piece is to look as it should. There should be no lumpy places, no wrinkles, and no irregularities of any kind in the muslin undercover; there *must* be no irregularities in the final cover.

When you cover an antique, match the cover fabric as closely as you can to the original. If you have any doubts, go to the library and browse through books about period styles or antique furniture in particular. There you will find information about the kinds of fabrics used during the period, and comments if not photographs of some of the typical pieces. This will prove a valuable reference as you work toward selecting the appropriate colors and fabric types.

In this chapter I continue to follow the pieces begun in Chapter 5. Notice that the sequence or order of steps in covering furniture are variable to some extent. In places where one step must follow another in a specific arrangement, the reasons are evident in the illustrations. Study them carefully and pay attention to all the details, the methods of application, the way tools are handled, and so forth.

CUTTING THE FABRIC

When you cover a piece that still has the original cover, you will probably have a pretty good pattern to follow. This will not always hold true, since an old cover can be so worn out or ragged that it is difficult to know just what the shape should be. You can usually tell how to cut the new piece.

If the piece has already been reupholstered at some time, and this is often the case with old furniture, the pattern may or may not be difficult to establish, depending on the quality of the first reupholstery. The cover fabric that you remove is important, since it will help you in cutting new pieces. In many instances it isn't critical that you follow the old pattern exactly. Just be sure to cut the new pieces big enough.

In Fig. 6-1 the old cover is spread on the new fabric on a cutting table. Cutting lines have been marked on the new fabric with tailor's chalk. They are not even very close to being the same as the dimensions of the original piece. The original piece is pretty ragged, and the cutting lines will make a larger piece. The old piece is used as a general guide only.

The situation in Fig. 6-2 is quite different. It is clear here that the old piece has been used accurately as a pattern for the new. In some instances, particularly in other than squared pieces, it is important to follow the old pattern as accurately as you can.

The cutting and sewing process illustrated here apply to the Victorian sofa begun in Chapter 5. This sofa will have three cush-

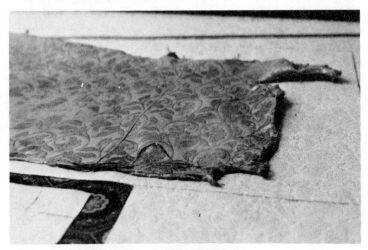

Fig. 6-1. The original fabric as a general guide.

ions in the seat, with welting around all the edges. There will also be welting on the arms, with one strip along the front skirt panel. In Fig. 6-3 welting strips have been marked with chalk and are being cut. It is convenient to prepare all such trim at once; simple measuring with a tape will quickly tell you how many feet or yards of welting or other trim you will need.

In Fig. 6-4 a wide stretcher or extension in the dark fabric is sewn to the cover fabric. Such an extension saves the expensive cover fabric. It may also be of a lighter weight, though not inferior in strength, and is sometimes easier to work with.

SOFA: SEAT COVER

Figure 6-5 illustrates the use of the wide extension. The seat is covered with this material, which will be covered by cushions when the sofa is completed. See the discussion and photographs in Chapter 5 for the way this piece is installed. This is one example of a situation where padding and installing a final cover are simultaneous in application.

When the extension is put on and the piece is connected according to the instructions in Chapter 5, the extension is pushed between the seat and back upholstery and between the seat and arm upholstery (Fig. 6-6). The extension is pulled through over the rail as shown in Fig. 6-7 and stapled to the rail. This extension must be pulled taut, but not so tightly that the fabric will tear when some weight is imposed on the sofa seat. Pull the extension through all along the back, returning to the front to check for a neat, correct fit before you begin stapling. When you begin stapling the stretcher to the rail, start in the center of the back, and work from the center toward each end. This will keep the fabric straight and in place as it should be. If you begin stapling at one end, no matter how careful you are to keep the fabric positioned properly, you will nearly always finish with a large error that will force you to remove all the staples and begin again.

The extension has been pulled through at the back and the ends in Fig. 6-8. At this point, make the cut that will permit the extension to fit neatly around the leg. You should never make the cut in advance. There is no practical way to measure for such a cut, so you simply wait until the work has reached the point where the cut must be made and then do it. Cut deeply enough to pull the extension properly around the leg, but not so deeply that the cut will show. These cuts, ideally, should be exactly the depth you need and no more. Since you are estimating, though, you will not always be able

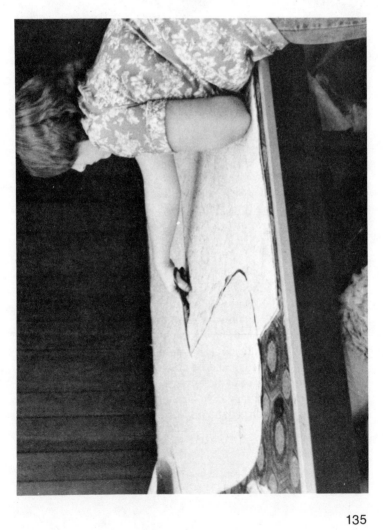

Fig. 6-2. The original fabric as a specific pattern.

Fig. 6-3. Cut welting strips of the same width.

to get them exactly right. Cut a little way, and then pull the fabric down. If you haven't cut far enough so that the fit on the inside corner of the seat is snug, pull it out and cut a little farther. Don't get impatient and start slashing.

With the extension stapled along the back and end rails, the fit over the seat padding is smooth and snug. The next step is evident. Pull the cover fabric down over the front panel in preparation for stapling it to the rail (Fig. 6-9). This is a particularly critical area where the final appearance is concerned. If you recall, this piece is pulled over an edge roll covered with a layer of felted cotton. The fit should be excellent.

Staple the fabric all along the front rail, beginning in the center and moving toward the ends. Only after the stapling is completed, with the fabric pulled taut with equal tension along the length, can you distinguish for certain whether there are any spots that aren't perfectly smooth. You may have to pull some of the staples, smooth some of the cotton padding, and staple the piece again.

This strip of fabric could be cut wide enough and pulled and stapled on the underside of the front rail. You may feel that it would be more attractive if this wide area is interrupted, so prepare a second strip with welting and install it as shown in Fig. 6-10.

SOFA: ARMS

The curved arms of this sofa are a bit tricky, but not so difficult if each phase of the project can be comprehended. First, the pattern

136

Fig. 6-4. Extension sewn to cover fabric.

is cut. The welting and front panel of the arm are sewn in (Fig. 6-11). Notice that the extension strip is a scrap of some other upholstery fabric.

The arm cover is fitted over the padded arm. In Fig. 6-12 the extension is pushed between the arm and back upholstery, and the arm and seat. When the extension is properly positioned, it is stapled to the bottom end rail (Fig. 6-13) and to the back (leg).

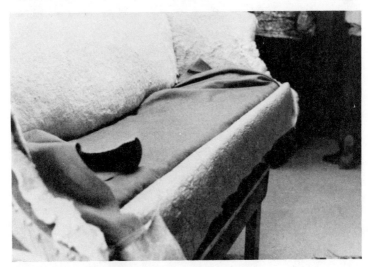

Fig. 6-5. Extension over seat padding.

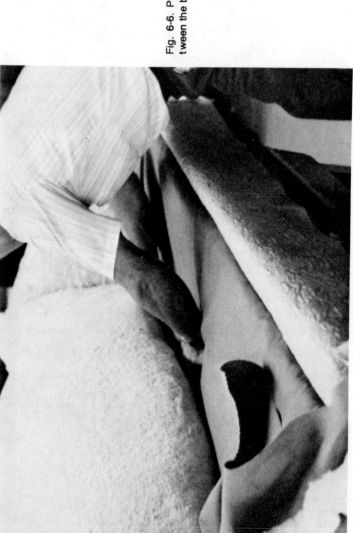

Fig. 6-6. Push the extension between the back and seat.

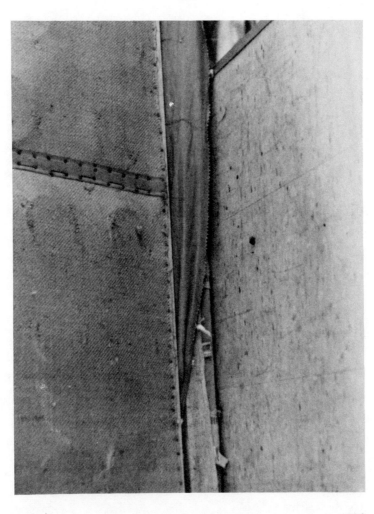

Fig. 6-7. Staple the extension to the rail.

139

Fig. 6-8. Make a cut in the extension to fit around the leg.

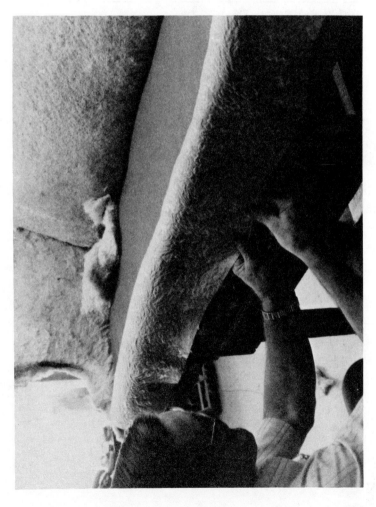

Fig. 6-9. Fit the cover fabric over the seat edge.

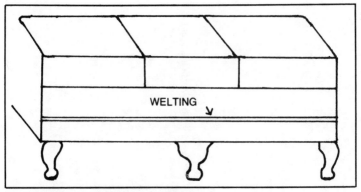

Fig. 6-10. Welting across the front panel.

Notice that the strip of welting had been continued far beyond the fabric of the arm cover. The reason for this will soon be clear.

As you can see in Fig. 6-14, the fabric being stretched over the front panel of the arm is much too wide. This extra width is pulled around and stapled to the outside of the arm. In order to fit it properly, this extra fabric must be notched because of the curve in the arm. If the arm is straight, notching will be unnecessary. The extra fabric is being stapled to the outside of the arm in Fig. 6-15.

The extended welting is stapled along the edge of the arm panel over the notched and stapled fabric. Figure 6-16 shows this step completed, and the front of the arm looks fine.

Now you must complete the outside end of the arm. There will be no stress in this area as the sofa is in use. No real padding is necessary. Something besides the cover fabric should be applied here.

A piece of heavy scrap upholstery material is stapled over the end of the arm first. It is stapled on the underside of the bottom end rail and stretched around the back and stapled there as well (Fig. 6-17). Then the final upholstery fabric is installed.

Beneath the curve of the arm, a tacking strip holds the fabric in a straight edged line (Fig. 6-18). It is folded under and carefully stapled along the curve in the arm (Fig. 6-19). This fabric is stapled on the underside of the bottom end rail and along the back part of the frame or extended leg (Fig. 6-20).

SOFA: BACK

Look ahead now to the photographs of the finished sofa. The back is covered with a single large rectangular piece of fabric.

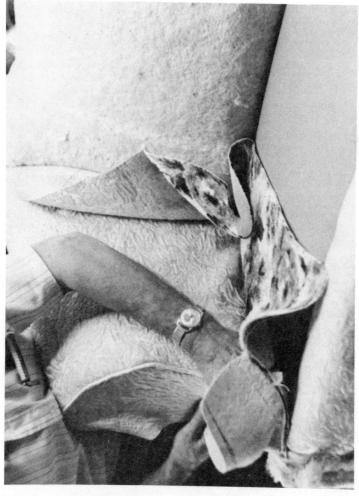

Fig. 6-11. Front panel of the arm with welting.

143

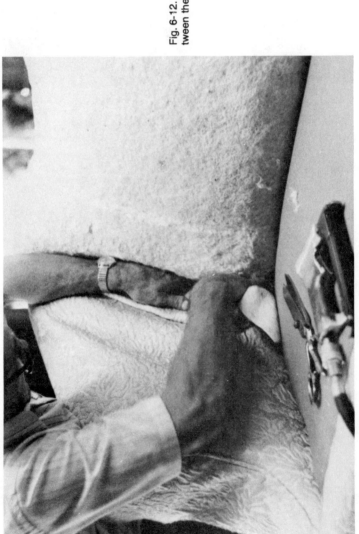

Fig. 6-12. The extension pushed between the arm and seat.

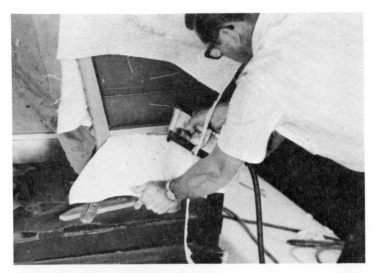

Fig. 6-13. Extension stapled to the rail.

First, the bottom of this back piece is pushed between the seat and back upholstery. It is stapled along the back to the bottom rail (Fig. 6-21).

The fabric is pushed between the arm and back upholstery next, with the extensions pulled through but not yet stapled (Fig. 6-22). With the fabric stapled along the bottom rail in the back, it is

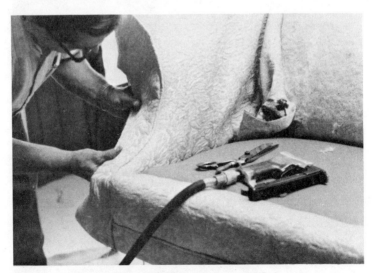

Fig. 6-14. Front arm panel is too wide.

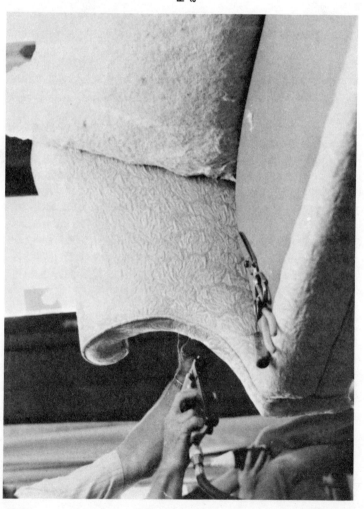

Fig. 6-15. Staple excess to the outer arm.

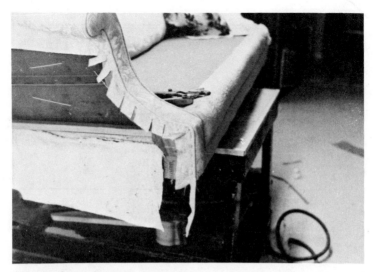

Fig. 6-16. Completed front arm panel.

stretched over the back padding and stapled to the frame, beginning at the high point in the middle. Again, because of the curves in the back, the fabric has to be notched so it will fit (Fig. 6-13). The fabric is worked into neat, small pleats where it stretches over a curve (Fig. 6-24).

All that remains of the sofa upholstery itself at this point is the back panel. Again, this is little more than a large rectangular piece of fabric, folded under and stapled to the back edge with the aid of tacking strips (Fig. 6-25). At the ends of the panel, the same process

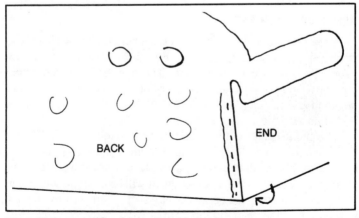

Fig. 6-17. Scrap padding fabric stapled to the frame.

147

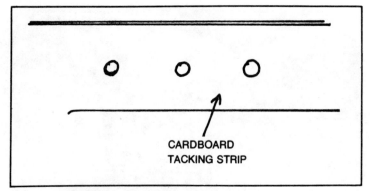

Fig. 6-18. Tacking strip.

is followed. The bottom edge is stapled along the underside of the back bottom rail.

CUSHIONS

The method of making cushions is quite easy, especially after the first try. A cushion for this sofa consists simply of two flat pieces of fabric the size of the foam form, one long strip of boxing to cover three sides of the cushion, and a boxing strip with a zipper sewn in for the fourth side. The making of cushions is discussed in detail in Chapter 7. In Fig. 6-26 the upholsterer is preparing the boxing strip containing the zipper, which is the only part of the process that can cause any problems at all. Study the section on cushions in Chapter 7 for a thorough understanding of the way cushions can be made for this beautiful Victorian sofa (Fig. 6-27).

ARMCHAIR: INNER BACK

The new fabric is cut first to fit the inner back of the chair. The shape of the piece is like that in Fig. 6-28, with a pull strip or extension sewn along the bottom. The new fabric is positioned correctly over the padding in the back of the chair, and stapling is begun in the center top as in Fig. 6-29. The edge of the fabric is folded under as it is stapled.

From the center of the back, the curve is followed. Stapling is continued toward each side. In Fig. 6-30 the upholsterer checks to be sure the fabric will fit properly around the arms before stapling is continued. When it is evident that the fit will be accurate, the cover fabric is pulled under the back. The pull strip is temporarily stapled to the back of the chair (Fig. 6-31).

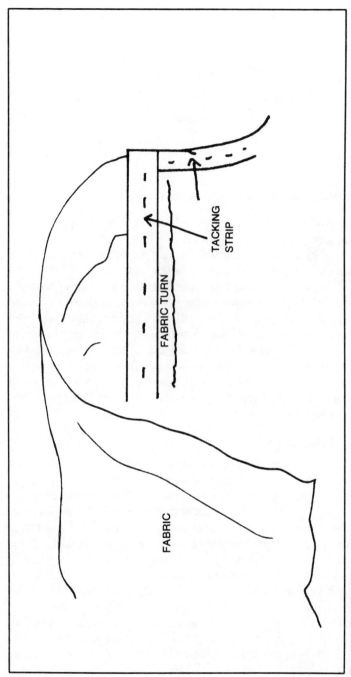

TACKING STRIP

FABRIC TURN

FABRIC

Fig. 6-19. Blind tacking.

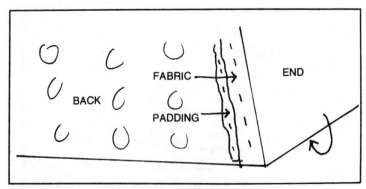

Fig. 6-20. Secure the fabric padding to the frame.

Notice in Fig. 6-32 that the upholsterer is making the cut in the fabric that will enable it to fit properly over the curve of the arm. Then in Fig. 6-33 the fitting and stapling of the cover fabric along the back and next to the woodwork can be continued.

As you install cover fabric, particularly around curved areas, be careful that you do not stretch the fabric as you work. When you are stapling the cover fabric along a straight surface, after it has been pulled over the bulge of the back padding, you will already have a lot of extra fullness to work in as you staple. This is accomplished by permitting a tiny bit of looseness between all the staples. Later, this will be covered by decorative gimp and will not show. Any extra fullness resulting from your inadvertent stretching of the fabric will only cause you more trouble.

ARMCHAIR: ARMS

The final cover fabric for the arms on this chair is an approximate square (Fig. 6-34). The fabric is placed over the curve of the arm and checked over to be sure that the fit will be accurate.

The first thing to be stapled on this arm is at the back (Fig. 6-35). Again, the fabric is folded under and stapled neatly in place. Then it is pulled toward the front and stapled again to hold it in place as the upholsterer is doing in Fig. 6-36. After the cover fabric is secured at each end, the rest of the fabric is stapled all along the length under the curve of the arm. With the fabric stapled under the arm and at the end, the extension or pull strip is stretched snugly beneath the arm and stapled to the frame as in Fig. 6-37. This stapling is temporary. The staples will be removed. The extension is pulled down and stapled to the bottom rail after the chair seat is in place.

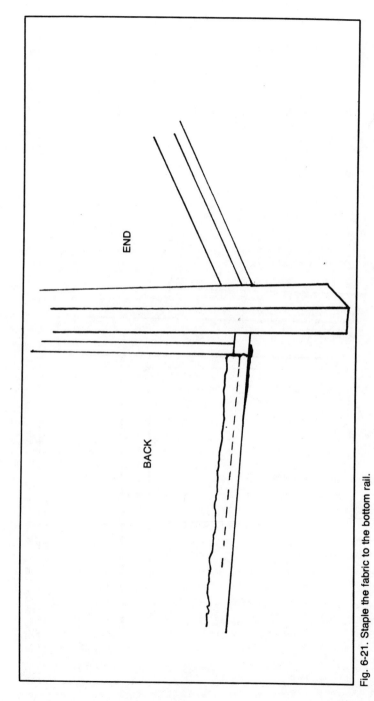

END

BACK

Fig. 6-21. Staple the fabric to the bottom rail.

151

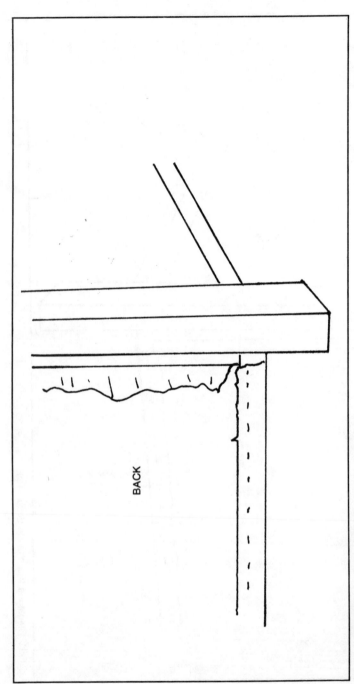

BACK

Fig. 6-22. Extension pulled between the back and arm.

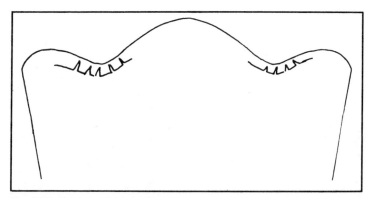

Fig. 6-23. Notch the fabric to fit.

Now that the arm cover is stretched and held in place, the excess fabric is pushed between the arm and back upholstery (Fig. 6-38). Notice the excess fabric in the corner of the chair seat. A cut will have to be made in this spot in order to permit the cover fabric to fit neatly around the back part of the chair frame.

Look at Figs. 6-39 through 6-45. These photographs show the complete sequence of activity in finishing the inner arms on this chair. The fabric is pulled around against the woodwork. The stapling is begun, in this case from the bottom to the top. The fabric is folded under. Staples are placed closely together, as there may be quite a lot of stress in this area on the chair. In Fig. 6-41 the upholsterer begins pleating the fabric around the curve. Such pleats should be small, neat, of equal size, and evenly distributed. At one point the upholsterer finds the pleat unsatisfactory and pulls the staples to redo the work. Finally, when the pleats in the top of the

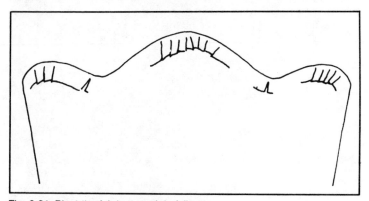

Fig. 6-24. Pleat the fabric to work in fullness.

153

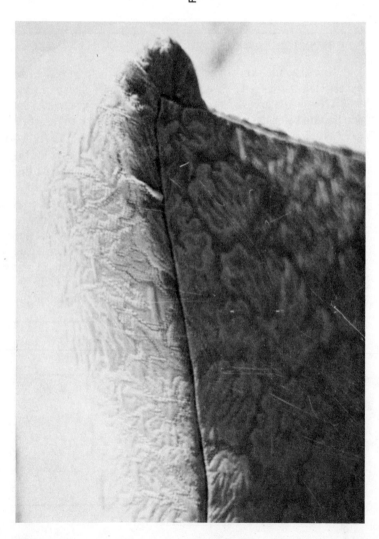

Fig. 6-25. Back fabric in place.

Fig. 6-26. Preparing the welting on zippered boxing.

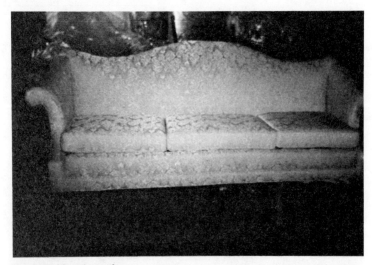

Fig. 6-27. Victorian sofa.

curve of the arm are completed, the upholsterer goes back over the area, applying additional staples to better secure the fabric. All these staples and the rough edges of the pleats will be covered with decorative gimp when the chair is finished.

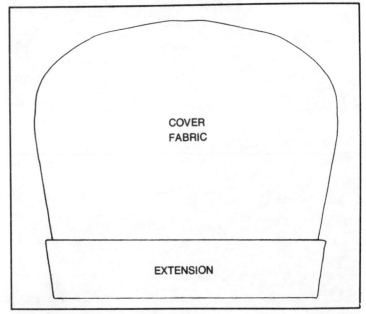

COVER
FABRIC

EXTENSION

Fig. 6-28. Fabric pattern for chair back.

Fig. 6-29. Begin the back in the center top.

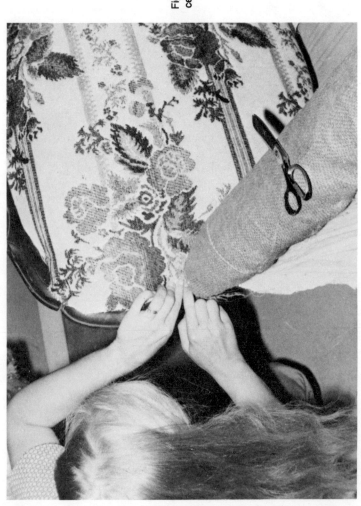

Fig. 6-30. Move from the center toward the sides.

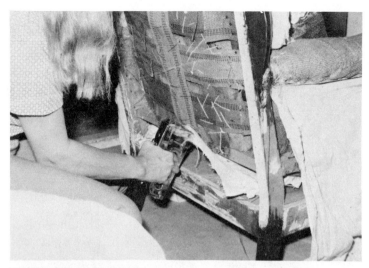

Fig. 6-31. Temporary stapling.

Fig. 6-32. Cut fabric to fit around the arm.

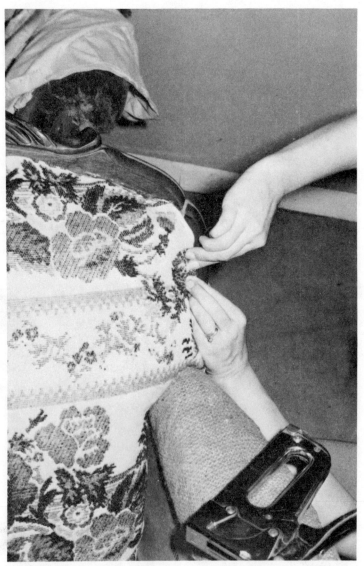

Fig. 6-33. Continue stapling sides.

In Fig. 6-44 the upholsterer is ready to begin the process of stapling and pleating on the opposite arm. The sequence is shown complete in Fig. 6-45.

With the inner arms and the front part of the arms completed except for the gimp, the chair is beginning to be attractive (Fig.

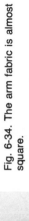

Fig. 6-34. The arm fabric is almost square.

161

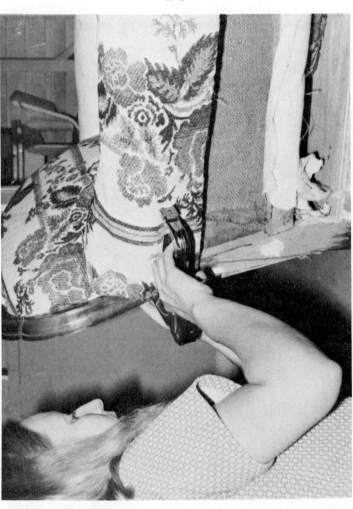

Fig. 6-35. Secure the fabric in place at the back.

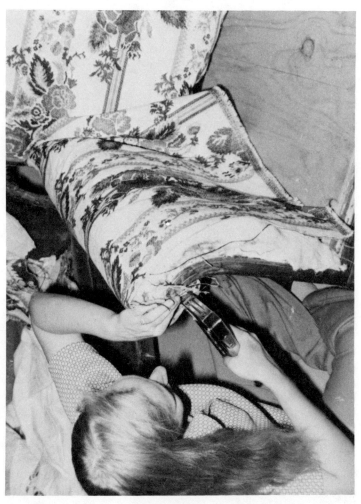

Fig. 6-36. Put a staple on the front end.

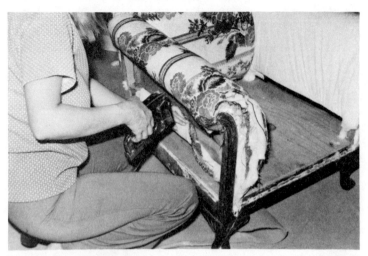
Fig. 6-37. Temporary stapling.

6-46). The outer arms, or the area beneath the curve of the arms on the outside of the chair, cannot be completed until the seat is put in place and covered.

In this particular project, the upholsterer did not do the seat padding until this point was reached. It can be done either way. The building up and padding of the chair seat is discussed and illustrated in the preceding chapter. In any case, whether the seating is done before the final covering of the back and arms or afterward, the seat must have its final cover in place before the arms can be finished.

ARMCHAIR: SEAT COVERING

The cover for this chair seat is a simple rectangle, most of which consists of an extension. The narrow band of upholstery fabric will cover the front panel of this part of the seat, and the extension will be covered by the cushion later (Fig. 6-47).

In Fig. 6-48 the upholsterer makes the cut that will permit the cover to be pushed between the seat and arm upholstery, and to be properly fitted over the front panel of the seat. The extensions are then pulled through to the outside of the chair on the sides and the back. In Fig. 6-49 the upholsterers check everything to make sure the fit will be accurate before the stapling begins. The fabric is again folded under and stapled very close to the woodwork (Fig. 6-50).

Finishing touches are put on this phase of the project in Fig. 6-51. The end of the panel is finished in a neat and attractive manner.

Fig. 6-38. Push fabric between the back and arm.

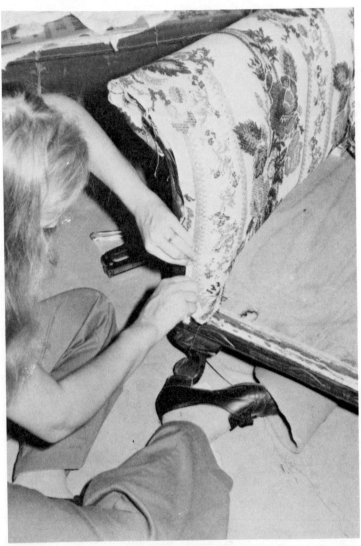

Fig. 6-39. Pull the fabric against the wood trim.

With the front of the seat properly stapled, neat, and straight, the extension on the back of the seat cover is pulled taut and stapled to the bottom rail (Fig. 6-52). After this extension is stapled, the temporary staples in the extension of the inner back cover fabric are pulled. This extension is also pulled down and stapled to the bottom rail, directly over the extension of the seat cover (Fig. 6-53).

The seat cover has been finished along the front of the chair and securely stapled along the back rail. In Fig. 6-54 the upholsterer pulls the extension at the side of the seat cover down, preparing to staple it to the rail on the side. Afterwards, the temporary staples holding the inner arm cover fabric will be pulled. This fabric will be

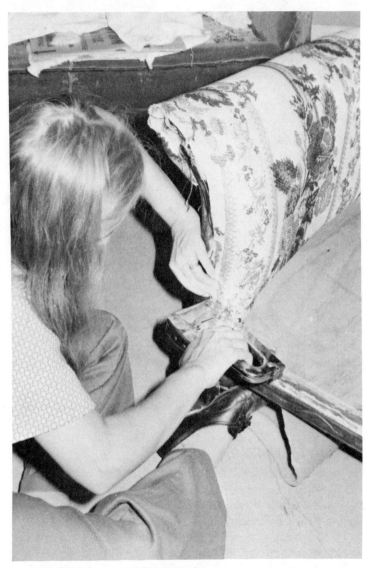

Fig. 6-40. Staple it very close to the wood.

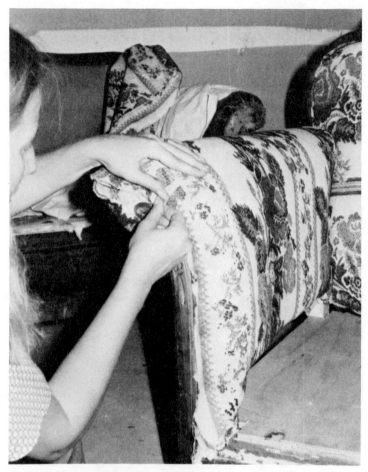

Fig. 6-41. Work in small pleats and staple them.

pulled down and stapled to the bottom rail directly over the extension on the seat cover (Fig. 6-55).

FINISHING THE ARMS

Now that the chair seat is completed, the arms can be finished. In Fig. 6-56 the lady receives some assistance in pulling the cover fabric of the arms a little more snugly and restapling it. The fabric on the inner back and inner arm is stapled more securely (Fig. 6-57).

The fabric which will cover the outer side of the arms is essentially a square piece. It must be attached at the top, directly under the curve of the arm. In Fig. 6-58 the cover is spread over the arm, right side down. The man measures a strip to determine the length of tacking strip that will be required. With the fabric for the outer arm lying right side down over the arm, a few staples are placed to hold the piece in place temporarily (Fig. 6-59). With this fabric held temporarily in place, a tacking strip is stapled across the area (Fig. 6-60). The tacking strip will keep the fabric straight along

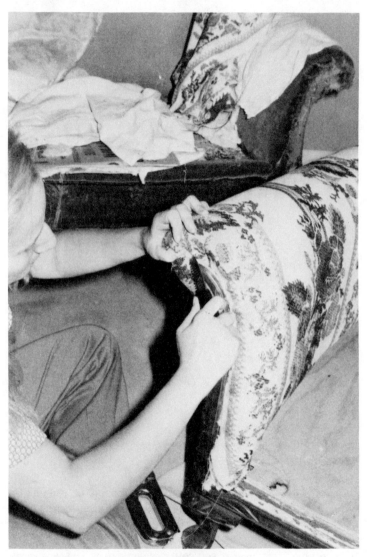

Fig. 6-42. Pull staples and redo to make pleats even.

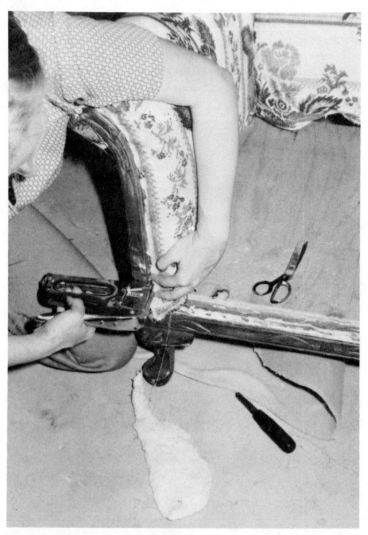

Fig. 6-43. Add extra staples as needed.

the top edge beneath the arm, even as it is pulled and secured at the bottom and along each side.

Before this process can be continued, a bit of padding is installed on this part of the arm. A piece of ordinary cardboard is cut to fit from under the curve of the arm to the bottom rail, and from the front to the back of the chair. This cardboard is covered with spray adhesive, and a thin layer of soft cotton is glued to it. The cardboard

Fig. 6-44. Fit the cover fabric close to the wood.

171

Fig. 6-45. Staple all pleats neatly.

is fitted over the area, cotton side out, and stapled in place (Fig. 6-61). Only at that point is the cover fabric stretched down along the bottom rail and secured. A couple of staples are put in the fabric at the bottom rail to hold it temporarily while the front edge of the fabric is folded under and stapled (Fig. 6-62).

With both the front and back edges of this outer arm stapled, the fabric is folded beneath the bottom rail. It is stapled there on the underside of the rail (Fig. 6-63).

Fig. 6-46. Arms and back are nearly finished.

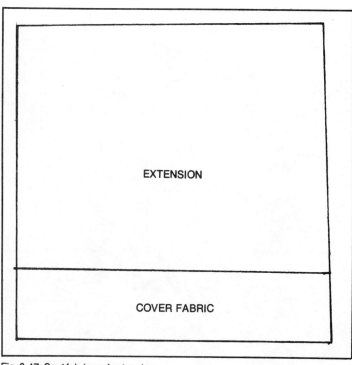

EXTENSION

COVER FABRIC

Fig. 6-47. Seat fabric and extension.

Fig. 6-48. Cut the fabric to fit around the leg.

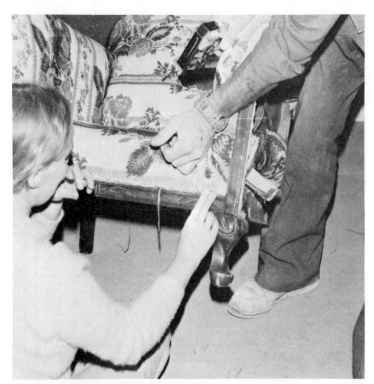

Fig. 6-49. Check everything for a good fit.

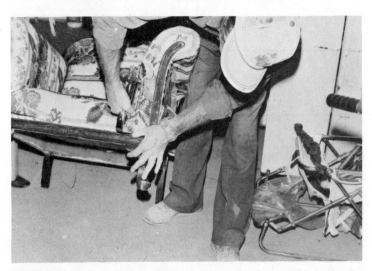

Fig. 6-50. Staple close to the wood trim.

174

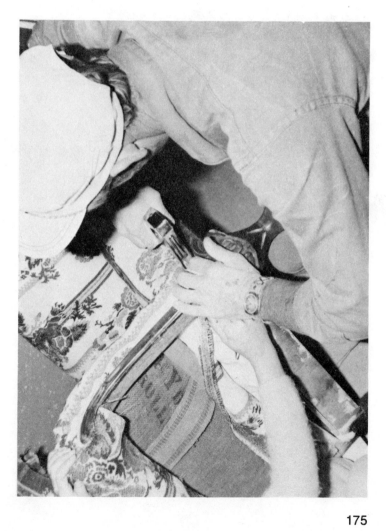

Fig. 6-51. Finish the end of the front panel.

175

Fig. 6-52. Staple the extension to the bottom rail.

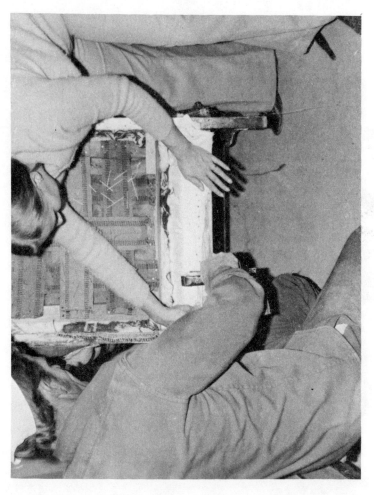

Fig. 6-53. Staple the back cover to the bottom rail.

177

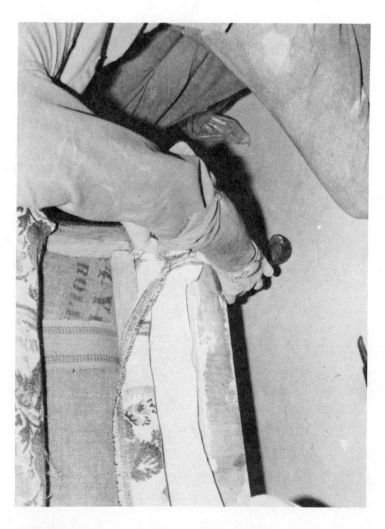

Fig. 6-54. Staple the seat cover extension to the rail.

The outer back of this chair is covered with a sheet of cardboard and a thin layer of soft cotton. The cover fabric is simply stapled over it with the sides turned under in a hem along the top and sides. At the bottom edge, the cover is pulled under the bottom rail and stapled.

The cushion for this chair is made according to the instructions given in Chapter 7. The gimp is then glued all around the woodwork, covering the staples.

This chair is now an attractive, functional piece of furniture. The little vanity stool in Fig. 6-64 is covered in a piece of the same fabric.

SMALL CHAIR

The small chair discussed in Chapter 5 will be continued here. The padding is neat and firm, and this makes the seat fairly easy to cover.

Begin by cutting a piece of cover fabric large enough to cover the seat, with a little surplus fabric to be trimmed off later. Lay the fabric over the padded seat, and staple it in the center of the front. Stretch the fabric snugly. Staple it in the center of the back. Do the same in the center of each side of the seat, keeping the fabric neatly aligned as you work.

From these center staples, continue stapling toward the corners. When you reach the corner, form a very neat pleat to fit the fabric over the corner. Pull it snug and staple it.

Fig. 6-55. Inner arm cover stapled to the rail.

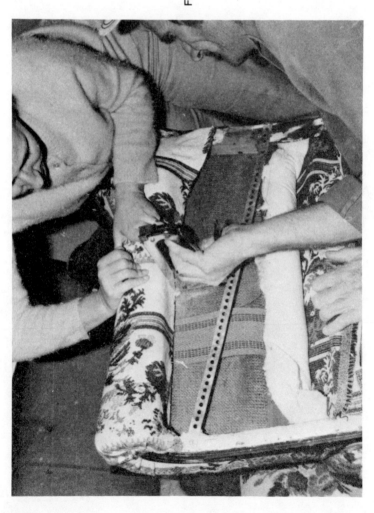

Fig. 6-56. Restaple any weak places.

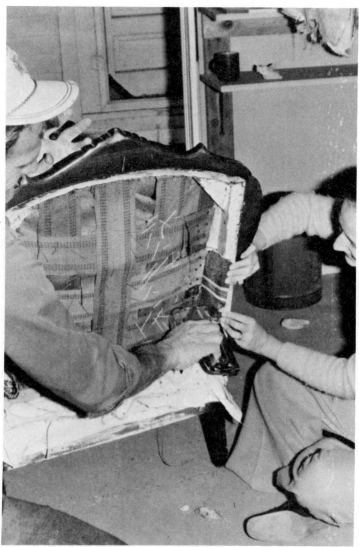

Fig. 6-57. Secure the inner arm fabric.

The chair in Fig. 6-65 has the cover in place and stapled all around. The next step is to trim the fabric close to the staples and glue the gimp in place.

The upholstered back panel is also simple to cover. The fabric is placed over the padding. It is stapled at the bottom and again at the top (Fig. 6-66).

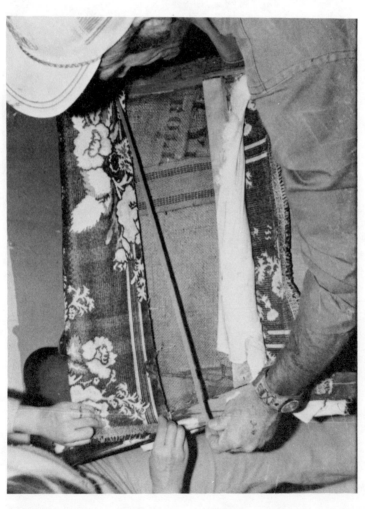

Fig. 6-58. Measure and cut a tacking strip.

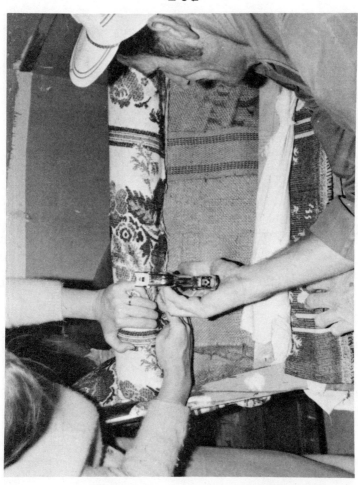

Fig. 6-59. Attach the wrong side of outer arm cover under the curve of the arm.

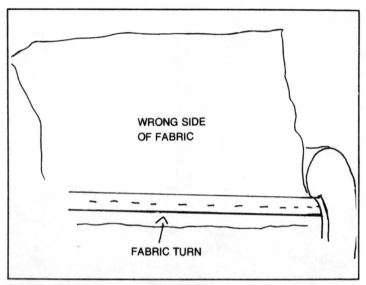

Fig. 6-60. Staple the tacking strip under the arm.

From this point, the stapling continues around the panel as in Fig. 6-67. This step is completed in Fig. 6-68. The surplus fabric is trimmed off close to the staples next, and the gimp is applied.

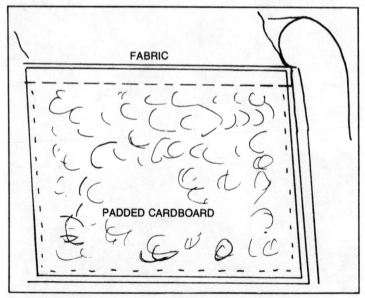

Fig. 6-61. Outer arm panels covered with cotton-padded cardboard.

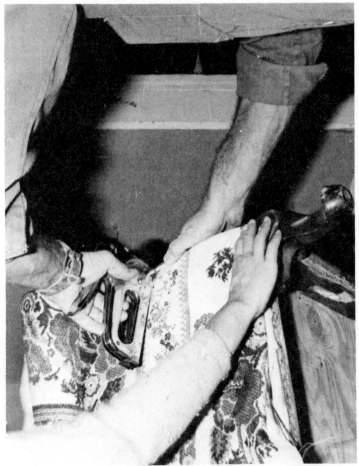

Fig. 6-62. Staple the front edge near the wood trim.

Fig. 6-63. Staple fabric on the underside of the rail.

Gimp can be tacked, stapled, or glued in place. Glue is usually the best choice. White polyvinyl glues work well, but temporary tacks may also be needed to hold the gimp while the glue dries. The ideal solution is that illustrated in Figs. 6-69 and 6-70. The upholsterer is using a hot glue gun to attach the gimp. This glue dries almost instantly, is easy to handle, and looks good.

Fig. 6-64. Vanity stool.

If it hasn't been done previously, a cambric dust cover is stapled over the webbing on the seat (Fig. 6-71). The small chair is completed (Fig. 6-72).

DROP-IN PADDED SEAT

This project is about as simple as upholstery can ever be. The old cover (Fig. 6-73) is removed, and a new cover is cut. The

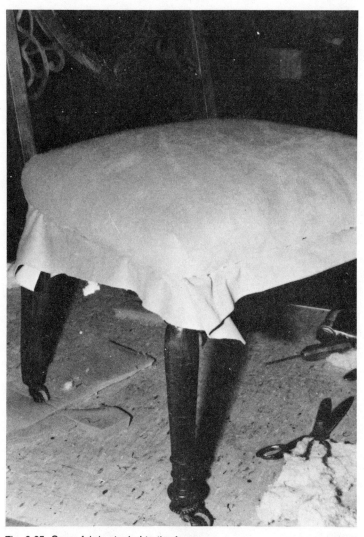

Fig. 6-65. Cover fabric stapled to the frame.

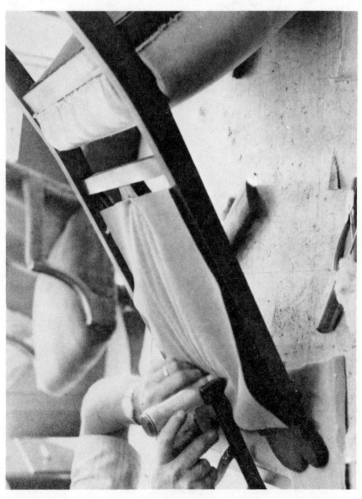

Fig. 6-66. Begin stapling at the bottom point.

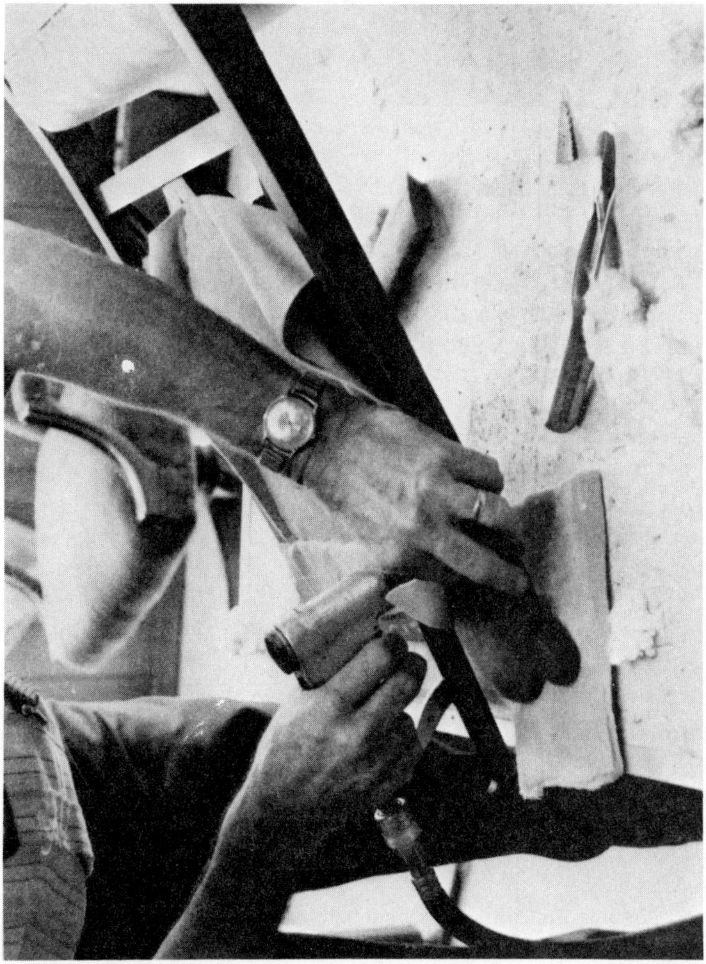

Fig. 6-67. Staple around the panel.

189

Fig. 6-68. Completed fabric cover.

padding is replaced on the wood insert, and the cover is positioned correctly over it (Fig. 6-74). The whole thing is carefully turned upside down, and tacks or staples are centered in the middle of each of the four sides. From the centers, the stapling is continued to the corners where the fabric is pleated and stapled in place. The seat is simply dropped back into the chair frame, and the drop-in padded seat is completed.

CHANNELING

Channeling is also often called *fluting* or *piping*. It is essentially the technique of covering (usually) the inner back of a chair or sofa with an equally distributed and stuffed series of channels. The technique is quite useful in that it can dramatically change the appearance of a chair or sofa. In addition, channeling can be used to make seat furniture more comfortable by affecting the slant of the backrest.

The visual effect of a channeled piece can differ in interesting ways as well. Long, narrow channels heighten a back, and wider channels make the piece appear wider and less high.

Channeling can be done in several ways. Any method takes quite a bit of time. Particular care must be given to see that all channels are of the same width and depth, and stuffed to the same consistency.

Assume that the chair has a padded back covered with burlap and a separate seat cushion. You can put a channeled back cover on

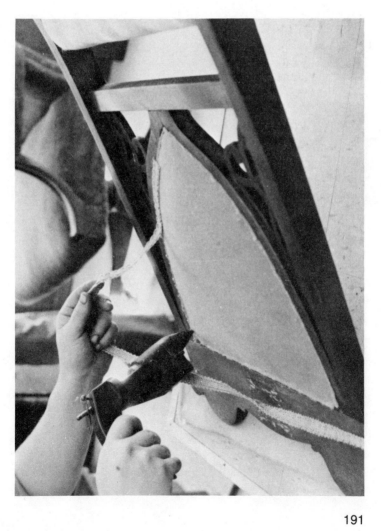

Fig. 6-69. Hot glue attaches the gimp.

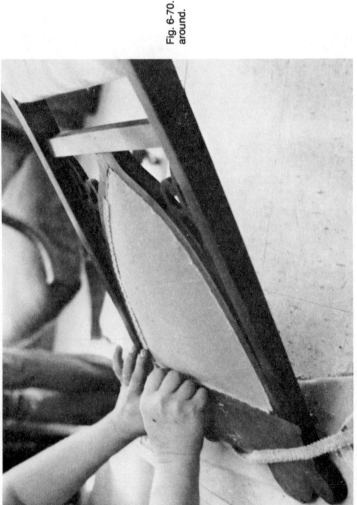

Fig. 6-70. Fit gimp neatly all the way around.

solid wood, but the spring or padded-back chair is more likely to be the type chosen for channeling.

A few decisions must be made before any actual work begins. You must decide how many channels to use, how deep they will be, and whether they will be deeper in the middle or toward the top or bottom. Ordinarily the channels should be from 2 to 3 inches deep, and of the same depth for the length of the channel. By making them deeper at one end or the other, you can affect the slant of the backrest (Fig. 6-75).

In this example the chair back is wider at the top than at the bottom, which means that the channels will also be wider at the top. Select the number of channels by measuring across the top of the chair and the bottom. Divide these measurements by an odd or even number until you find a satisfactory width. Assume that there will be a total of nine channels. The odd number means that one channel will be centered directly down the midpoint of the chair back, rather than having a valley between channels occurring there (Fig. 6-76).

Making a Pattern for the Channel Casing

Now you must make a pattern for the channel casing. Measure from the top to the bottom of the inner back. Then add plenty of extra length to staple the ends over the backs of the top and bottom rails. Determine the required width of each strip of channel casing by the following method.

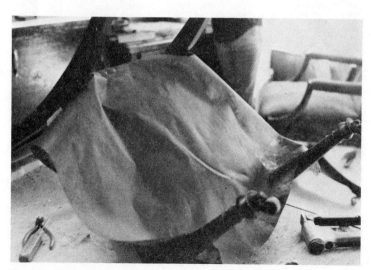

Fig. 6-71. Cambric dust cover.

Fig. 6-72. Completed chair.

Draw a pattern of one channel on a piece of paper, 4 inches wide at the top and 3 inches at the bottom, and of the actual length of the inner back from top to bottom. Measure the depth of the chair cushion, and mark this point on the drawing (Fig. 6-77). Take some flexible material (wire, a steel measuring tape, or a thin plastic belt and arch it from one side of your pattern to the other, near the top. The center of the arch should be 2 inches high, if your channels will be 2 inches deep. Measure and record the exact length of your measuring tape from one line to the other. Repeat this process near

194

Fig. 6-73. Original cover.

the bottom end of the channel, but *above* the cushion line you drew. Remember that if the curve is not of the same *depth* on each end, the slant of the chair back will be affected.

Assume that the curve measured 6½ inches at the top of the channel and 5½ inches at the bottom of the channel. Add 2 inches to each measurement (for a seam allowance) to get 8½ inches and 7½ inches.

Take a strip of pattern paper (wrapping paper, newspaper) long enough for the channel pattern, and fold it lengthwise. From the fold, measure *half* the top width you have determined (½ of 8½ = 4¼) and make a mark there. From the fold above the cushion line,

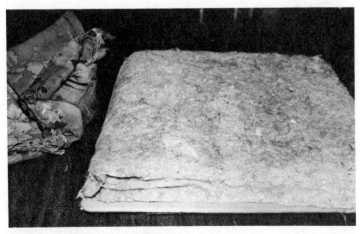

Fig. 6-74. Reassemble the seat padding.

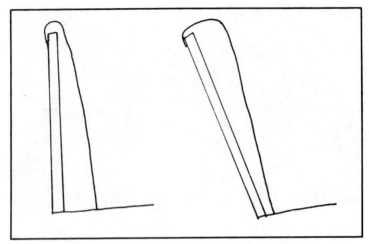

Fig. 6-75. Depth of channels affect the slant of the backrest.

measure one-half of the bottom width (½ of 7½ = 3¾) and make a mark.

Take a straightedge like a yardstick and connect these two marks in a straight line. Cut the folded paper along the line, unfold it, and you have a precise pattern for each channel (Fig. 6-78).

Use this pattern to cut the appropriate number (9 in the example) of muslin casings for channels. Make 1-inch seams. Sew them

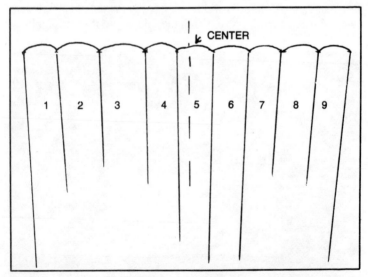

Fig. 6-76. An odd number places a channel over the center of the back.

together side to side. Press the seams, but do not press them *open.* Lay the whole piece, seam allowances up, with the center channel in the center of your ironing board. Press the seam on each side of the center channel *outward* (Fig. 6-79).

Stuffing and Sewing the Channels

Lay the chair on its back. Measure and mark the locations of the channels on the burlap (Fig. 6-80).

Spread the muslin casing over the chair back, and sew the fourth seam allowance (from either right or left) to the corresponding line on the burlap (Fig. 6-81). Fill between this seam and the next line with any kind of resilient stuffing (hair, polyester, or foam). You will need to experiment a bit to stuff the first channel just right. When it feels right, fold that channel casing over it (Fig. 6-82) and pin it to the corresponding line on the burlap. Pin through the seam allowance; now it is evident why you pressed the seam allowances on each side of the center, toward the outside of the chair back.

When you are satisfied with the stuffing in the channel, sew that seam allowance to the line and remove the pins. Continue stuffing and sewing the channels, one at a time. Leave the ends, both top and bottom, open.

When all channels are stuffed, examine them for loose or lumpy spots. If you find places that need to be adjusted, you can often use a long, thin tool (a regulator or an improvised tool) to insert into the channels and move the stuffing.

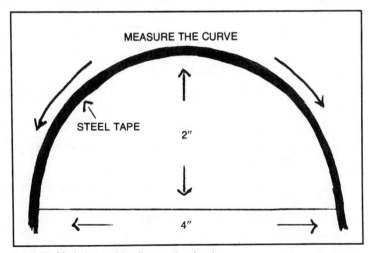

MEASURE THE CURVE

STEEL TAPE

2″

4″

Fig. 6-77. Mark the cushion line on the drawing.

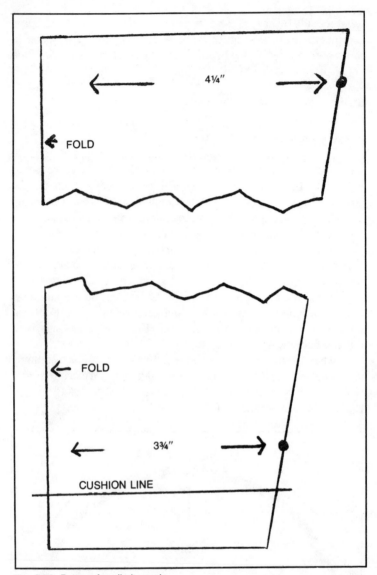

Fig. 6-78. Pattern for all channels.

At the lower end of the channels you must decrease the depth gradually, so the seat cushion will fit as it should. When the bottoms are right, pull the extra tacking length through to the back and staple it at the seams. Gather or pleat the excess fabric of the curve neatly and staple it.

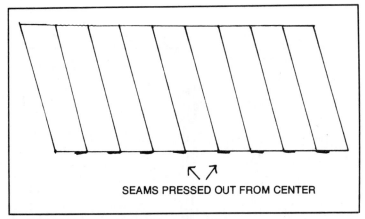

Fig. 6-79. Press seams outward from the center.

At the bottom of channels, follow the same procedure. Let the stuffed channels curve over the back. Then staple the tacking length to the rail, and pleat or gather the excess fabric neatly.

Final Cover

The final cover to go over the channels is cut and assembled just as the muslin casing was done. Instead of pressing the seams, open them and place a length of strong cord (spring tying cord is

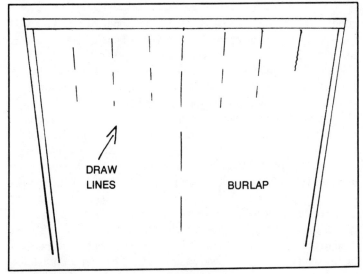

DRAW
LINES

BURLAP

Fig. 6-80. Mark channel locations on the burlap.

Fig. 6-81. Sew the seam allowance to the burlap.

good) between the two parts. Use your zipper foot to sew very close, but not into the cord. Use enough cord so that several inches will extend at each end of every seam (Fig. 6-83).

Begin at one of the center seams. Drive a tack halfway into the air back above the already stapled muslin casing on the bottom, and another just below it on the top (Fig. 6-84).

Spread the final cover over the chair back, and push the cord at the bottom end between the seat and back. Go to the back of the chair and pull this cord through. Tie it around the tack (Fig. 6-85).

Hold the cord at the top end. Press that seam of the final cover into the valley between the cased channels. Pull the cord snugly over the top of the chair back. Tie it to that tack.

Prepare to do the same with the next seam. Place a layer of soft cotton over the muslin casing. Fit the final cover over it. Tie the cord to the bottom, tack, work it into the crease between channels, tie the top end of the cord, and so forth until the cover is completely installed.

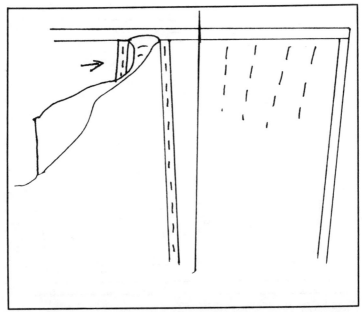

Fig. 6-82. Stuff the channel and sew the second seam allowance to the burlap.

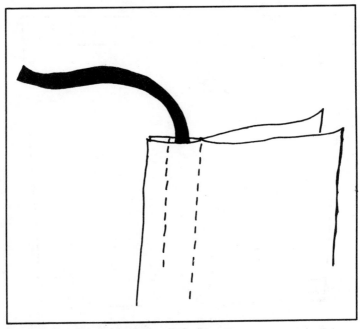

Fig. 6-83. Sew the cord inside the seam allowance.

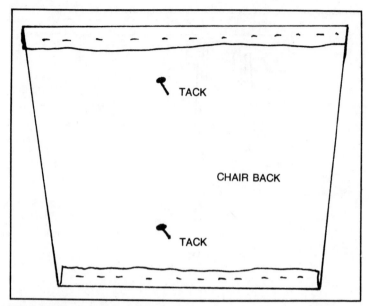

Fig. 6-84. Put tacks in the chair back.

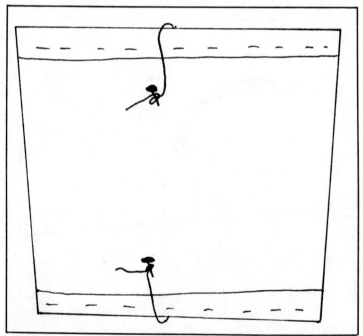

Fig. 6-85. Pull the cord through to the back and tie it around the tacks.

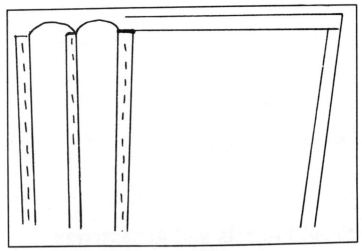

Fig. 6-86. Separate channels.

Gather or pleat the surplus fabric at the top of each channel neatly, and staple it to the chair back. Drive the tacks all the way in.

At the sides of the chair, staple, sew, or tack the fabric edges. The way you handle the edges will depend on the methods you employ for the rest of the upholstery.

Channeling Without the Muslin Casing

You can also do channeling, omitting the muslin casing. Just do it the same way—use the cover fabric as you did the muslin casing, sew it the same way, and so on. There is more opportunity to make irreparable mistakes this way, because the final cover is the only chance you have. Any mistakes that you correct will damage this fabric to some extent. After you have done one casing project using muslin casings, it will not be too difficult to try again and not use the casing at all.

A Third Method

A third method is also possible. The measuring and cutting essentially proceeds the same way, except that you make a *complete* casing for each channel, stuff it, and then attach it to the chair back. Make another complete channel, stuff it, and sew it on (Fig. 6-86). This method probably takes a little more time; on the other hand, it is convenient to be able to handle each channel as you stuff it. The most important thing, aside from neat, durable work, is that all the channels be uniform in size and consistency.

Small Projects and Accessories

While the projects to be discussed in this chapter are not actual upholstery, they are important skills for you to learn. They will provide satisfactory and financially rewarding activities for the professional shop as well.

These projects are closely related to upholstery and require many of the same materials and equipment, as well as identical or similar techniques. When you develop some of these skills, you have more freedom in actual upholstery for your home. The finishing touches in home decorating are these very projects. Therefore, you can feel free to use fabrics in colors and textures that differ from what you customarily have, because you can finish the room in complementary cushions, pillows, draperies, and so forth.

The instructions to follow are not difficult, but they do require thoughtful study and careful measuring and assembly. Be sure that you understand the directions before you proceed. Soon you will have both the competence and the confidence to accent your upholstery work in the precise way that it should be done.

CUSHIONS

A cushion can be made in practically any shape you desire. Cushions differ from pillows in that they have a boxed edge, while pillows do not. Figure 7-1 shows the parts of a cushion.

You must decide what your cushion will be filled with. You may go to a dry goods store and buy molded foam forms in a variety of shapes and sizes. Should the size or shape you want not be available, many shops will cut one to your specifications from the large sheets

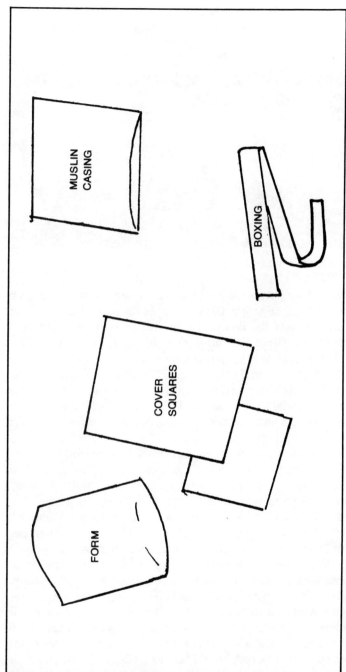

Fig. 7-1. Parts of a cushion.

Fig. 7-2. Foam padding.

of foam they have available (Fig. 7-2). When you buy foam from sheets like those shown, you pay for it by the inch. Therefore, have a good idea of the dimensions needed to avoid waste. If shop proprietors will not cut a form for you, buy a piece of a suitable size, draw the pattern on it, and cut your own.

Other ready-made forms are also available. These forms consist of a cloth cover already stuffed with shredded foam or some similar material. Such forms are also easy to make for yourself. You can make your own cover and stuff it with any of a variety of fillings available in department stores.

Once you have a form prepared, whether a solid foam form or a stuffed form, you are ready to measure and cut the cover. You should always make not only the outer cover, but also a casing. Casings are usually made of muslin. This material is inexpensive and easy to work with. A muslin casing will make a cushion look nicer, primarily because it will help the cushion to retain its shape. It will also aid you in installing the outer cover in an attractive way.

Your muslin casing and outer cover will be cut to the same dimensions. If your form is a single piece of foam rubber, the covers, both casing and outer cover, should be cut to the same measurements as the form itself without any seam allowance. Ordinarily you will run ½ inch seams throughout the project. When you have sewn the casing, its dimensions will be somewhat smaller than the form. Perhaps it sounds odd, but this is desirable. It will cause you to struggle just a bit as you put the form inside the casing, but once it is in place, the foam will be slightly compressed. It will fit neatly inside the cover.

If your forms will be stuffed casings, cut the cover, casing and outer cover both, to the dimensions of the form itself, plus a ½-inch seam allowance all the way around.

You will find it most helpful to measure your form in diameter, depth, and circumference (see Fig. 7-1 again). Add a ½-inch seam allowance for filled forms, and transfer these measurements to a sheet of newspaper or similar material to make a pattern. Making a paper pattern to guide you in cutting the material is always a good idea.

As in most sewing projects, you will ordinarily place the pattern on the lengthwise and crosswise grains of the material. This will depend on the pattern of the material you are using and on whatever eventual design you wish to create. Therefore, there will be occasions when you will want to cut the material on the bias. The true *bias* of any fabric is the diagonal line which bisects both the lengthwise and crosswise grains (Fig. 7-3).

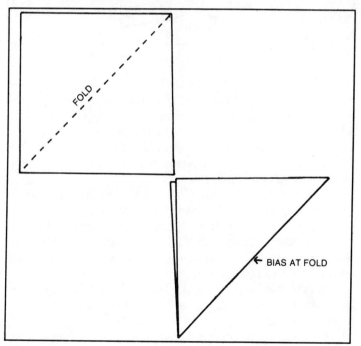

Fig. 7-3. True bias.

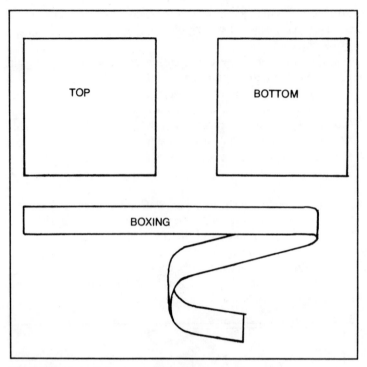

Fig. 7-4. Basic parts for a square cushion.

Whatever the eventual shape of your cushion, the steps in cutting and assembly are essentially the same. Measure the diameter, depth, and circumference of the form. Add a ½-inch seam allowance if the cushion is to be the filled type, and make a pattern. Pin the pattern to the fabric. Cut it. You should begin with the casing. Should you make any error, it is best to do so with the inexpensive muslin.

The parts for the simplest kind of square cushion consist of two squares, plus one long boxing strip (Fig. 7-4). Begin at a corner of one square and at one end of the boxing strip, and pin the right sides of both together as shown (Fig. 7-5). Sew the strip to the square, all the way around. When you reach the corner where you begin, connect the ends of the boxing strip.

Pin and sew the second square to the strip in the same manner as you did the first, but only on three sides. Leave one side open in order to place the form.

Turn your muslin cover inside out. Place the form inside it, and close the open side by hand or machine.

If the muslin cover fits the form properly and is straight and neat, cut the outer cover to the same dimensions as you did the muslin cover. Assemble it in the same manner, leaving one side open to place the form. Fit the form inside the outer cover, close the opening, and the simplest cushion is completed.

There are several options in making cushions that will add to their suitability and attractiveness. These are all quite simple to achieve; they require a few more materials and a bit more time.

Zippers

A zipper closing for your outer cover will permit you to remove it for laundering. There are different ways to add a zipper to a cushion cover. You may have examples of different methods on cushions already in your home. The simplest one is that where the zipper is centered in a section of the boxing strip.

This zipper may be of whatever length you desire. Make sure it is long enough to provide a sufficiently wide opening to remove the form. This depends on the size of the form and how snugly it fits inside the cover. It is a good idea to permit the zipper to extend the length of one side of the cushion, and slightly beyond on each corner.

A boxing strip is ordinarily a single piece of fabric. Adding a zipper will require that the strip be of three pieces. Determine the required length of the boxing strip, and add 2 inches for seam allowances. Cut the piece that will contain the zipper first. This piece will be the length of the zipper itself, plus 1 inch for a ½-inch seam allowance on each end. It must also be 1½ inches wider than

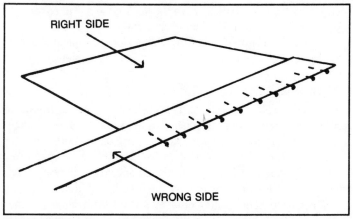

RIGHT SIDE

WRONG SIDE

Fig. 7-5. Pin boxing to the cover.

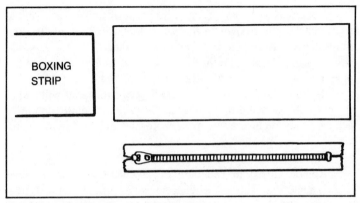

Fig. 7-6. Boxing strip for the zipper is wider.

the rest of the boxing strip to provide seam allowances for the zipper (Fig. 7-6).

Fold this strip, right sides together, and pin it. Three-fourths inch from the folded edge, baste the pieces together and cut along the fold (Fig. 7-7). Fold the seam open. Press it flat.

Your zipper should be 1 inch shorter than the piece you have just assembled. Place the zipper, precisely centered on the seam, right side down. Pin it in place and sew it. Then pull out the basting threads. Check to see that the zipper is properly aligned and operates smoothly.

At this point you have two pieces of boxing strip, one with a zipper and one without. Place the ends of two strips, right sides together, and sew them. Open the zipper and attach the strip to the squares as previously discussed. Remember to place the zippered section properly in relationship to the square, so it will cover one end and extend a bit beyond on each corner.

Turn the cover inside out through the zippered opening, insert the form, and close the zipper. The cushion is complete.

Puffed Boxing

Puffed boxing is pretty on any cushion as long as the fit is accurate. All steps are accomplished in the same manner as in the preceding discussion, except the boxing strip on the outer cover.

Prepare the muslin casing, fit the form, and close the open side. Cut the two squares. The depth of the boxing strip will remain the same as in the previous type; only the length is different.

The difference in length of the boxing strip will depend on the amount of fullness you desire in the puffed boxing, and on the kind of

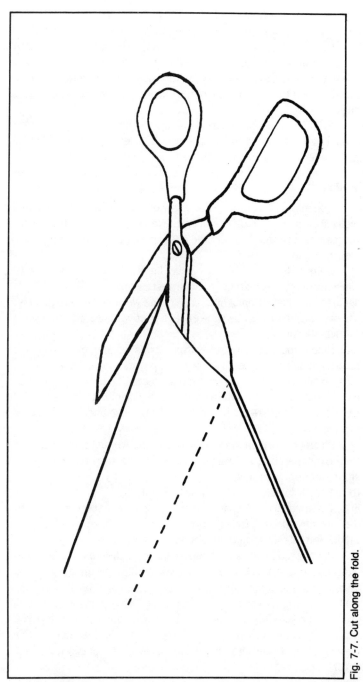

Fig. 7-7. Cut along the fold.

fabric you are using. A good length to observe on a first effort is to make the boxing strip twice as long as it would otherwise be.

Gather both edges of the boxing strip, by hand or machine, until the edges are the same length as the circumference of the squares. See that the gathers are equally full throughout the circumference of the strip. Pin the edge to one of the squares, and sew as previously directed (Fig. 7-8).

Attach the second square, leaving one side open unless you are adding a zipper. Insert the form, close the opening, and the cushion with puffed boxing is completed.

Welting

You may add welting to the edges of your cushion. You will find welting cord in department stores in a variety of thicknesses. Select the size of cord that best fits the cushion you plan, and prepare the welting strip.

Remember that this welting can be in the same fabric as your cushion cover, or a matching or contrasting color. Refer to Fig. 7-3 again for an illustration of bias, and cut the welting strip on the bias. The welting strip must be wide enough to cover the cord and leave a ¾-inch allowance.

Since you are cutting welting strips on the bias, you will probably have to connect two or more pieces to get a long enough strip. When you do so, connect the strips as illustrated in Fig. 7-9. By connecting the strips diagonally, you will avoid a thick spot in the finished welting. Always press the welting seam open for the same reason.

Place the cord on the wrong side of the welting strip. Fold the strip over the cord, keeping the edges of the strip together. The zipper foot on your sewing machine will permit you to sew closely to the cord, but avoid actually sewing into it.

When you have prepared welting of a sufficient length to finish the cushion edges, place it on one side of the boxing strip (Fig. 7-10). Sew the welting to the strip.

Pin the edge of one of the squares to the boxing strip and welting, and sew them together. As you do this, the material should be placed so the boxing strip with welting sewn on is on the top (Fig. 7-11). By doing so, you can follow the first seam you made. This will prevent the possibility of one of the seams showing on the cover when you turn it. You will find it necessary to clip the edges of the welting strip at corners to prevent a bunched appearance (Fig. 7-12).

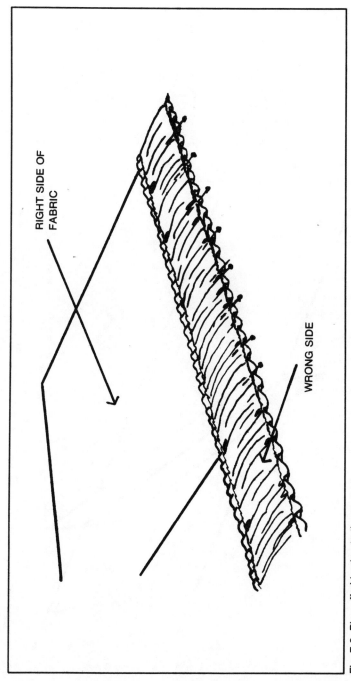

RIGHT SIDE OF FABRIC

WRONG SIDE

Fig. 7-8. Pin puffed boxing to the cover.

213

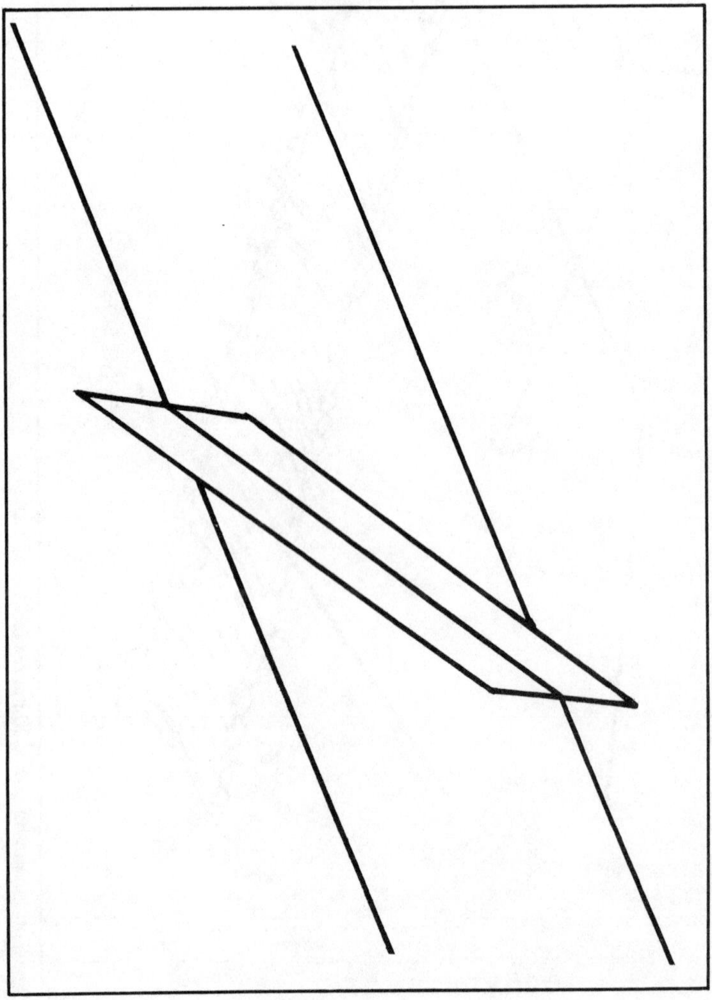

Fig. 7-9. Connect welting strips diagonally.

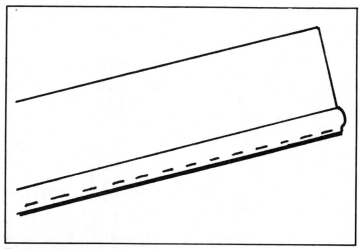

Fig. 7-10. Pin welting to the boxing strip.

Visit dry goods and department stores. Examine the many kinds of decorative trim available. Adding such trim in the seams of cushions is often a nice touch.

PILLOWS

The notable difference between a pillow and a cushion is that the pillow has no boxing. The squares or two pieces of covering material are joined to one another, forming a sharp edge.

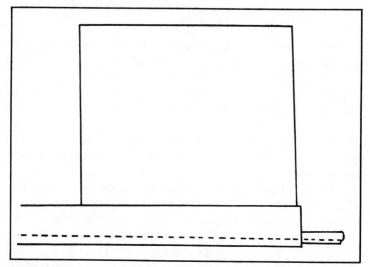

Fig. 7-11. Sew over the first seam.

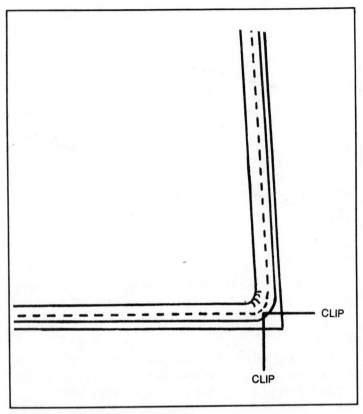

CLIP

CLIP

Fig. 7-12. Clip the welting at the corners.

Most of the directions for making pillows will be the same as those for measuring, cutting, and assembling cushions. Pillows, like cushions, can be made in any shape you wish. You may find molded forms, ask to have forms cut to your specifications, or buy foam and cut your own forms. Forms for pillows may also be made with a stuffed muslin casing.

In some respects, pillows are more simple to make than cushions. You can design the shape in any number of ways and make your own paper pattern.

For the simplest pillows, you will need to cut only two pieces of fabric in muslin and two in cover fabric. These will be of the same dimensions. Sew the two pieces of muslin together, observing a ½-inch seam allowance, and leave an opening to place the form.

Clip the corners as illustrated in Fig. 7-13. Turn the cover and fit the form inside. Close the opening.

Your cover fabric will be assembled in the same manner. This completes the simplest pillow, but there are ways to add extra decorative touches.

Zippers

Since a pillow has a sharp edge rather than boxing, the zipper must be installed in the seam. Cut the two pieces of fabric just as you would without a zipper. Baste the pieces together the length of the zipper, right sides together. Press the seam open, aligning the zipper directly over the seam, right side down. Pin it in place. Sew the zipper to this seam. Then pull out the basting threads and see that the zipper is properly placed and works smoothly. Open the zipper.

Join the remaining circumference of the cover. Turn it through the zippered opening. Fit the form and close the zipper. Additional touches like welting, trims, or ruffles can be added.

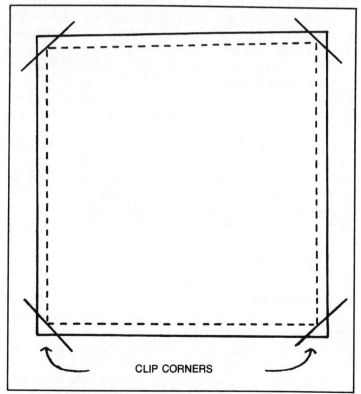

CLIP CORNERS

Fig. 7-13. Clip corners of the casing.

Ruffled Edges

As with other trims, ruffles for a pillow can be of matching or contrasting colors. A simple and attractive way to make your own ruffles follows.

Measure the circumference of your pillow, and double this measurement to obtain the length of the ruffling strip. Decide how wide you want the completed ruffle to be. Double this width, and add 1 inch for seams. Cut the fabric along the crosswise grain if possible. This isn't absolutely necessary, but it does make ruffling easier and smoother.

Fold the strip, wrong sides together, down the center. Keep the cut edges together and press the fold, seeing that there are no wrinkles and that the folded strip is neat and squared. Sew the cut edges together near the edge.

One-half inch from this cut and stitched edge, begin gathering the ruffle. If your machine has a ruffler attachment, you will find this very convenient. You may gather the ruffle by hand about as well. If you gather it by hand, take even stitches. Make the length of this strip the same as the circumference of the pillow, plus a 1-inch seam allowance where you will connect the ends of the strip.

When the strip is gathered to the proper length, distribute the ruffling evenly from one end to the other. Place the ruffled strip along the right side of one edge of the covering square, and sew it to this cover piece. Join the two ends of the ruffling strip together neatly.

Pin the second piece of cover fabric, right side in, along the edges of the other piece with ruffle attached. Place the material on your machine with the piece you just added on the bottom. This will permit you to see and follow the seam you made earlier, avoiding the possibility that the seam will show on the outside when you reverse the cover. Leave a large enough opening to fit the form inside.

Turn the cover, fit the form inside, and close the opening. The ruffled pillow is completed.

MAKING DRAPERIES

The choice of draperies for your home is second only to the furniture itself in the decorating project. The ability to make draperies (or the lack of it) can greatly affect the planning and the success of the actual upholstery. The reason is simple. Suppose you want very much to upholster your furniture in a particular fabric, but you cannot find suitable draperies anywhere. Unless you can afford to have draperies custom-made (which is terribly expensive) or are able to make your own, you have no choice but to compromise in your selection of upholstery fabrics.

Such a compromise will not be necessary if you make your own draperies. It is unlikely that you will have any difficulty in finding suitable drapery *fabric*. An abundance of drapery materials is available in department stores. You are almost certain to be able to find what you need.

Making your own draperies involves many steps if they are to be properly done. As you read through the steps, do not be deterred by the sometimes lengthy directions. Read through the discussion a time or two as needed to grasp a broad view of the overall project. Then return to the beginning and carefully study each step in the process.

Once you have a pretty clear idea of the sequence and the techniques, you can do the necessary measuring and acquire the fabrics. You will find the instructions easier to comprehend and follow when you have the actual materials at hand.

Some decisions must be made before actually buying materials. You must choose a fabric type and color. Decide whether the draperies will cover the actual window only, or be extended beyond the window to create some spatial effect. Plan for panel drapes (fixed position) or draw draperies (requiring traverse rods). Choose to make lined or unlined draperies. Decide whether to make your pleats or to use pleating tape. Decide just what kind of drapery hardware (curtain rods) you will use. These decisions are made first so you can measure accurately.

Straightening Fabric

No matter what kind of draperies you choose to make, there are some essential preparatory steps. If the draperies are to hang smoothly, there can be no guesswork in aligning and cutting along lengthwise and crosswise fabric grains. You will sometimes find that because of the manner in which the fabric is wound on the bolt, the grain will be stretched out of shape. The first thing to do, then, is to determine whether it is straight.

The crosswise grain is that perpendicular to the *selvage*. Pull a thread of the crosswise grain near the cut end of the piece. This pulled thread will create an easily seen line, showing the *true* crosswise grain. Fold the fabric lengthwise, and pin it together along the line where you pulled the thread. Smooth the folded fabric on your worktable. With the folded fabric pinned together along the true crosswise grain, the selvages will match if the fabric is straight. If they are not together (Fig. 7-14), this means that you must straighten the grain.

This is accomplished by stretching the fabric gently along the bias, in whichever direction will properly align the grain. Straight fabrics will have the lengthwise and crosswise grains at right angles to each other. Pull the fabric gently along the bias until it is straight and the selvages are together, with the pinned line where you pulled the thread smooth and squared.

Your drapery fabrics will not always require such straightening. Never begin cutting, however, until you have determined and possibly corrected the alignment of the grain. Otherwise, you may find that your draperies will sag at one corner or another.

Matching Patterns

If your fabric is of a solid color, a vertical stripe, or otherwise patterned in a manner that won't create problems in matching, you won't need to read this section. If your fabric has a specific design, you must be sure that the design in each panel occurs at the same vertical spot.

In order to match the design, you will need a little extra fabric. If you will lay out a piece of the fabric and measure from the center of one design to the center of the next or adjoining one, this will be a sufficient amount to add to each panel to match the designs.

Most seamstresses, in arranging the design on draperies, lay out and cut the fabric so that the beginning edge of a design occurs at the fold representing the bottom edge of the completed drapery.

When making draperies, never overlook the need for matching the design patterns in adjoining panels. An unmatched pattern in drapery panels can destroy the total decorating scheme in a room.

SIMPLE PANEL DRAPERIES

The easiest draperies of all to make are those with neither pleats nor lining. These draperies are simply gathered onto the curtain rod.

By the time you have decided what kind of draperies to make, you will know which rods to use. Either install the rod now, or mark the window frame for the exact location when you do install it.

You must decide what the finished length of your draperies will be. Ordinarily, there are three acceptable lengths. One is that which barely touches or misses touching the *windowsill*. Draperies might also properly extend beyond the sill, reaching the bottom edge of the apron (the wide board attached directly to the wall beneath the sill). The third acceptable drapery length is that which barely touches, or better, barely misses touching the floor.

There are other measurements that are considered more or less standard. These do not have to be observed to the inch; you can make slight adjustments with no harm done. The most important thing is to be consistent in your measurements throughout the project. Following are some of the most often observed measurements.

The bottom hem should be 3 inches long. The top hem will include the thickness of the rod and any heading above it, plus the length to be folded to the inside for the hem. Usually this will require about 10 or 12 inches of fabric (above the bottom of the rod).

Measure from the bottom edge of the rod to whatever length you have chosen. To this length, add the 3½ inches for the bottom hem and the 10 to 12 inches for the top hem, heading and all.

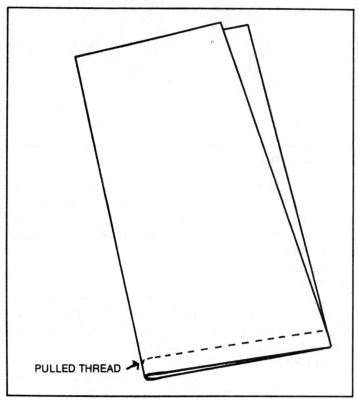

PULLED THREAD

Fig. 7-14. The fabric grain must be straightened.

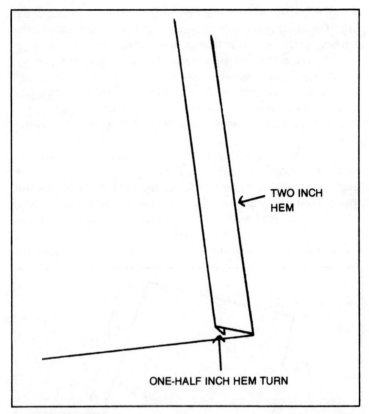

TWO INCH
HEM

ONE-HALF INCH HEM TURN

Fig. 7-15. Hem and turn.

Measure for the width of each panel next. This will be determined in large part by the size of window to be covered. For instance, you would want two panels for the average double-hung window (the one where one sash slides vertically in front of the other to open the window).

Measure the total width of the window frame, from the outside edge of one casing to the outside of the other one. To this measurement, add approximately 10 inches. This will permit four 2-inch hems, and four ½-inch turns on the hems (Fig. 7-15). Since all draperies should extend around the curve of the rod to touch the wall, you will add approximately 4 inches more to accommodate this curve at each side of the window.

You must also allow for fullness. With these simple gathered draperies, you have some option in this measurement. The extra width necessary to provide the desired fullness is one which you must estimate for yourself. This will depend upon the type of fabric you will use, and how fully it can be gathered and look nice. A beginning point, but one with which you must experiment, is to add the width of the window frame again. An example: you have calculated the width *excepting* that for fullness. Assume that the window frame is 40 inches wide. To this 40 inches, add four for the curve around the ends of the rod. Add 10 inches for the hems and turns, and then add 40 inches again for fullness. The total is 94 inches required width for two panels, or 47 inches per panel.

Lay the fabric out on your cutting table, and pull a thread near the end. This will establish your first cutting line. Determine whether the grain is straight. Straighten it if necessary. Remember to match design patterns in adjoining panels, and then cut the fabric for length. Always cut the selvages off. Measure and cut for the correct width.

In these simple draperies, complete the side hems first. Measure accurately. Press the folds before you sew. Turn the edge ½ inch under and press it, and then turn 2 inches for the hem and press again. Do this on both sides of each panel.

You can straight stitch these hems with your machine, but the draperies will be more attractive if you either slip stitch them by hand or blind stitch with your machine.

When the side hems are sewn and pressed, do the top hem. Be careful to match designs. Fold the fabric ½ inch and press it. Machine stitch this fold near the edge (Fig. 7-16). Make the second

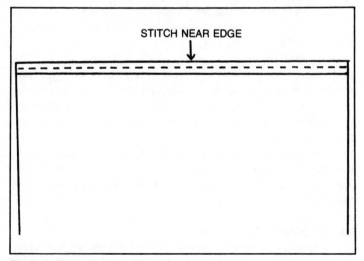

Fig. 7-16. Stitch near the edge.

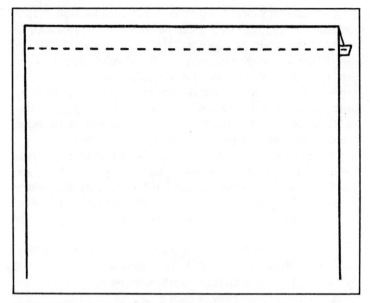

Fig. 7-17. Make the ends of the hem fit neatly.

fold which includes the width of the rod, the heading, and the inside of the hem.

Stitch the hem on your machine. The seam will not show; it will be concealed in the fullness. Be sure the ends of this hem are neat. Avoid the situation illustrated in Fig. 7-17.

Measure up from the hem seam the width of the rod, plus enough fullness to accommodate the rod. Mark this line and sew it on the machine (Fig. 7-18).

Insert the rod in the run you just made, and hang it in place. All your measurements should be correct. It is always wise to measure the length of the drapery after it is hung in order to be certain that the bottom hem will occur at the proper place. Mark the fold for the bottom hem on each panel so they are precisely the same, and pin the hem in place.

You could finish the hem now, but it is usually a good idea to leave the hem unfinished without pressing a fold or doing any stitching. Thus, if the drapery shrinks after the first laundering, you can adjust it and then finish the hem.

PLEATED DRAPERIES

Measuring for length and width of *pleated drapes* is done in the same manner as in the preceding discussion, except for one point.

There is no guesswork necessary for the width measurement in these panels. You will be able to figure exactly how much fabric is required.

You will probably choose either the *pinch pleat* or the *box pleat*. In either kind the pleats should be spaced approximately 4 inches apart, and each pleat will require about 5 inches of fabric. These figures are approximate and can vary slightly. Consistency in size and placement of the pleats is more important than the actual size of the pleats.

You must plan the pleats in order to get the right width measurement. If you are making panel draperies, measure 2 inches from the center edge of the panel, and mark for the beginning of the first pleat. From this first mark measure approximately 5 inches, and mark for the second edge of the first pleat (pins are fine) (Fig. 7-19). The second pleat you make or plan will fall, when the drapery is hung, right at the end of the rod. No pleats will be placed in the part that extends around the curve and to the wall. Measure the depth of this curve, and mark for the outer edge of the first pleat on this side at that point. Measure 5 inches farther and establish the other edge of this pleat.

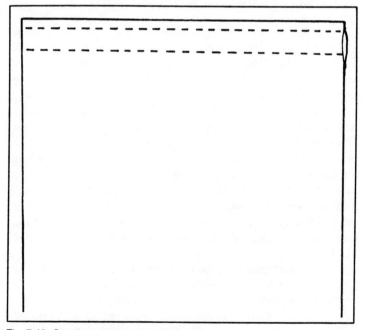

Fig. 7-18. Sew the seam to enclose the rod.

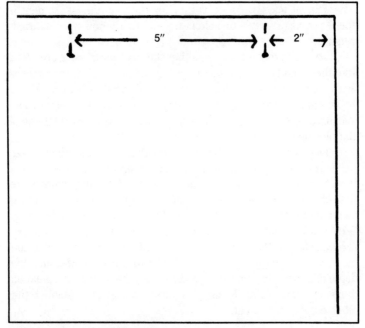

Fig. 7-19. Mark for pleat locations.

The number and spacing between the rest of the pleats will be determined by the remaining space between the two pleats you have established. Measure the space and divide it into the appropriate number of pleats. Space the pleats equally. Use the same amount of fabric for each one.

When you make draw draperies to be used on *traverse rods*, the panels overlap about 2½ inches when the draperies are closed. When they *are* closed, the distance between the inside pleat on each panel should be the same as that between other pleats throughout the panels. This means that the first pleat must be more than 2 inches from the center edge. If you intend to space your pleats at 4 inches, establish the outer edge of the first pleat 3¼ inches from the edge. When the draperies are closed, there will be a 4-inch space. Otherwise, measurements for pleats will proceed as in the preceding discussion.

When your panels will be very wide, requiring that you seam two lengths of fabric together, be sure to allow for this seam in your width measurements. Allow generally ½ inch for each length.

There are two ways to prepare the drapery heading for pleats. The simplest way is to use *pleating tape* which you can buy at department stores. This material is stiff enough to support the pleats and has evenly spaced narrow runs in which you insert the prongs of pleater pins. This automatically forms attractive pleats. The use of pleating tape will affect the length measurements, because the tape will take the place of the wide hem fold at the top.

Place your fabric on the worktable, right side up. Lay the pleating tape near the edge of the fabric. The tape should extend the full length of the completed drapery, but it should not be folded in the side hems. If your side hems will use 2½ inches of fabric each, cut the pleating tape 5 inches shorter than the total width of the panel. Place it as shown in Fig. 7-20. Trim the end of the pleating tape. Place it so the first pleat on the outer edge of the panel will occur at the end of the rod, but not in the curve.

Sew the top edge of the pleating tape to the fabric. Fold the pleating tape to the inside (Fig. 7-21). Press the fold of the fabric. The bottom edge of the pleating tape must now be sewn to the fabric.

The side hems are completed next. When you fold the hem 2½ inches to the inside, you will find that there is considerable thickness at each corner. If this is too bulky, trim some of the hem away

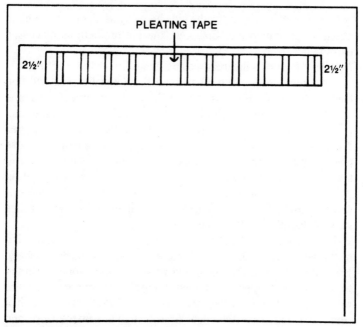

Fig. 7-20. Pleating tape is not folded into side hems.

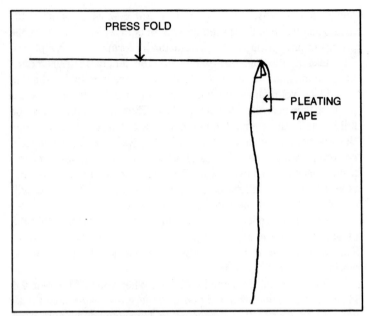

PRESS FOLD

PLEATING TAPE

Fig. 7-21. Fold the pleating tape to the inside.

before sewing it. Slip stitch the side hems by hand, or use the blind stitch on your machine. Complete the bottom hem as discussed earlier.

The draperies are ready to be hung. Insert the pleating pins into the runs on the tape. Distribute them equally. You will find many types of pleater pins at your drapery department. Examine each type and decide which will be most suitable for your draperies.

Another way to prepare the heading for pleats in unlined draperies is to use a strip of *crinoline* to provide the stiffness necessary to support the pleats and keep them looking nice. The strip of crinoline will be as wide as the top hem. Like the pleating tape, it will be cut so that it will not be folded into the side hems. If you will use 2½ inches for each hem, cut the crinoline 5 inches shorter than the width of the fabric.

If you have chosen to make a 4-inch top hem, fold the top edge of the fabric 4½ inches to the inside (½ inch for turning under). Press the fold to create a crease at what will be the top edge of the finished drapery. Open the folded and pressed hem now, and place the crinoline strip along the crease as in Fig. 7-22. Fold the ½ inch of remaining fabric over the edge of the crinoline. Sew the fabric and crinoline together on your machine.

Refold the hem at the crease. This conceals the crinoline strip. Tack it at intervals. It is not necessary or desirable to sew here, for the hem is secured when the pleats are installed (Fig. 7-23).

Now the heading is prepared for pleats. Finish the side and bottom hems as discussed earlier. Pleats must now be made before you complete the bottom hem.

Refer to the earlier discussion of measurements for pleats. Mark the edges of each pleat with chalk or pins. Remember to place the outside pleats first, and then distribute the inner pleats.

Fold the fabric so that the two edges of a pleat are together, and sew them from the top edge of the heading to slightly below the hem. When you have sewn all the plates in this manner, it will look like Fig. 7-24.

In order to make pinch pleats, fold the single large pleat into three small ones. Tack them together at the bottom (Fig. 7-25). To make box pleats, fold the large pleat so that it is equally wide on each side of the seam. Tack it along the top, concealing the stitches (Fig. 7-26). This completes the drapery. You may insert the hooks and hang it prior to finishing the bottom hem.

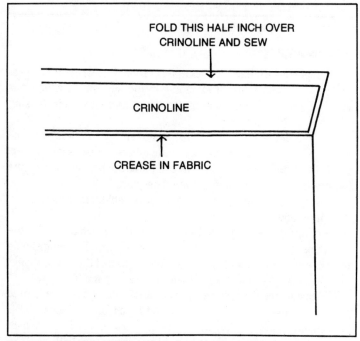

Fig. 7-22. Place the crinoline next to the crease.

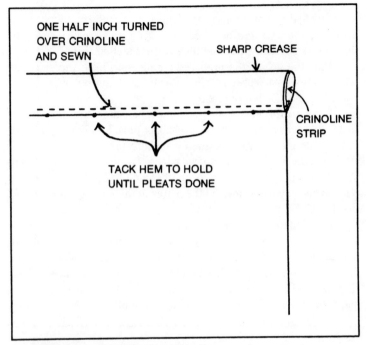

ONE HALF INCH TURNED OVER CRINOLINE AND SEWN

SHARP CREASE

CRINOLINE STRIP

TACK HEM TO HOLD UNTIL PLEATS DONE

Fig. 7-23. Pleats will hold the hem securely.

LINED DRAPERIES

Draperies are lined for several reasons. Primarily, lining prevents the drapery fabric from fading in the sunlight to which it is usually exposed. Linings also create softer, more luxurious looking draperies if they are properly done.

Lining draperies is not difficult. Finish the top hem with the crinoline inner facing for support of the pleats as discussed earlier. Finish the side hems, too. Do not complete the bottom hem on the drapery fabric, but do fold and pin it in place.

Lay your drapery panel on your worktable, right side down. Straighten and smooth it neatly.

Lining for a drapery panel should be wide enough to overlap the side hems and the top hem approximately ½ inch. The lining should overlap the bottom hem slightly, but the bottom of the lining should be at least 2½ inches shorter than the drapery itself.

Measure the drapery panel from the inside of one side hem to the inside of the other side hem, and add 1 inch for a ½-inch overlap on each side. Add another inch to this measurement for a ½-inch turn on each side of the lining fabric. Measure from the bottom of the

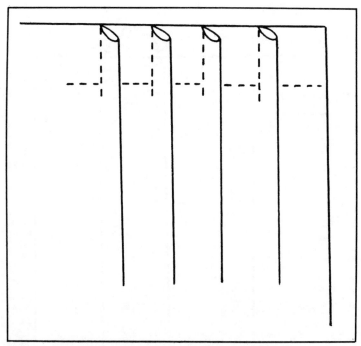

Fig. 7-24. Sew from the top edge to just below the hem.

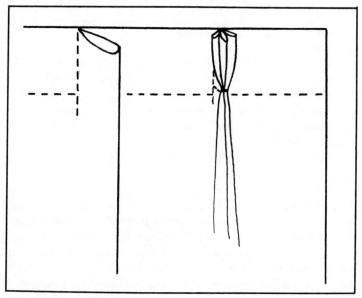

Fig. 7-25. Tack the three pleats at the bottom.

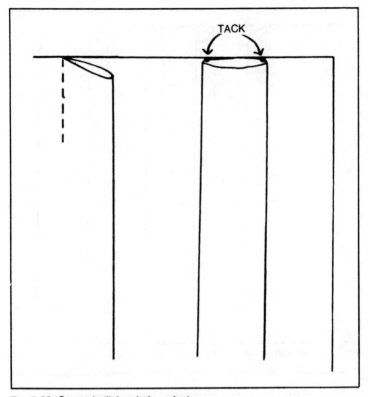

Fig. 7-26. Conceal stitches in box pleats.

hem to the top of the bottom hem. Add 1 inch at the top for a ½-inch overlap and a ½-inch turn on the lining. Add enough at the bottom end for a hem (2 inches is all right) so that the hemmed lining overlaps the top of the bottom hem slightly (Fig. 7-27).

Straighten your lining fabric if it is needed, and cut it on the lengthwise and crosswise grains. Hem the bottom according to your plans. Machine hemming is fine. Fold both sides and the top under ½ inch. Press these folds.

A drapery lining can be sewn to the drapery by machine, but it is probably better done by hand with a slip stitch. Lay the lining fabric, wrong side down, on the drapery panel that you have spread on your worktable. Place it so that the lining fabric overlaps the top, side, and bottom hems slightly. If the panel is not very wide, you may simply slip stitch the lining to the hems on the drapery along the top and sides. If the panel is very wide, it is advisable to tack the lining to the drapery fabric.

To do this, find the center of your lining fabric. Fold it back (Fig. 7-28). Be careful to pick up only a few threads of the drapery fabric, and tack the lining to the drapery in several places along the folded length (Fig. 7-29). When you have completed this step, repeat it once more halfway between the center and one edge, and then halfway between the center and the other edge. Then slip stitch the sides and the top of the lining to the side and top hems of the drapery fabric. This step is necessary on very wide panels to prevent the lining from eventually hanging unattractively below the bottom of the drapery material.

Do not finish the bottom hem of the drapery panel until you have pleated the heading and hung the drapes, so that your measurements will be precise. When you are satisfied that they are accurate, finish the bottom hem. Do not attach the bottom of the lining to the drapery. It is attached only at the sides and top, and in wide panels at vertical intervals as just described.

BEDSPREADS

Bedspreads may be the quickest and easiest projects in this book. Yet relatively few people make them. Why? Probably the single most effective deterrent is the *size*.

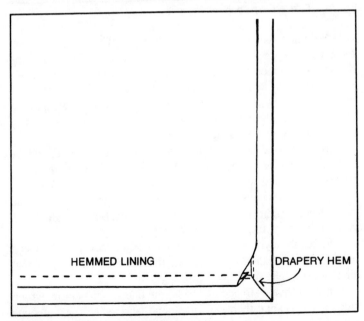

Fig. 7-27. The lining overlaps the bottom hem.

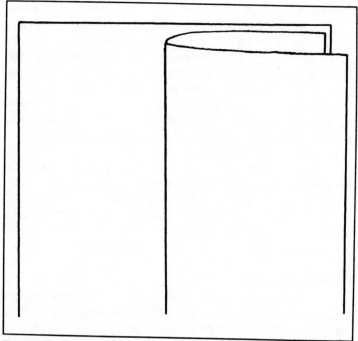
Fig. 7-28. Fold the lining back at the center.

Making a bedspread is fast and easy. There are different techniques, depending on the type of spread and the fabric, but some things are common to the making of all bedspreads.

See that the fabric type and color are suitable to the occupant of the room where the spread will be used. It isn't usually wise to use dry-clean-only fabric in a boy's room. Few teenage girls will really enjoy a spread of bold-striped denim.

When you measure for a dust ruffle, do so with all covers off the bed. In other measurements for the spread itself, keep the usual covers on the bed while you measure.

When you choose the fabric, remember to get thread and needles of the right color and size for that fabric. Buy enough so that you can match patterns when necessary.

If the fabric you want is not wide enough to cover the bed side to side, plan a single width down the middle. Then add equal amounts to each side (Fig. 7-30).

If the spread is to be lined baste the lining to the fabric, wrong sides together, and then sew lining and fabric seams at the same time. This is not a good idea for lining ruffles; I explain later.

Dust Ruffle

Take all covers off the bed. Measure the length and width of the mattress (or the box spring). Make a pattern of the curve at a corner of the mattress by placing a piece of cardboard between the mattress and springs, and drawing around the curve (Fig. 7-31).

To both the length and width measurements, add 2 inches for a wide seam allowance. Cut (and seam, if necessary) a muslin cover to these measurements. Use the cardboard pattern that you made. Draw the curves at the corners, 1 inch from the edge.

Measure from the top of the spring to the floor. Add 2 inches to the measurement, which is the length of the ruffle, plus a hem and a 1-inch seam allowance.

The yardage required for the ruffle will depend upon the kind of fabric you will use. For medium-weight fabrics, four times the length measurement is usually sufficient. Sheer fabrics will require perhaps half again this amount. Cut the pieces for the ruffle and sew them together end to end. Hem the complete length of the ruffle strip, making a simple double-fold hem (a ½-inch turn and a 1-inch hem).

Ruffle the fabric 1 inch from the top edge. With large projects like this, you will appreciate a ruffler on your sewing machine.

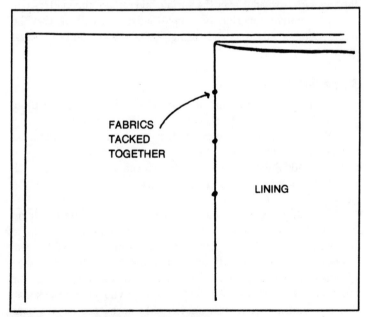

Fig. 7-29. Tack the lining to the drapery fabric.

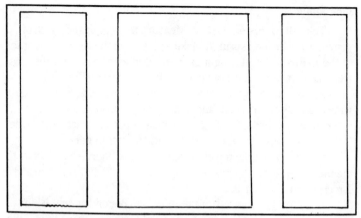

Fig. 7-30. For narrow fabrics, use three lengths.

Remove the mattress from the bed. Spread the completed project over it. To keep it in place so you don't have to keep taking the mattress off to straighten it, make a 6-inch *return* at each corner at the head of the bed. Pin the ruffle to the flat muslin sheet, 6 inches from one corner, around the corner and all around the sheet, to finish with another 6-inch return opposite the first (Fig. 7-32). Sew the ruffle on, spread it over the spring, and replace the mattress. A quilt, decorative coverlet, or simple bedspread will overlap the intersection of mattress and spring, and show off the pretty *dust ruffle*.

Simple Bedspread

In most cases the simple bedspread will have to be three pieces. The first thing to do is measure for length and width.

With covers and pillow on the bed, measure from the mattress behind the pillow, and over the pillow, to the foot of the bed and to the floor. Add 3 inches for a ½-inch turn and a 1-inch hem at each end, and approximately 15 inches for tucking the spread under the pillow.

To obtain the width measurement, measure from the floor, over the bed and covers, to the floor on the opposite side. Add to this measurement 3 inches for hems and 4 inches for wide seam allowances where you will sew the three pieces together. The pieces will look like Fig. 7-33. Seam them together. Place the spread correctly on the bed. Just as though you were marking an ordinary hem, mark one corner at the foot where it touches the floor (Fig. 7-34).

236

Remove the spread. Cut the surplus off, making a neat curve at the corner. Then fold the spread lengthwise. Cut the other corner in the same curve. Hem the spread. The simple spread is complete.

Plain Bedspread

This is another very easy spread requiring three or four lengths of fabric. Both possibilities are shown in Fig. 7-35. In one drawing the center section falls over the foot of the bed to the floor, and the side sections reach the foot of the bed only.

For a real fitted or tailored look, cut the foot extension as a fourth piece. Accent the edges, sides, and foot with welting.

For either possibility the length measurement is obtained in the same way as for the simple bedspread. The side lengths are measured only to the foot of the bed, and for the possibility described in the previous paragraph you must add an extra 2 inches for the welting seam.

Coverlet

A *coverlet* may be a simple spread, but one that reaches *just below* the top of the spring to reveal the dust ruffle. It may be a pretty quilt. The coverlet is used to match or accent the dust ruffle.

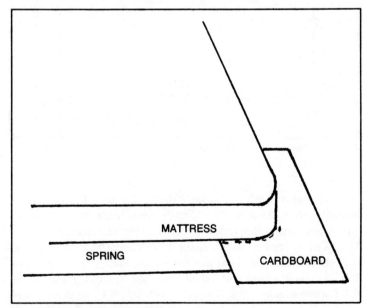

Fig. 7-31. Make a pattern of the curve.

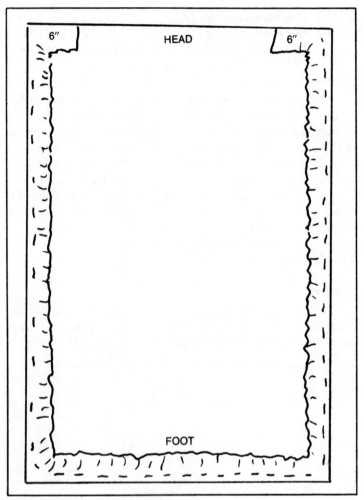

Fig. 7-32. Make returns at the head end.

Welting

Welting is one of the most familiar trims on bedspreads. It consists of a cord encased in either the same fabric or some matching or contrasting one, and sewn between two pieces at the seam.

Welting cord can be obtained in most department stores. The size of cord will depend on the weight of the fabric you are using and the way you want the finished piece to look. Generally, the lighter fabrics use smaller cord. Cut welting strips on a bias of sufficient width to cover the cord. Leave an adequate seam allowance.

Ruffled Bedspread

Ruffled bedspreads are also relatively simple to make. They require more time and more fabric than the simpler spreads; otherwise, there is little difference.

Measure from the mattress behind the pillow, over the pillow, and to the foot of the bed. To this measurement, add 2 inches for a hem at the top and a seam allowance for the ruffled skirt at the bottom. Add about 15 inches for tucking the spread under the pillow. Measure from one side of the mattress to the other for the width of the sheet part of the spread.

The spread can have either a single long ruffled skirt or a gathered skirt with a narrow ruffle at the bottom. For the skirt without a ruffle, measure from the top of the bed with covers to the floor. Add 1 inch for a seam allowance and 1 inch for the hem. The ½-inch turn on the hem will lift the skirt barely off the floor.

In medium-weight fabrics such as polished cotton, you will need approximately twice the length measurement to make a nicely gathered skirt. Sheer fabrics will require more length.

Seam the pieces together for the skirt, and then hem the whole length. Ruffle the skirt 1 inch from the top.

Pin the gathered skirt to the sheet, right sides together, beginning at one end. Pin it all the way around, and then sew it to the

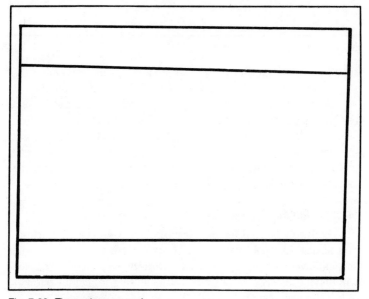

Fig. 7-33. Three-piece spread.

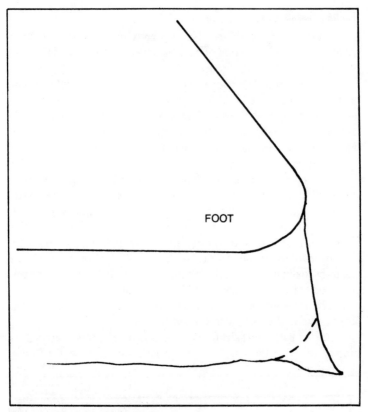

Fig. 7-34. Mark the corner curve.

sheet. Hem the ends of the gathered skirt and the top end of the sheet part, and the simplest kind of ruffled spread is complete.

Add a ruffle, 2 or 3 inches deep, to the bottom of the skirt for a really pretty ruffled spread. The skirt will be 2 or 3 inches shorter. The ruffle is cut, seamed, hemmed, gathered, and sewn on, just as the skirt was. If you doubled the length measurement of the spread to get the right length for the skirt, then double the length of the skirt to get the best length for the ruffle.

Machine-Quilting Bedspreads

Bedspreads can be quilted beautifully on your sewing machine. You can use a straight stitch to make square, triangular, or diamond shapes. If your sewing machine has a variety of stitch patterns, you will find these particularly attractive in quilting around the outlines of large fabric designs.

In order to produce the nice puffy appearance, you will need some kind of soft lining or padding. There are several choices of padding materials in most department stores. You might use two layers of flannel.

Before precise cutting of the bedspread pattern is done (quilting will have a slight effect on the measurements), baste the two layers of flannel to the wrong side of the fabric. Baste a few seams along both the lengthwise and crosswise grains. This keeps the fabric and padding in place as you quilt.

If you use a straight stitch and a simple pattern, mark the first line—diagonal, vertical, or horizontal—on the padding after it is basted to the fabric. Begin in the center of the piece. Work from the center line toward each side or end. If your machine has a quilting foot, you will appreciate it. It will be easier to maintain the correct spacing between lines of stitching. The adjustable space guide is set on the first line of stitching and follows it as you sew the second and succeeding lines (Fig. 7-36). If you use some kind of decorative stitching where you outline a floral or other design, do the sewing with the fabric side up.

SLIPCOVERS

Slipcovers must be well made, with a good fit and a pleasing appearance, if they are to be worth the time and effort. Covers can

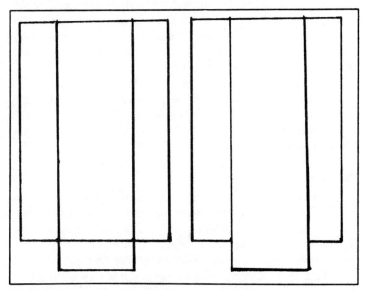

Fig. 7-35. Three or four-piece spread.

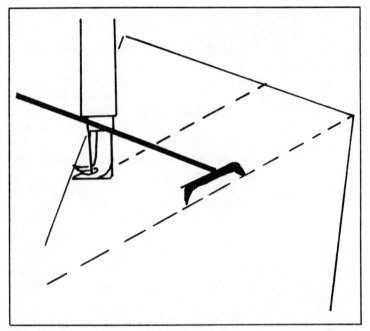

Fig. 7-36. The space guide maintains correct seams.

be changed with the seasons or for any special occasion. They certainly add to the life of the cover fabric on the furniture. They are practical in homes with small children, because they can be removed and laundered. The single most pleasing thing about nicely fitting slipcovers is that you can change the mood, or the overall effect, of your furniture in a short time.

There may be small variations where different furniture styles require them, but slipcovers are nearly always made in the same basic way. Unless you are already experienced at this project, make a pattern of inexpensive muslin first. You cut the fabric for the slipcovers from this pattern.

Measuring

The chair in Fig. 7-37 is a rather simple one. Where the sofa or chair for which you want to make a slipcover differs from this one, you can easily make the adjustments by following the same basic principles in measuring and cutting.

Measure and record in the same sequence expressed in Table 7-1. These are actual chair measurements. Make a similar chart for your chair and record the measurements.

On every piece, 4 inches or 2 inches are added to the width and length measurements.

In many cases this may be too much. It is a good idea to have some surplus on your first effort. The surplus and the waste will only apply to the muslin pattern, not the cover fabric. The surplus is advisable; it will absorb errors in measuring and some irregularities in the furniture itself.

Please note the use of the words length and width in Table 7-1. Their use is deliberate. In order to estimate the amount of yardage in muslin, add all the length measurements except the boxing length. The total in Table 7-1 is 188 inches. Since no width measurement is more than 36 inches, if you divide the total you reached by 36, you have a fairly accurate estimate of yardage required. Add an extra yard for any welting you might decide to do, and there should be enough surplus to make the boxing strip.

Cutting and Fitting the Pattern

There is a second reason for the use of the terms length and width in Table 7-1. All the length measurements are cut on the lengthwise grain of muslin (and fabric, later), and all the width measurements are cut on the crosswise grain.

Be sure the muslin is straight; and then cut the pieces according to your chart. In this example the first piece to cut is the top back, which is a rectangle 5 inches on the lengthwise grain and 26 inches

Table 7-1. Sample Chart for Recording Chair Measurements.

A-A	top back length	$\underline{5''}$ + 4″ seam allowance
B-B	top back width	$\underline{26''}$ + 4″
C-C	outside back length	$\underline{26''}$ + 4″
D-D	outside back width	$\underline{21''}$ + 4″
E-E	inside back width	$\underline{26''}$ + 4″
F-F	inside back length	$\underline{18''}$ + 4″ =__″ + 3″ tuck
G-G	seat length	$\underline{20''}$ + 4″ =__″ + 3″ tuck
H-H	seat width	$\underline{26''}$ + 4″ =__″ + 6″ tuck
I-I	front panel length	$\underline{8''}$ + 4″
J-J	front panel width	$\underline{26''}$ + 4″
K-K	inside arm length	$\underline{15''}$ + 4″ + 3″ tuck =__″ cut two
L-L	inside arem width	$\underline{20''}$ + = ″ + 3″ tuck
M-M	outside arm length	$\underline{18''}$ + 4″ cut two
N-N	outside arm width	$\underline{24''}$ + 4″
O-O	front arm length	$\underline{18''}$ + 4″ cut two
P-P	front arm width	$\underline{5''}$ + 4″
Q-Q	cushion length	$\underline{20''}$ + 2″ cut two
R-R	cushion width	$\underline{26''}$ + 2″
S-S	boxing depth (width)	$\underline{3½''}$ + 2″
T-T	boxing strip length	$\underline{92''}$ + 2″
U-U	arm back length	$\underline{18''}$ + 4″ cut two
V-V	arm back width	$\underline{5''}$ + 4″
W-W	back end length	$\underline{12''}$ + 4″ cut two
X-X	back end width	$\underline{5''}$ + 4″

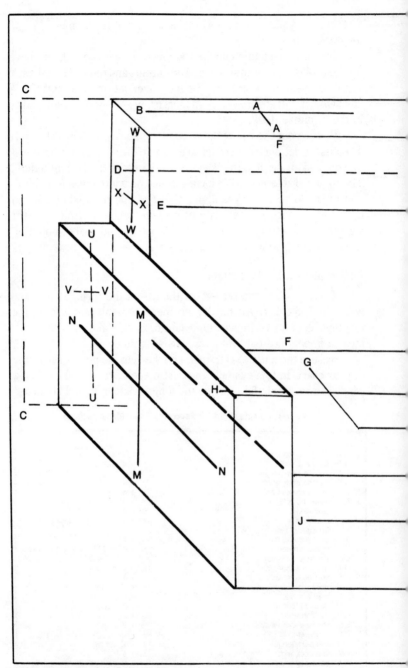

Fig. 7-37. Measure all the parts of the chair.

244

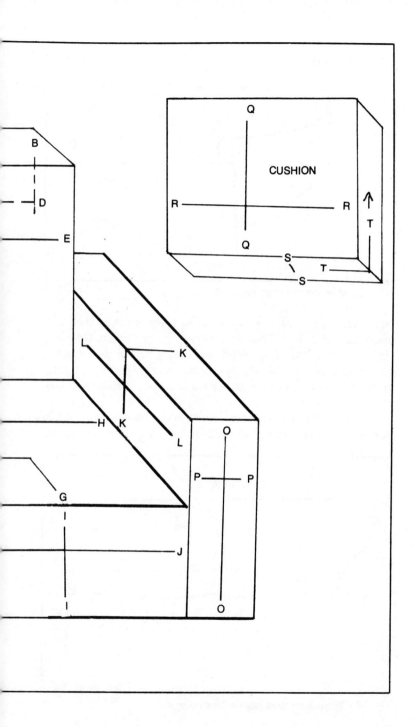

CUSHION

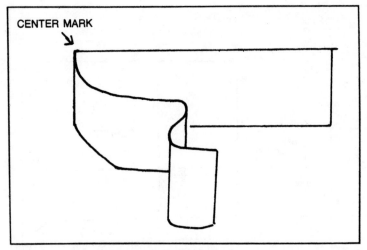

Fig. 7-38. Mark the center on the lengthwise grain.

on the crosswise grain. As soon as this piece is cut, it should be folded as in Fig. 7-38. The center is notched or marked. Do every piece this way. Find the exact center of the top back on the chair, and pin the muslin piece on the two center marks. If it is correctly measured and cut, there should be a 2-inch overlap all the way around (Fig. 7-39).

The outside back is cut next, which in the example is a piece 26 inches on the lengthwise grain and 26 inches on the crosswise grain.

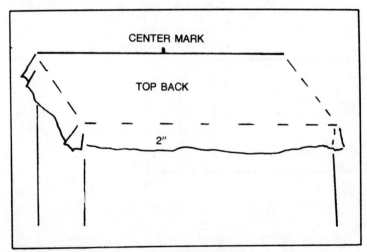

Fig. 7-39. The piece should have a 2-inch overlap.

246

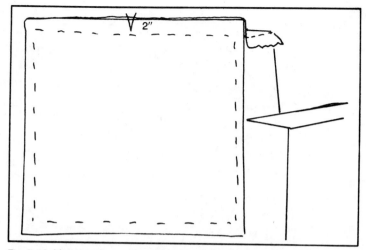

Fig. 7-40. Match center marks and pin the back to the chair and the top.

Immediately mark or notch the center on the top, match it, and pin it to the center mark on the first piece. You have cut the pieces with a 2-inch seam allowance all the way around, so pin them this way. Almost certainly you will find an error, and the extra 2 inches will be absorbed. Just pin the pieces at this point; don't do any trimming of excess seam allowances yet.

Pin the second piece to the first as described. Pin it to the chair as well (Fig. 7-40).

As you continue this process of cutting and pinning, you find, on nearly any piece of furniture, that you must trim excess fabric, or at least notch it, to make it fit around curves. See the wing chair in Fig. 7-41. This muslin pattern should be fitted pretty closely, so trim or notch when necessary.

In Fig. 7-41 you find curves in the other direction, where fullness must be gathered or worked in. On the final fabric cover you gather this fullness with a needle and thread to get the fit accurate. As you prepare the muslin pattern, however, just work the fullness in with your pins.

Now cut and pin the inside back, and then the seat. There is an extra 3 inches on the length and on the width of the seat, as well as the back, for tucking between the seat and back upholstery. See that only a 2-inch seam allowance remains at the front edge of the seat (Fig. 7-42). Cut and pin the front panels (I-I in Table 7-1).

Cut and pin the inside arms. These will be pinned to the back and the seat. Pin them to the chair.

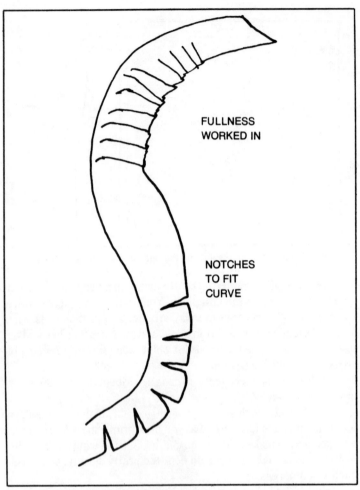

FULLNESS
WORKED IN

NOTCHES
TO FIT
CURVE

Fig. 7-41. Curves must be gathered or notched.

Outside arm pieces are next. Then the inside and outside arm pieces are joined when you add the front panel of the arms (front arm, O-O and P-P in Table 7-1).

The cushion is next. You may save it for last if you like. At any rate, it is cut and pinned in the very same way (Fig. 7-43).

All that remains is to cut and pin the backs of the arms (to the inside arm at the top, the outside back, and the outside arm). Cut and pin the ends of the back (W-W and X-X in Table 7-1).

Go over *every* pinned seam. Loosen or tighten the seams until the fit is snug and neat all over.

Fig. 7-42. Notice the tucking fullness.

Identify every piece by writing on it (Fig. 7-44). You might use colored chalk or a pencil. If you use a pen, be sure the ink isn't penetrating and marking the chair upholstery.

Use good, sharp shears, and trim all the seam allowances to approximately 1 inch. Use sharp scissors to notch the center of every lengthwise piece.

Now mark the seam lines. Hold the seam open with the fingers of one hand, and mark both pieces where they are joined by the pins (Fig. 7-45). When all the seam lines are marked, the seam allow-

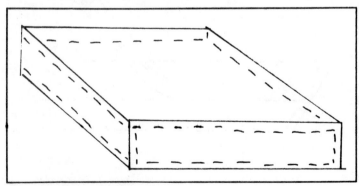

Fig. 7-43. Pin the cushion pieces.

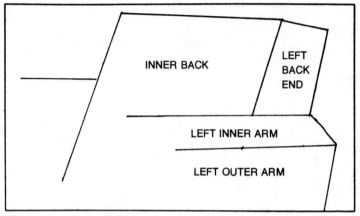

Fig. 7-44. Identify every piece.

ances trimmed, the center notched, and all pieces are identified, you can remove the pins, taking the whole job apart.

Cutting the Slipcover Fabric

Lay out your slipcover fabric right side up. Place the muslin pattern pieces right side up on it. Remember the grain directions. Cut out the pattern, reproducing the center notches.

Pin the cover fabric on the chair, just as you did the muslin pattern. It will be much quicker this time. When you have the fabric pinned on, right side out, mark the seam lines as you did on the muslin pattern.

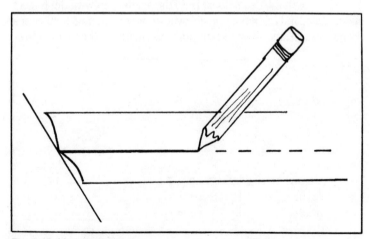

Fig. 7-45. Mark the seam lines.

250

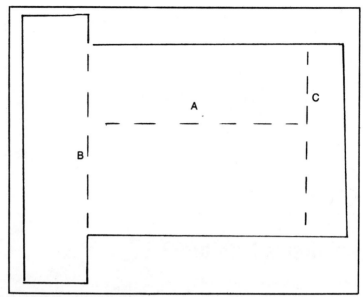

Fig. 7-46. Use logic in seaming.

If there are curves around which fullness must be gathered, do it by hand now, while the fabric is pinned in place. Do any necessary notching for opposite curves very carefully.

You cannot write on your cover fabric, so write the identifications on pieces of scrap muslin. Pin them securely to the fabric. Once this is done, you may remove the pins.

Most slipcovers have welting in the show seams. If you add welting, pin it to one piece, sew it, and then sew the second piece as instructed earlier.

Sewing the Slipcovers

Simply place the pieces right sides together, and join them at the seam lines you marked. Think ahead, following a logical order in this assembly. In other words, when seams will cross one another as in Fig. 7-46, logic determines that seam A is sewn first.

Follow the seam lines you made, even if they seem a bit irregular. They probably will be irregular in places, especially on used furniture, but they must be if the slipcovers are to fit. If you have measured, cut, pinned, and marked with care, the slipcovers should fit snugly.

Children's Furniture

When you become interested in furniture upholstery and furnishings, the children's room offers some exciting opportunities. The children's room is especially fun to work with in ways that differ from other rooms.

The needs and preferences of children continually change. You can easily visualize a room as first a nursery and then as a bedroom-playroom, a bedroom-study room, and finally as the private retreat of a young adult.

REASONS FOR REDECORATING A CHILD'S ROOM

Redecorating a child's room is extra fun because the child can help, and I don't mean by running errands while you do the work. Children are not hampered by the sometimes rigid notions and inhibitions that most adults have. This freedom permits children to envision many delightful ways to arrange a room. An example of this was expressed well by a child of my acquaintance. He was 8 years old at the time and was fascinated by height. He wanted a tree house but there was no place for one. He asked for a bed near the ceiling.

Impractical? Not really. The father happened to be handy with tools, and the boy's room was a bit on the small side anyway. They built the bed shown in Fig. 8-1. The bed was structurally sound and safe, the boy loved it, and this arrangement provided lots more play space than he originally had. The only real handicap was that of changing sheets and making the bed, and the boy did these tasks happily.

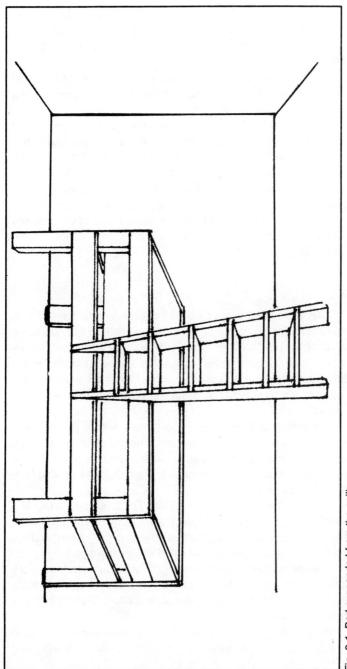

Fig. 8-1. Bed suspended from the ceiling.

253

Encourage your children to make suggestions and become involved in the planning and the work. Children have nimble fingers and eager enthusiasm, in addition to the unique approach that produces ideas.

Children must have every reassurance of security that you can provide. Giving a child a room that is definitely and uniquely his own is one way to offer him privacy.

You can redo a child's room with some upholstery and curtain material, foam and cotton padding, paint, adhesive-paper, and sometimes a few boards. Make use of throwaway things. A sheet of old, worn pegboard from my own "junk" became the foundation for a beautiful wall panel that finished the decorating in a bedroom. By making the most imaginative use of all sorts of odds and ends, you can redecorate a child's room without going broke in the process. Following are suggestions and ideas for making a child's room interesting.

BEDS

There are many ways to build or arrange beds for children. While there are problems in novel arrangements, such as space management, most of these problems actually add to the fun by presenting challenges to your imagination. Since the bed is generally the primary piece of furniture in a child's room. I consider a few ways to create interesting beds and add accessory articles to complete a theme.

A sleeping nook gives most children a secure feeling and a sense of privacy. Such an *alcove* can be built, but often there are odd-shaped rooms already suited to such an arrangement. What if the bed doesn't quite fit? If the space is big enough for the child the bed is no problem.

Suppose the alcove is 5½ feet long. To make a bed to fit, cut a slab of the appropriate size from plywood, Brace it in many ways (Fig. 8-2). Then cover the plywood with high density foam padding. This will be comfortable and an excellent back support.

I can almost hear someone saying, "The sheets won't fit." They won't. Anyone with a little time, a sewing machine and some bleached muslin, though, can make perfect fitted and flat sheets in any shape or size.

Bunk beds of the same kind are perfect in alcoves (Fig. 8-3). A really big space of any shape can become a home-made king-size bed (Fig. 8-4).

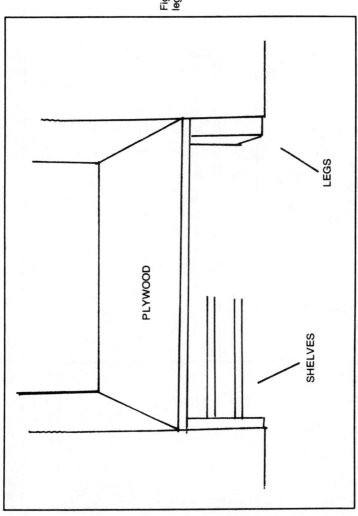

Fig. 8-2. Brace the plywood with legs, shelves, etc.

PLYWOOD

LEGS

SHELVES

255

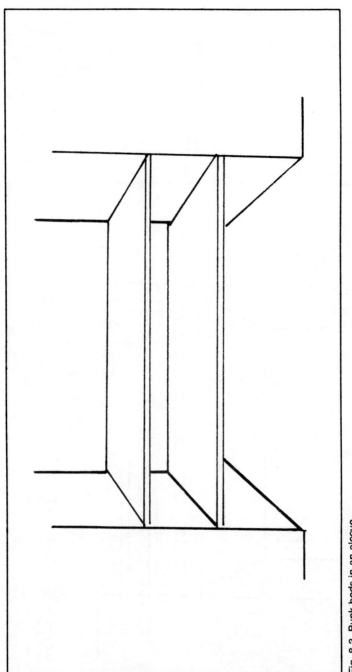

Fig. 8-3. Bunk beds in an alcove.

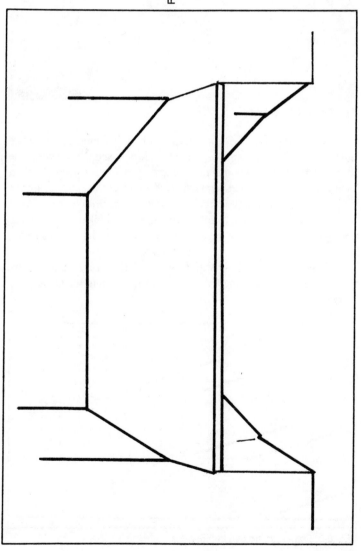

Fig. 8-4. Odd-shaped bed.

Fig. 8-5. Multilevel bed.

The bed in Fig. 8-5 is a multilevel bed designed by a teenage girl. It is really quite simple, though a bit of space is required. The frame is built of plywood (Fig. 8-6) and each level is padded with a foam mattress. This bed is imaginative, comfortable, and has lots of space for pajama party guests. Sometimes space problems are a real nuisance and frustrating to solve. You probably think of bunk beds as being one directly above another. What if you need three in a room, but there's no space for more than two?

There are a couple of ways to approach this problem. Make two beds "stacked" and hang the third from the ceiling, or arrange all three on the wall (Fig. 8-7).

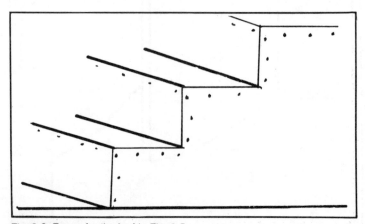

Fig. 8-6. Frame for the bed in Fig. 8-5.

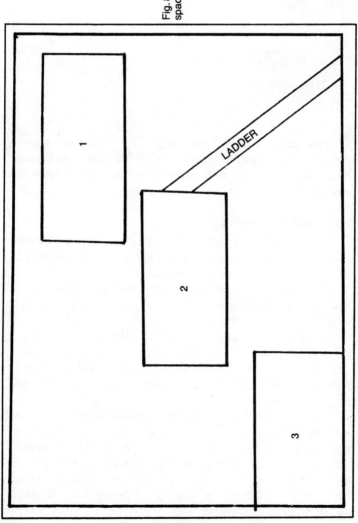

Fig. 8-7. Use novel arrangements for space efficiency.

Fig. 8-8. Spray adhesive.

How about "ordinary" beds? Again, there are many ways to dress them to complement the rest of the room and add interest. One of the best ways is to make headboards or to cover the headboard that is attached to the bed frame.

Bed Without a Headboard

The bed without an attached headboard is truly fun to work with. Assuming that you have, say, four bedspreads for this bed, you can easily have four matching headboards.

Begin with a thin, lightweight slab. I have used old pegboard. Paneling works well. Heavy cardboard is also good if you handle it carefully while you work.

Cut the panel to whatever shape you like. Then pad it with a layer of cotton. Use spray adhesive (Fig. 8-8) for quick, easy handling. Cut a piece of fabric like that of the spread—or in some other complementary color or design—the shape of the panel, but 3 inches bigger all the way around.

Spread the fabric on a worktable, right side down, and lay the padded panel on it (Fig. 8-9). Make a ½-inch turn in the fabric, finger-pressing it, and then fold the fabric over the edge of the panel. Staple it to the panel (Fig. 8-10). The fabric can be attached with something besides staples, but staples will permit you to remove this cover for laundering or to apply a different cover to match another spread.

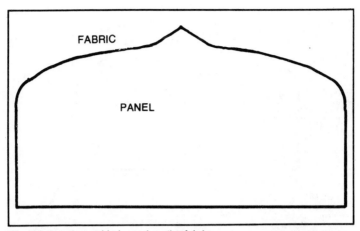
Fig. 8-9. Lay the padded panel on the fabric.

Select a couple of wall hangers appropriate to your own walls. Attach them and hang the pretty headboard over the bed (Fig. 8-11).

This same technique can be used to further decorate the room. Make small panels covered in the bedspread fabric for wall hangings (Fig. 8-12).

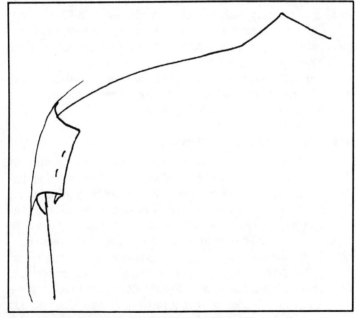
Fig. 8-10. Fold the fabric and staple it to the back of the panel.

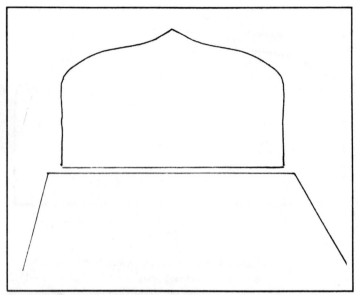
Fig. 8-11. Hang the headboard on the wall.

Another very pleasing headboard for this kind of bed can be made with a sheet of foam padding. The technique is actually that of making an ordinary cushion which was discussed in Chapter 7.

Cover the foam with the same fabric as the bedspread or in some other complementary fabric. Use welting, or cording, if the bedspread has seams finished that way.

You will need to sew some narrow loops into the top back seam. Then hang this padded headboard(s) from an attractive curtain rod attached to the wall (Fig. 8-13).

Accenting the Attached Headboard

The simplest attached headboard to work with is the straight, flat panel type. If your attached headboard has other features, they can be either taken off (if you don't mind permanently affecting the headboard) or worked around. This is an interesting advantage to buying bed frames at sales, auctions, and such places. Even if the headboard is scarred beyond repair, it can always be covered.

To *permanently* cover a plain headboard, cut a piece of thin foam padding, two layers of an old blanket, or a similar material, to fit the panel. Foam can be permanently attached with spray adhesive. If you use a blanket or similar padding, or if you don't want to permanently change the headboard, the padding should be fitted.

Fig. 8-12. Wall hanging of the spread fabric.

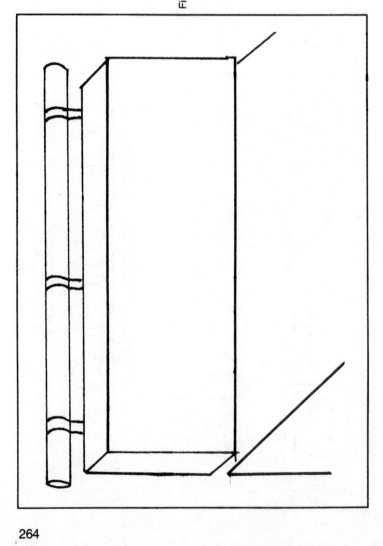

Fig. 8-13. Foam cushion headboard.

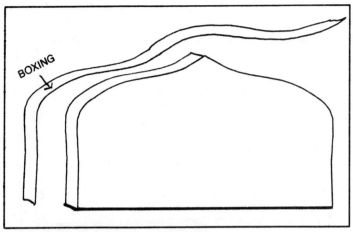

Fig. 8-14. Cut a boxing strip to cover the edge.

Baste two layers (or more for softness) together. Cut another piece the same size for the back of the headboard.

Cut a boxing strip to fit over the top and down the sides of the headboard (Fig. 8-14). Sew the padded front section and the back section to the boxing. This can be done by hand or machine.

Simply slip the padded cover over the headboard. Make a fabric cover to fit over it. The fabric cover should be finished with seams like those in the bedspread.

You can usually add decoration to even the more ornate headboards like the one in Fig. 8-15. Cover the center panel with a soft

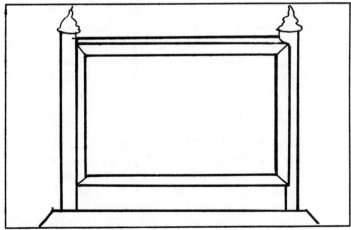

Fig. 8-15. An ornate headboard.

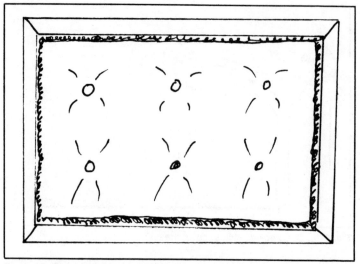

Fig. 8-16. Cover the staples with gimp.

layer of cotton first. Then cut a fabric cover to fit the panel, with sufficient excess fabric for a turn-under around the edges. Tack or staple the cover around the edges. Cover with complementary gimp (Fig. 8-16).

Never buy fabric for bedspreads until you have looked the room over for more accenting possibilities. Some possibilities are slipcovers for the bedroom chair, cushions covered in the bedspread fabric, draperies, hassocks, and wall hangings.

HASSOCK

A *hassock* may be used for sitting or for a footrest. In a child's room hassocks may serve as seating for guests or, as in one little girl's room, chairs for a tea table. The manner of making any such item will often depend upon the expected use, but the hassock in Fig. 8-17 can be used for years and take some rough treatment.

Plastic Bucket

The framework is a simple plastic bucket similar to those in Fig. 8-18. Restaurants buy pickles, dehydrated onions, and other things in these big plastic containers. You may be able to get the buckets for the asking. A second source is a farm. The plastic buckets shown here once contained transmission fluid for farm equipment. With a little scouting, you should be able to find some buckets.

Fig. 8-17. Hassock.

Remove the wire bail first. Then wash the bucket thoroughly to remove odors and any foreign matter that might prevent adhesive from sticking to it.

The container can be left empty if you like. If you do leave it empty, it will be very light in weight, but it will also fall over easily. If this seems undesirable, the bottom can be weighted. One solution is to mix a couple of pounds of building plaster and pour it into the bucket. When the plaster has set up and dried, finish filling the container with any material at hand. The plaster is sure to break up later if the hassock is treated roughly, so the filler will keep the weight in the bottom of the hassock. Tightly packed excelsior is a good filler, but any lightweight material that will keep its shape fairly well will do.

Fig. 8-18. Plastic buckets.

267

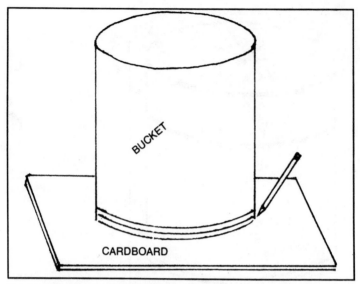

Fig. 8-19. Draw a circle around the bucket.

Allow the plaster a day or two to dry before filling. It will become hard in 30 minutes or so, but it will still contain a lot of moisture.

The lid should fit tightly on the bucket. If it does not have a good, snug fit, spread glue around the top before closing it.

Foam Padding

You will need some ½-inch foam padding (available in most dry goods shops), cardboard, and either spray adhesive or a bottle of white glue. Draw a circle around the top of the bucket, on cardboard, as illustrated in Fig. 8-19. Cut the circle out. Spread glue on the side of the round cutout, and affix it to the top of the bucket (Fig. 8-20).

Measure the length (or height) of the bucket, top to bottom. Mark this measurement accurately on the sheet of ½-inch foam, if the bucket sides are vertical.

The bucket you use may have vertical sides, or they may be slanted. If they are vertical, there is no problem. If the sides are angled, the ends of the foam cutout will be like that in Fig. 8-21. Cut the foam a little wider than the height of the slanted bucket, and trim the excess after drying.

Cut the foam with a single-edge razor blade for the best results. Cut about halfway through the first time; complete the separation with the second cut.

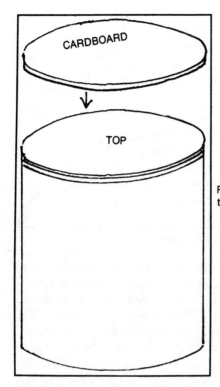

Fig. 8-20. Glue cardboard to the top of the bucket.

Glue the foam to the sides of the plastic bucket. If the end cuts are square, there will naturally be a triangular-shaped gap where they meet. This is easy to prevent by cutting the ends at angles, so they will meet in either of the two ways shown in Fig. 8-22.

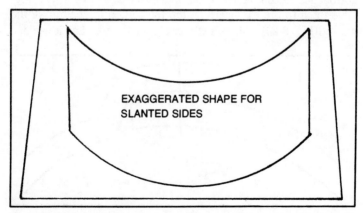

EXAGGERATED SHAPE FOR SLANTED SIDES

Fig. 8-21. Angled cutout.

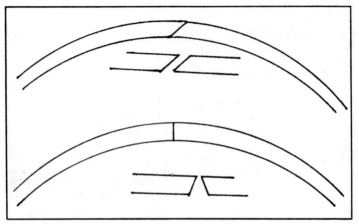

Fig. 8-22. Ends of the foam should fit together.

An alternative to this method of fitting the cut edges is to follow the procedure used in matching linoleum patterns at a seam. Hold the foam in place, firm but not stretched, and cut through both layers at the same time (Fig. 8-23). You will need an extra pair of hands and perhaps some practice on scraps to do this accurately.

Spread a thin layer of white glue (or spray adhesive) over all sides of the bucket, and permit the glue to become slightly tacky. Press the foam onto the plastic, wrapping it snugly around and fitting it carefully. You may secure it in place for drying with masking tape or with a needle and thread, taking quick, loose stitches.

When the adhesive has dried, draw a pattern of the bucket bottom and top on the foam. Cut these round pads very carefully. Glue them to the cardboard on the top and on the bottom of the bucket (Fig. 8-24). Cut an extra circle for the top. Lay it aside.

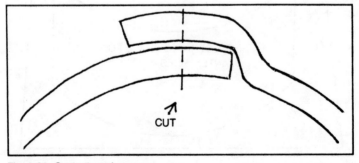

CUT

Fig. 8-23. Cut both ends at once.

Welting

The hassock will be more attractive with welting in the same fabric as the cover material, or in matching or contrasting colors. Welting is not at all difficult to make.

Select a cord of a thickness appropriate to the cover material and pattern. This cord is available at dry goods or upholstery stores. You will need enough cord to circle the hassock three times.

Cut strips of the material to be used for the welting. These strips should be long enough to avoid seams if possible. If seams are necessary, make them diagonal (Fig. 8-25). Press them open. The strips must be wide enough to cover the cord and provide a ½-inch

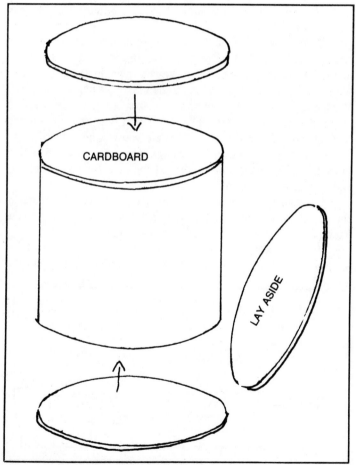

Fig. 8-24. Glue foam to the bucket ends.

271

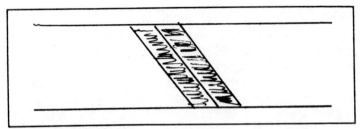

Fig. 8-25. Diagonal seams.

seam allowance at least. Place the cord on the wrong side of the welting strip, fold it over, and sew with your zipper foot, snugly against the cord (Fig. 8-26). Make only enough welting to circle the hassock once. Welting for the other two times is more easily done in another way.

Cover a button for the center top of the hassock. Upholstery buttons are available where other such materials are sold. If you have a button box somewhere, make your own. Find a large button with holes in it, and thread a long cord through the holes (Fig. 8-27). Pad the upper part of the button with cotton or foam, and lay it on a scrap of your cover fabric. Fold the fabric over the button, and estimate the size of the circle of fabric you will need to cut.

Sew by hand ½-inch from the edge of the fabric circle, making a drawstring (Fig. 8-28). Pull the drawstring snug, tie with a slipknot, and you have a covered button. Lay it aside and proceed.

Cut your cover pattern next, being careful to center or match the design as needed. The top cover must be the same size as the foam pad, plus at least a ½-inch seam allowance.

If the bucket sides are vertical, the side covering will be simple. If the sides are slanted, the easiest method is to cut the

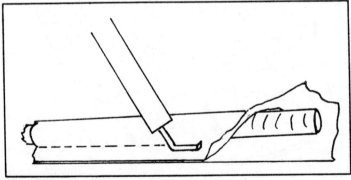

Fig. 8-26. Sew close to the cord.

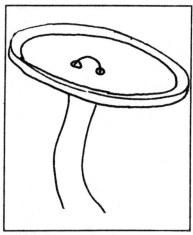

Fig. 8-27. Thread a cord through button holes.

material square to fit the biggest end, and run darts to make the narrow end fit (Fig. 8-29). Cut the side covering 8 inches longer than the height of the hassock.

Turn the side cover fabric inside out and seam it to fit (Fig. 8-30). At this point, the circumferences of the top cover and the top edge of the side cover opening should be the same.

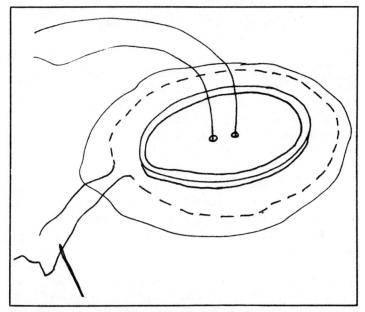

Fig. 8-28. Make a drawstring in the fabric.

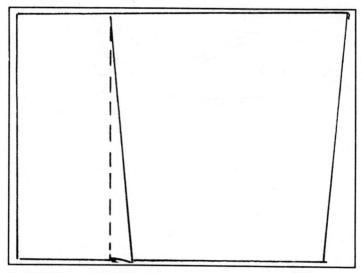

Fig. 8-29. Run darts to fit the cover.

Sew the welting to the right side of the top cover (Fig. 8-3). Overlap the fabric at one end of the welting cord over the opposite end (Fig. 8-32), sewing it tightly.

Hand or machine baste the side and top covers together. Check them for a neat appearance before doing the final sewing.

Button

Now for the button. Thread both ends of the cord through a large needle. Fit the foam circle (that you laid aside earlier) into the top cover. Find the exact center of the top, and run the needle and cord through from the top.

Make a small ball of cotton. Place it *between* the two cords, pull them firm, and tie securely.

Fitting and Closing the Cover

At this point your upholstery cover will be just a bit bulky, but not really a problem. The next step can be omitted, but it is an attractive touch. The only difficulty is that of accurate measurement.

Select a spot, perhaps 6 inches from the top welt. Mark it clearly all the way around the outside (right side) of the cover. Simply fold the cover over the welting cord. Sew it snugly with your zipper foot, basting by hand first if you prefer. Use a needle and

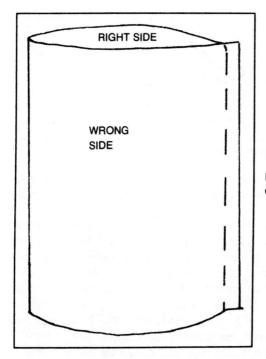

Fig. 8-30. Seam the cover to fit.

thread to connect the two ends of the cord when you approach the spot where you began.

Fit the cover over the padded bucket. This is the hardest part if the cover you have made fits well. Work slowly, depress the foam

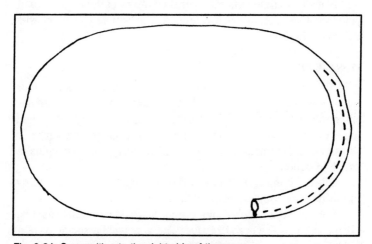

Fig. 8-31. Sew welting to the right side of the cover.

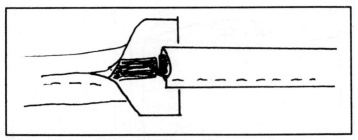

Fig. 8-32. Cover the ends of the welting cord.

padding, and fit it neatly. When you have the cover in place, mark it all around the bottom edge for the location of this bottom welting. (You can do this without fitting, removing, and then refitting the cover if you measure carefully. If you do so, be sure to allow for the stretching or pulling tight of the cover over the bottom of the hassock.) If you fit the cover on for marking, remove it. Put the final bottom row of welting on as you did the second row.

When the bottom row of welting is in place and the cover is fitted over the hassock, you are ready to close the cover. Pull it snug all the way around, and pleat as shown in Fig. 8-33. These pleats can be tacked in place with needle and thread or stapled to the plastic.

When all the pleats are in place, measure the diameter of the bottom of the hassock. Cut a circle of fabric about 1 inch smaller. This fabric may be the same as that of the cover or some other strong material. Fold it over. Stitch the edges (Fig. 8-34) to prevent raveling.

Place this circle of fabric over the bottom of the hassock, and hand sew it securely all the way around. The completed bottom will look like Fig. 8-35.

STORAGE CHEST

Children, particularly while they are small, need a lot of floor space. Any storage chest has a built-in handicap which is the temptation to use it as a catchall for junk, broken toys, dirty socks, and apple cores. If you and your child will recognize and agree to withstand such temptation, the storage chest can be a real plus in the child's room.

The chest in Fig. 8-36 is a good beginning. It is old, very sturdy and made with rough lumber and nails.

For the older child's room, the chest would be suitable as it is, except that it isn't very attractive. The young child should have a padded chest.

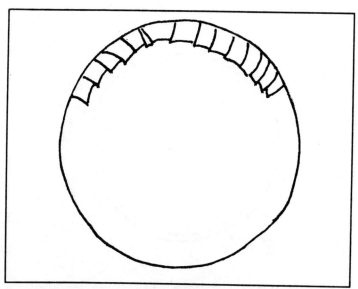

Fig. 8-33. Pleat the fabric around the bottom.

To cover this or any similar chest, begin with padding. This can be of foam, a thick layer of cotton, or various other materials that can be attached most simply with adhesive. As you reach the corners, overlap the padding so corners won't remain sharp.

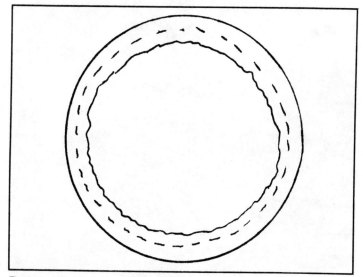

Fig. 8-34. Hem the edge of the circle.

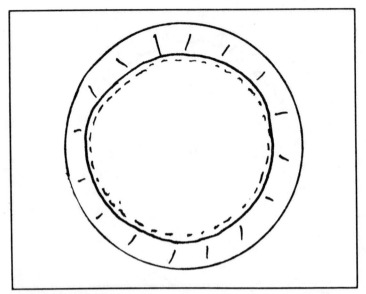

Fig. 8-35. Completed bottom.

Fig. 8-36. Wooden chest.

278

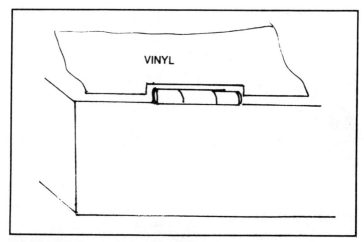

Fig. 8-37. Fit vinyl around the hinge.

It may be possible to cover the outside of the chest with a single strip of fabric or vinyl, or four pieces may be used. If a single piece is used, make the seam in the center back or at either back corner.

If more than one piece is necessary, cover the ends first. Vinyl and some heavy fabrics can be attached to foam padding with spray adhesive; otherwise, you will need to overlap the end corners and staple, tack, or stitch the fabric in place. Front and back covers can be blind-tacked or stapled.

The lid can be covered with the same kind of padding, and it should cover the edges as well. The fabric or vinyl cover is pleated neatly at each corner, folded under, and fastened with staples or tacks. The cover must be fitted around the hinges in back. If you use vinyl, simply cut the vinyl so it fits around the hinge as in Fig. 8-37. Tack or staple it to the inside of the lid. Fabrics should be bound around the cutout.

The same basic techniques can be used to make a chest/window seat. Padded window seats might also be storage shelves.

SOFA-BED

A basic wood box can be the frame for a sofa-bed for the child's room. High density foam on the top becomes a mattress or sofa cushion. One, two, or more of the foam headboards discussed earlier in this chapter will make a comfortable, attractive backrest.

Chair Seating

There are three common methods of reweaving chair seats: *caning, rushing,* and *wood splinting.* Anyone with some patience and enthusiasm, a chair, and the seating materials can reseat a chair by one of these methods—or even with baling twine.

CANE

Cane for chair seating is a thin, hard bark which is taken from the rattan palm. It is cut into narrow strips and is bought in hanks of varying widths to suit any chair. Cane can also be bought in prewoven panels. These panels are used in chair seating and in many decorative ways which I consider later. The simplest method of cane seating is that using the prewoven panels. The most intriguing is hand weaving the cane strips through holes in the chair frame.

You must first determine the width of cane needed for your chair. The suitable size depends upon the diameter of the holes and the spacing between holes. Use Table 9-1 for this determination.

TOOLS AND MATERIALS

When you buy the cane, you should get a strip that is wider than the rest. This wider strip is called a *binder.* It is used to make a neat border around the seat, which will neatly cover the holes.

Besides the cane and the chair, you will need a small tub of warm to hot water, scissors, an awl, and either golf tees or dowels to use as pegs. Optional tools will be helpful such as weaving needles, which you can buy or fashion from wire. Additionally, a sealer should be applied to the finished seat. *Tung oil* is excellent. Some people prefer varnish, lacquer, or other hard finishes.

PREPARATION FOR WEAVING

The cane must be soaked in water to make it pliable enough to work with. Warm water will soften the cane much more quickly than cold, in perhaps 15 or 20 minutes. As you weave the cane, it dries and shrinks. It is necessary to dampen the woven parts every now and then as you work. This is especially true when you are working on the first project or two, while you are still somewhat slow.

You should wind several strips of the cane into a coil and place them in the water. When the cane has softened sufficiently, remove it. Put more in the water. It will do no harm for cane to remain in the water longer than the 15 or 20 minutes needed for softening.

The cane has a glossy (outer) side, while the inside is fibrous and rough. Always weave with the glossy side up, or showing. When the job is finished, even this glossy side will have a very fine fuzz on it. Take care of this later.

As you weave the cane, try to maintain an equal tension throughout. Do not weave tightly. Remember that the cane is shrinking as you work. You should weave the first front to back and side to side layers, so that you can rather easily press the weave down about an inch from level.

Before you actually begin the step-by-step weaving process, all the rows of back to front and side to side cane should be parallel. If the chair seat is square or rectangular, this will happen naturally. If the seat is narrower across the back than the front, which is a familiar design, skip some of the holes at the back sides to keep the back to front strips parallel. Without too much detail just yet, this process is illustrated in Fig. 9-1. While these instructions assume a square or rectangular seat, for clarity of drawings, the splayed shape will present no difficulties as long as you keep Fig. 9-1 in mind. It will become obvious as you work.

SIX STEPS TO CANE WEAVING

Remove a strip of softened cane from the water. If the seat is squared, you should begin at a front corner hole. If it is narrower or

Table 9-1. Chart for Determining Cane Width.

Cane Width	Hole Size	Between Holes
superfine or carriage	⅛ inch	⅜ inch
fine-fine	3/16 inch	½ inch
fine	3/16 inch	⅝ inch
medium	¼ inch	¾ inch
common	5/16 inch	⅞ inch

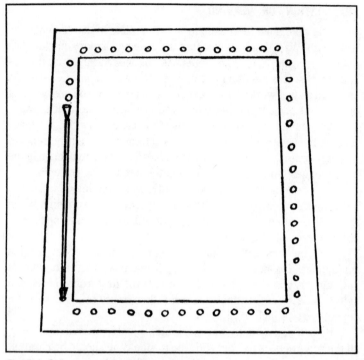

Fig. 9-1. Skip some of the holes at the sides.

rounded in back, begin at the front and back center holes and work toward the outer sides (Fig. 9-2).

Step One

From the top of the seat, thread one end of the cane through the hole. Pull it through from the bottom, 3 or 4 inches, and tap a peg (dowel, golf tee) into the hole to hold the cane in place. Again from the top, thread the other end of the strip down through the opposite hole in the back, then up through the next hole, and forward and down through the opposite front hole (Fig. 9-3).

When you come to the end of the strip, leave the excess cane again hanging *down* through the hole. Secure it with a peg (Fig. 9-3).

Check to see that you have maintained fairly equal tension, that you have the glossy side of the cane showing, and that you haven't missed any holes. When all looks as it should, tie the ends hanging from the underside of the seat. Tie with an overhand knot (Fig 9-4). Pull the knot snug. Trim it to about an inch. This completes the first step in cane weaving.

Step Two

The second step is essentially like the first, except that it is side to side weaving. Begin at the front corner hole, leaving 3 to 4 inches extending through on the bottom of the seat. Tap the peg in place to secure it. As you did in step one, thread the strip through the opposite hole on the other side, along the frame, and up through the next hole (Fig. 9-5). All the side to side weave crosses *over* the front to back weave. Take the strip across to the hole next to the one where you began step two, down, along the frame and up through the next hole, and so on.

When the side to side weaving is completed, tap a peg in the last hole. Check your pattern, tension, and position. Tie the loose ends. The dotted lines in Fig. 9-6 indicate how the cane is moved from one side to another as you weave.

Step Three

Now for step three. This step is the same as step one. You will thread the cane through the same holes from front to back, peg, and

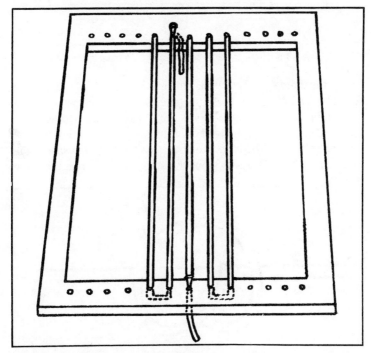

Fig. 9-2. Begin at the center, front, and back.

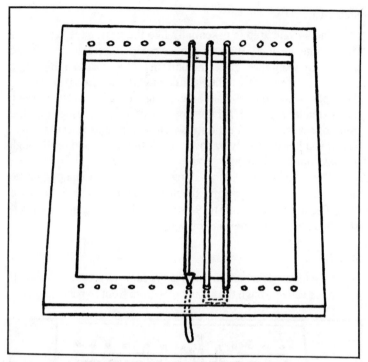

Fig. 9-3. Weave from front to back, across, and then back to the front.

finally tie them exactly as you did in step one. This is simply a second strand of cane in the same holes and the same pattern. The only difference is that the second strand will naturally cross over the side to side strips. Instead of placing this second front to back strip directly over the step one strip, position it to the *side* of the first strip (Fig. 9-7). Always put the step three strip on the same

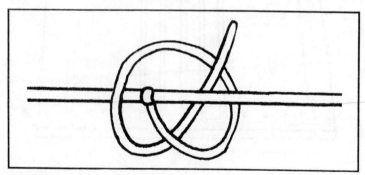

Fig. 9-4. Overhand knot.

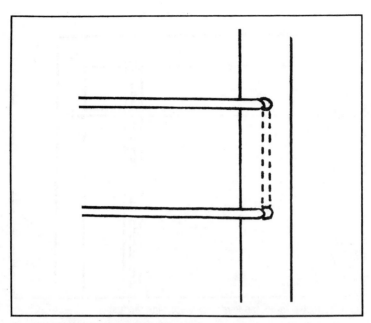

Fig. 9-5. Move the weave across the seat.

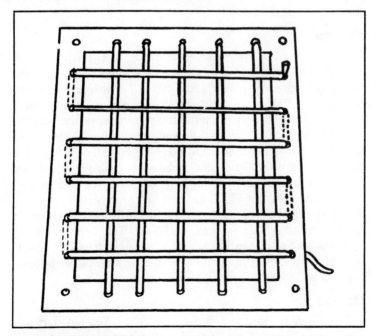

Fig. 9-6. Step two completed.

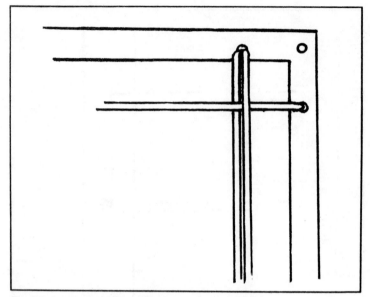

Fig. 9-7. In step three, the third strip lies beside the first.

side of the step one strip, either all on the right side or all on the left side.

Step Four

The first *actual* weaving is done in step four. You will thread the end of the strip through the same hole where you began step two. Tap a peg in the hole to secure it. As you weave from left to right, run the strip *under* the strip from step one, and *over* the strip from step three (Fig. 9-8). Continue this pattern across the seat, and thread the strip down through the opposite hole. Run the strip along the frame on the underside to the next hole, bring it up through the hole, and return to the left side of the seat. Weave over the step three strip and under the step one strip. When step four is complete, the seat will look like Fig. 9-9.

If you haven't already done so, you will probably need to dampen the cane with a warm, wet towel. This depends on the aridity of your work area, but keep the cane from drying too fast. If parts of the weave dry and shrink too soon, the weaving will become too difficult. A seat of uneven tension can result.

Step Five

Step five begins the first diagonal weave. You can start this weave at any point. Begin at the front left corner again.

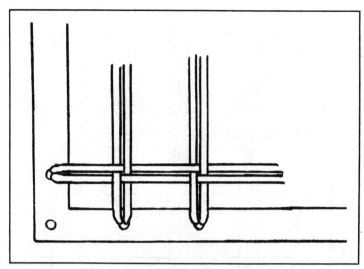

Fig. 9-8. Go under the step one strip and over the step three strip.

Thread the cane through a hole, as you did in the preceding steps. Thread the other end through the hole diagonally opposite (Fig. 9-10).

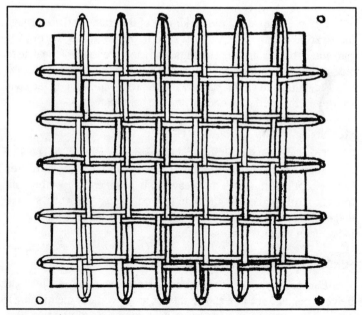

Fig. 9-9. Step four completed.

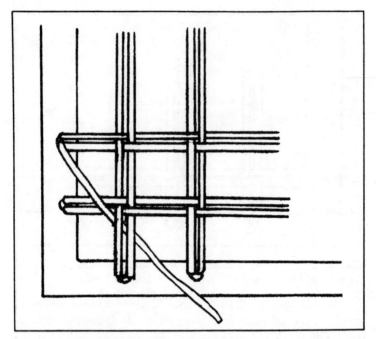

Fig. 9-10. Thread through the hole diagonally opposite.

Run the strip along the underside of the frame and up through the next hole (Fig. 9-11). The weave is quite simple. Thread the cane *under* both front to back strips, and then over both of the side to side strips. When the first diagonal weave is finished, it will look like Fig. 9-12. Check the pattern and the tension. Dampen the cane while you tie the loose ends with overhand knots.

Step Six

The sixth and final step in cane weaving is another diagonal, at right angles to the first. Proceed in exactly the same way as in step five, except that this time the weaving strip will cross *over* the front to back strips and *under* the side to side strips. When the second diagonal weave is complete, check your pattern and tension. Tie the loose ends when you are satisfied.

FUNCTION OF THE WEAVING NEEDLE

Earlier in this chapter I mentioned that a weaving needle might be very helpful, but I've shown the six steps without mentioning it again. The function of this tool is best shown by illustration.

At the beginning of step four and through steps five and six, a length of heavy (hard to bend) wire can be inserted through the pattern to hold the strips apart for quicker weaving (Fig. 9-13). Be sure there are no sharp ends on the wire to snag the cane.

A weaving needle does about the same thing, or the two can be used together. The function of the weaving needle is illustrated in Fig. 9-14. A little practice and experience will best teach you which tools will be most useful for you.

The cane weaving is finished, but the binder must be installed now. Select the binder strip, hopefully a little longer than the perimeter of the seat itself.

BINDING THE EDGE OF THE SEAT

All of the holes now have several strips of cane through them. Perhaps they seem a little crowded. With the awl, you can open the holes a little by separating the strips of cane enough to permit the securing of the binder.

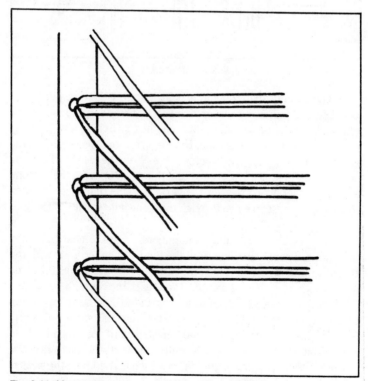

Fig. 9-11. Move horizontally on the underside of the frame.

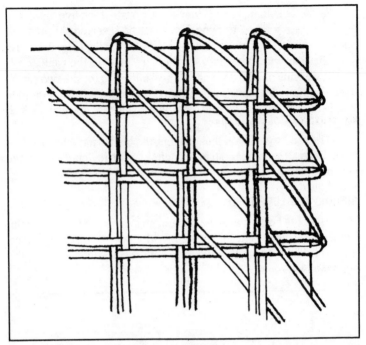

Fig. 9-12. The first diagonal weave is finished.

The binding strips should be a little longer than the perimeter of the seat. Begin in the center of the back of the seat, and thread one end of the binder through the hole from the top. Secure it with a peg.

Choose a thin strip of cane. Knot it on one end, or secure it to an adjacent woven strip. Three or four holes from the center where you secured the binder strip, thread this thin strip up from the bottom. Pull the binder strip snug, cross over it with the thin strip, and then thread this thin strip down through the same hole you just brought it up through (Fig. 9-15).

Run the thin strip along the underside to the next hole, and bring it up through the hole. Pull the binder snug, cross it with the thin strip, and then thread the thin strip back down through the same hole. Continue in this manner until you reach the center back again.

Remove the peg that holds the end of the binding strip, and run the other end of the binding strip down into the same hole (Fig. 9-16). Continue securing with the thin strip until you reach the hole where you began with it. Run the end of the thin strip through to the bottom. Wrap the excess around an adjacent strip, and the seat is completed.

Before the completed seat dries, you can use a blue (smoke-less) flame to singe the fuzzy spots off the seat. When the seat has dried, it is possible to sand it lightly to get it smooth.

Seal the dried seat on both sides with varnish, shellac, tung oil, or whatever sealer you prefer. The cane can also be stained before sealing.

PREWOVEN CANE SEATING

Perhaps you have a chair that once had a cane seat, but of a different sort than the kind just discussed. The chair with a prewoven cane seat has a groove all the way around the opening.

Prewoven cane panels or webbing are available in several widths. You need sufficient width to cover the seat opening. Get the cane 2 or 3 inches wider than the opening to allow for working space.

The *spline*, a long strip of cane in a wedge shape, is fitted into the groove to hold the webbed seat in place. Spline comes in different thicknesses. Measure the width of the groove to determine the thickness you need, but remember that one thickness of the webbing must also fit into the spline groove. Measure the circumference of the groove, and get the spline a few inches longer.

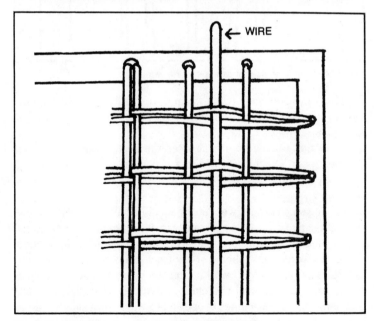

Fig. 9-13. A smooth wire will hold the strips apart.

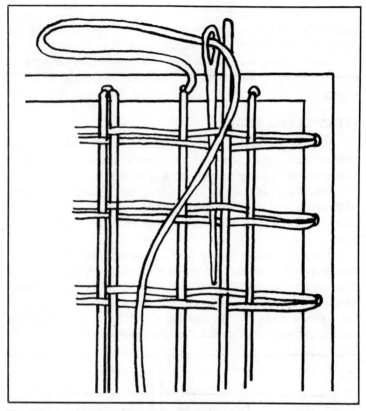

Fig. 9-14. A weaving needle can speed the work.

Soak the cane webbing in warm water until it becomes pliable. Do not bend or fold it to soak; if necessary, lay it in the bathtub. Put the spline in water to soak.

Lay the softened webbing over the seat. Trim it so that it extends about ¾ inch past the spline groove all the way around. Be sure that the pattern is properly aligned, particularly along the front rail.

Using some kind of wooden wedge, like half a clothespin press the webbing into the spline groove (Fig. 9-7). Begin in the middle of a rail, usually the front rail, and work toward either side in equal distances. When the webbing at the front rail is neatly tucked into the spline groove, begin working on the opposite back rail, again from the center toward the ends. When the front and back are finished, begin at the center of one side. Switch from side to side to keep the pattern straight with the frame.

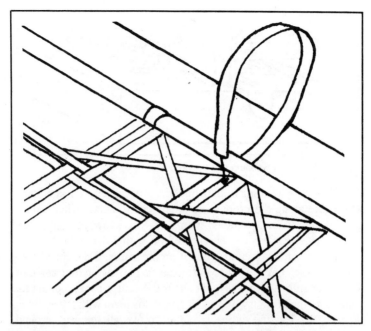

Fig. 9-15. The thin strip comes up, over the binder, and back down.

Once the webbing is pressed into the groove all the way around, use a sharp chisel or knife. Cut the webbing in the groove at the bottom outer corner (Fig. 9-18).

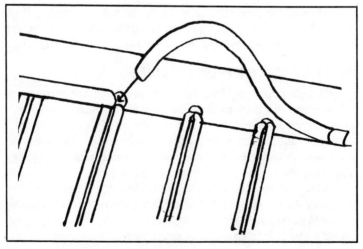

Fig. 9-16. Finish off the binder strip where you began.

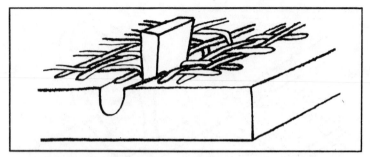

Fig. 9-17. Press the webbing into the groove.

When the webbing is all trimmed, spread a generous amount of white glue along the groove. As in all such projects, when excess glue exudes from two joined members, you know you have used enough glue. Excess can be cleaned off with a damp cloth.

Remove the softened spline from the water. If the corners are very sharp, you may want to miter the corners using four separate lengths of spline. Otherwise, begin at the center back, tapping the spline into the groove with a mallet until it is level with the webbing (Fig. 9-19). Tap the spline into the groove all the way around, working it around the corners.

When you reach the center back again where you began, mark the spline (Fig. 9-20). Cut it in two, and tap it into the groove against the other end. Singe the fibrous fuzz off the seat while it is still damp. Use a blue, smokeless flame. Be careful not to scorch the cane seat.

When all the cane dries, it will be tight and comfortable. If all excess glue has been thoroughly removed, the cane can be stained and/or sealed with some appropriate material such as tung oil.

DECORATIVE USES FOR PREWOVEN CANE

Prewoven cane webbing can be used to alter the appearance and the effect of any room. It can be applied to furniture, walls, and doors. Headboards can be easily and cheerfully decorated with prewoven cane, as can lampshades, hampers, and even walls or sections of walls. Cane can be cool and airy or warm and comforting, depending upon application, coloring, and so forth.

Prewoven cane webbing can be attached dry to most surfaces with glue, staples, or both. Edges are usually covered with molding which can be obtained in various styles, materials, and colors. Cane can put a new face on an old chest or dresser, or it can give new life to a worn or scarred piece.

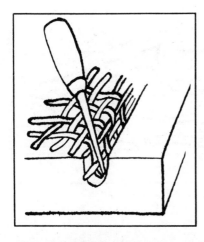

Fig. 9-18. Cut the webbing at the bottom outside corner.

RESEATING WITH RUSH

Natural *rush* consists of leaves twisted into a strand while wet. This material isn't used too often any more when reseating chairs. An artificial rush is used instead. Artificial rush is usually made of paper. Other materials are also available, and these substitutes for natural rush are strong and easy to work with.

Heavy twines or narrow ropes are also used in place of rush, and seats are woven of these materials in the same familiar X pattern. The technique isn't hard to learn or practice. Rushing proceeds rather rapidly. Besides the chair and rush, you need tacks and a hammer, some stuffing material, and some type of dull tool to force the strands of rush tightly together. This tool might be a heavy wood ruler or something like a large, dulled screwdriver.

Seats aren't often square; most are narrower in back than in the front. The difference in technique for a square or rectangular seat becomes obvious as you study the following illustrations.

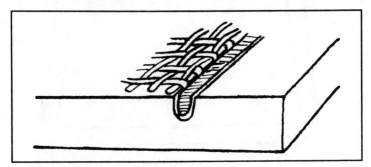

Fig. 9-19. Tap the spline into the groove.

Fig. 9-20. Mark the spline. Cut it to match the other end.

Weaving the Front Corners

Measure the front and back rails, from the inside of the posts (Fig. 9-21). Subtract to determine the difference in lengths. Then divide this difference and mark it on each end of the front rail (Fig. 9-22. The excess, or difference, must be woven first. This is done with short lengths of rush.

The length of the first piece will depend upon the kind of seat you are working with. Study the directions for the first piece. Then you can estimate the necessary length.

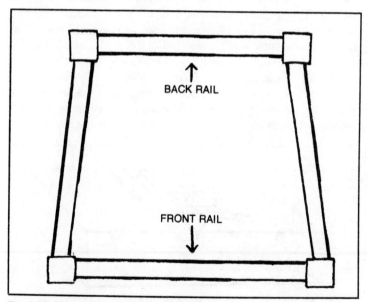

Fig. 9-21. Measure from inside the posts.

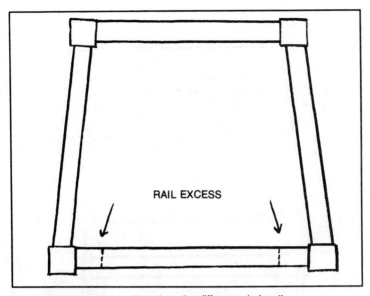

Fig. 9-22. Mark the front rail to show the difference in length.

Tack the end of the first piece to the inside of the left rail near the post. Then wrap the cord around the rails (Fig. 9-23). Run the cord across the seat, and wrap it around the rails at the opposite

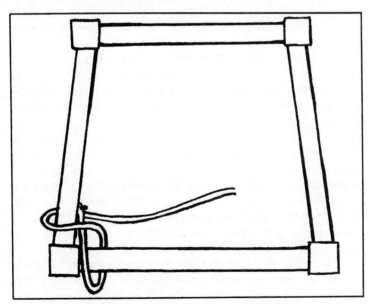

Fig. 9-23. Wrap the cord around the rails with one end secured.

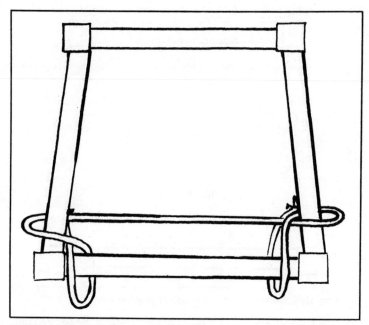

Fig. 9-24. Make the sides match one another.

corner. Tack this end to the inside of the right rail, at the same distance from the post as the left one. Figure 9-24 shows the first step completed, except that the rush *must be* pulled snug in every step.

Tack the end of a second cord just behind the first. Wrap it snugly next to the first cord, and tack it on the opposite side (Fig. 9-25). Notice that because a little extra length is required each time you tack a new piece on, each piece must be just a little longer than the preceding one.

Continue in the same manner, adding new lengths of rush. With every six pieces, use the dull tool, a regulator, to force the strands of rush together, prevent gaps, and maintain as straight a line across as you reasonably can (Fig. 9-26). This is important in assuring the overall strength and function of the seat. Also, you will soon begin stuffing between what has now become three layers of rush. If the strands are not pressed together, the stuffing will show through the gaps or empty spaces.

Finally you will reach the two marks on the front rail, and the tacked ends may have reached the rear posts (Fig. 9-27). If you measure it, you should find the unfilled space on the front rail equal in length to the back rail.

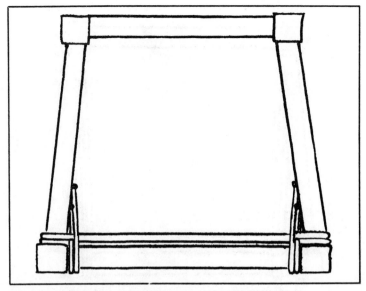

Fig. 9-25. Keep each row of cord snugly against the last one.

Continuous Weave

You can work with a longer cord, but more than 20 feet will be too much aggravation. Begin by tacking one end to the inside of the left rail next to the rear post (Fig. 9-28).

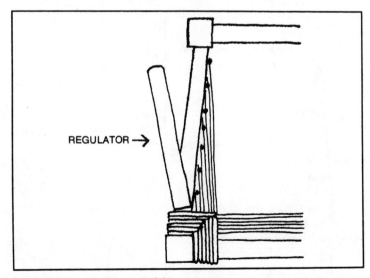

REGULATOR →

Fig. 9-26. Keep the line as straight as you can.

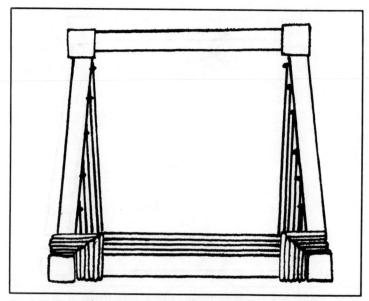

Fig. 9-27. The unfilled space should match the length of the back rail.

Bring the cord to the front, over, and then back under the front rail. Bring it to your left, over the left rail, and then back under it (Fig. 9-29). Pull the cord taut, and keep it close against the already woven ones as you work. Bring the cord across the seat, over the

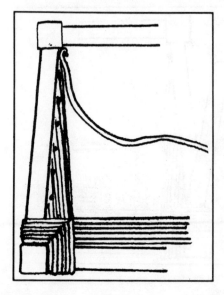

Fig. 9-28. Tack one end to the inside of the left rail.

right rail and back under it, then up and over the front rail, and back under and toward the back rail (Fig. 9-30).

The rush is woven at the rear corners just as at the front. Wrap the cord over the rail and tight against the post, back under the back rail, and then up over the right rail and back under (Fig. 9-31).

Bring the taut cord across to the left rail. Wrap it over the left rail against the post, back under, then over and back under the back rail, and return to the front (Fig. 9-32).

Stuffing

This pattern is followed until the shorter (usually side) rails are filled. Before you reach this point, you should pause and do some padding. The padding is not an absolutely necessary step. But it does help the rush to wear longer, and padding also gives the seat a full appearance. Proceed with the padding as follows.

When you have woven several strands of rush around the rear corners, pull the cord down and tie it *securely* around a chair rung and leg (Fig. 9-33). If the cord isn't tight, the work that you've done keeping the weave uniformly snug and taut will be wasted.

A variety of stuffing materials can be used. Keep any stuffing materials of the same color as the rush, or the eventual color. In

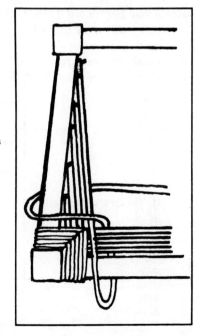

Fig. 9-29. Begin the continuous weave.

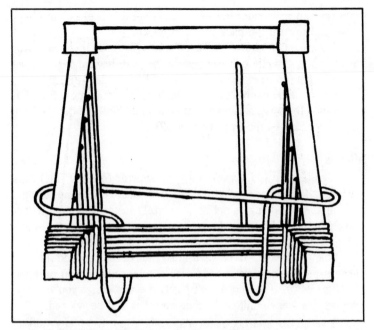

Fig. 9-30. Continue the continuous weave as indicated here.

spite of your best effort, there may be small spaces or cracks where the stuffing will show through.

You may use scraps of rush, stuffing it between layers of the woven rush with your regulating tool. Brown paper is sometimes twisted and stuffed as well. A third method is to cut pieces of

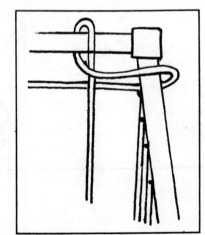

Fig. 9-31. The continuous weave.

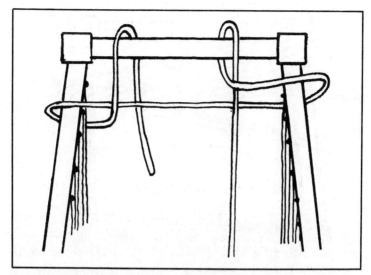

Fig. 9-32. Last step in the continuous weave.

cardboard, insert them between layers, and then weave over them (Fig. 9-34). Whatever method you select, pad the seat until it appears nicely full and smooth.

Once you have stuffed the woven areas, you may return to the weaving. You will need to tie on a second length of rush. Tie the two

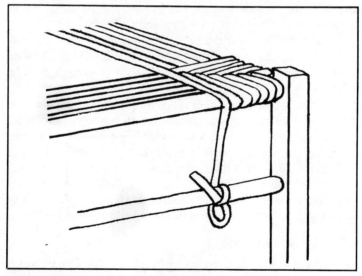

Fig. 9-33. Tie the cord securely whenever you must stop.

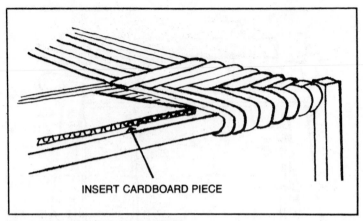

INSERT CARDBOARD PIECE

Fig. 9-34. Cardboard makes good filling.

pieces with a square knot as shown in Fig. 9-35. Be sure to make the knot where it will be covered by further weaving, on a pass from front to back or side to side. Remember to use the regulating tool often to force the woven cords tightly together.

Figure Eight Weave

Eventually the shorter side rails will be filled. Unless the seat is square, there will still be an open space (Fig. 9-36). When the shorter rails are filled, bring the cord up through the narrow crack that will naturally appear in the center of the seat. Begin filling from back to front by weaving in a figure eight pattern.

Wrap the cord over the back rail, bring it under and forward, and up through the crack at the center (Fig. 9-37). Wrap it forward over the front rail, back under and up through the center again (Fig. 9-38).

Continue filling the center space with this figure-eight weave, pushing the weave tightly together at every two rows or so. When the seat is completely filled, wind the cord tightly over the front rail. Turn the chair upside down to tie this cord. Tie it with half hitches as in Fig. 9-39, at least three on each side of the center, while you hold the cord tight. When you are satisfied with the knots, tuck them out of sight into the weave. The chair seat is finished. The rush seat can be sealed with materials available at building supply centers.

WOOD SPLINT CHAIR SEATING

People used to make their own furniture as an ordinary part of everyday living. Chair seats were woven from very thin, narrow

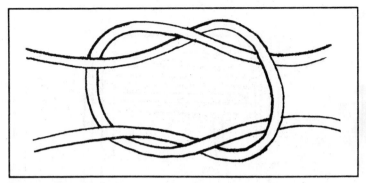

Fig. 9-35. Square knot.

strips of wood. These wood strips were usually called *splits*. The same technique is followed today with few modifications. One such change is in the name; the wood strips are called *splints* instead of splits. The furniture maker cut his own splits or splints; now you can buy them already cut. Cutting your own splints is not a difficult thing to do. The technique is definitely worth considering.

Preparing Your Own Splints

You will need wood with a very smooth, straight grain. The old-timers selected either white oak or ash.

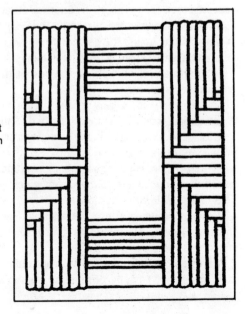

Fig. 9-36. If the seat isn't square, you'll still have an open space.

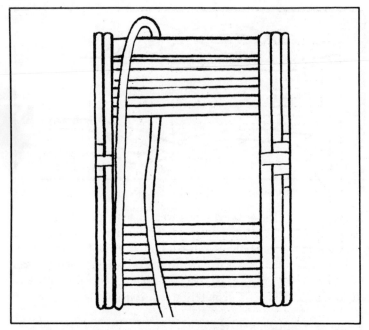

Fig. 9-37. The narrow crack in the center is the cross for the figure eight weave.

Find a sapling about 6 inches in diameter. This sapling should have at least 7 feet without any knots or other irregularities. Before cutting, examine the tree carefully to be sure it is smooth enough. When you have found the perfect sapling, cut a long block from the smoothest part—from 6 to 10 feet long.

Split this block in half, and then split the halves. The block is now in four sections.

The heartwood in any tree is darker in color and of a denser construction than the rest of the wood. Split the heart from each quarter of the block and lay it aside; you won't be using it in this project (Fig. 9-40).

Split the remaining quarters in half, and then split the eighths in half. You now have 16 pieces from which you obtain your splints. The pieces will be quite narrow.

With a knife, cut into the wood as shown in Fig. 9-41. The thickness of this cut should be the thickness of the annual growth rings.

Lightly tap the knife into the wood until you have separated the strip far enough to get a good, solid grip on it with your hand (Fig. 9-42).

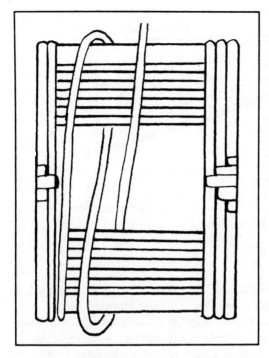

Fig. 9-38. The figure eight weave.

The rest is easy. Grasp the strip firmly, and simply peel it from the block. It does work if the wood is smooth and the grain is straight.

Continue peeling the strips—splints—from the block until you have all you need, maybe 15 for an average sized chair. Don't waste

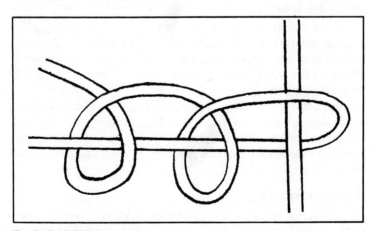

Fig. 9-39. Half hitch.

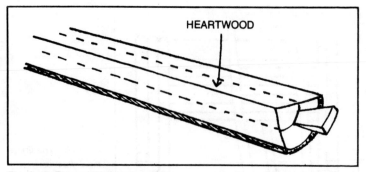

Fig. 9-40. Discard the heartwood.

any of the splints. Use whatever is left from the chair seat to weave some very beautiful and unique place mats, flower baskets, or wall hangings.

Modern Splint

You can buy *ash splint* that has been commercially prepared. It comes in 6 foot strips and in a couple of different widths. This machine cut material doesn't differ appreciably from that which you might cut for yourself, except that the measurements will be more precise. The overall appearance will be a little more uniform. Whether you buy or cut your splints, the method of weaving an ash splint chair seat remains the same. You will need a utility knife or similar tool, two thumbtacks, scissors, and something to soak the splints in.

Connecting Splints

Since splints are thin strips of actual wood, connecting them requires quite a different approach than for cane or rush. Begin by cutting, with your scissors, at the end of a splint. The shape is simple and easy (Fig. 9-43). This arrow on the end of one splint locks into the slot at the end of another (Fig. 9-44), which you can cut with a utility knife. The two are locked as in Fig. 9-45, and in the actual weaving the show side is Fig. 9-45B.

When the ends of a few splints are prepared, put six or so into warm water to soften. Add others to water as you remove and use some.

Weaving: First Step

Begin the weaving process by lightly tacking the end of a splint to the rear of the left rail (Fig. 9-46). Bring the splint forward,

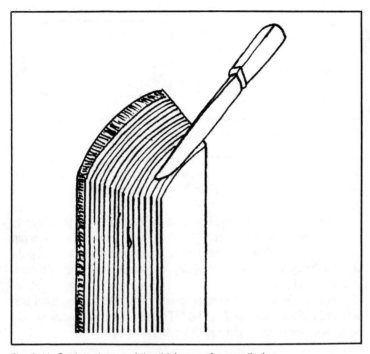

Fig. 9-41. Cut into the wood the thickness of a growth ring.

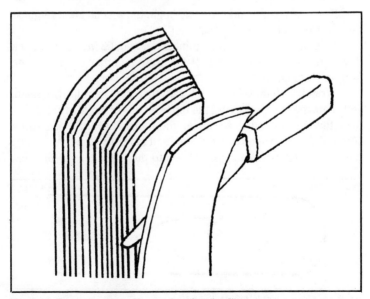

Fig. 9-42. Grasp the split with your hand and pull.

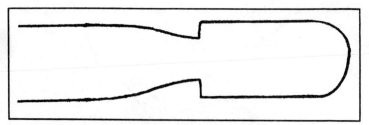

Fig. 9-43. Cut an arrow on one end.

wrapping it over the front rail. Wrap the connected splints around
the front and back rails in a continuous strand. Remember to connect the splints as shown earlier, with the arrow end on the inside of
the weave.

Do the weaving neatly. Do not crowd the rows of splint tightly
together; there must be narrow cracks between them. Do not wrap
the splint tightly. Like the cane discussed earlier, the wood splints
are wet. They will shrink as they dry, drawing the completed woven
seat taut and smooth.

When you have finished wrapping the splint around front and
back rails, it will look like Fig. 9-47. The end of the last splint should
be tacked under the right rail (Fig. 9-48).

Weaving: Second Step

Turn the chair upside down to begin the second step. Begin at
the left front, close to the front rail.

Fold the end of your first splint under about 2 inches, and hook
it over the second splint (Fig. 9-49). Run the other end under the
first splint (Fig. 9-50).

Wrap the splint over the left rail, turn the chair upright again,
and begin the weaving across the top front. Go under the first splint,
over the second and third, under the fourth and fifth, and so on
across the seat. When you reach the right side, turn the chair upside
down. Continue weaving back across to the left side. For the best

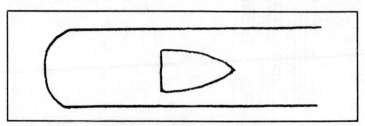

Fig. 9-44. Make a slot in the next piece.

310

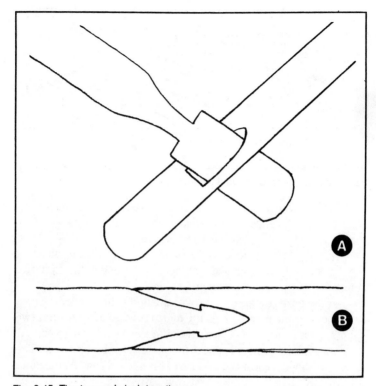

Fig. 9-45. The two ends lock together.

appearance, have all the connections appear on the bottom of the seat. You may have to cut some splints shorter, but the final appearance is worth the small waste.

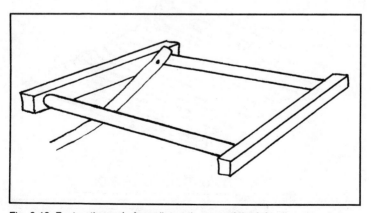

Fig. 9-46. Fasten the end of a splint at the rear of the left rail.

311

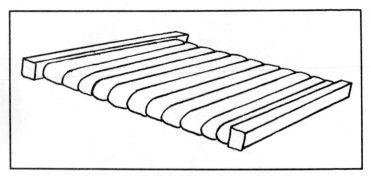

Fig. 9-47. Splint wrapped around the front and back rails.

Remove the thumbtacks as you approach them, and simply work those loose ends into the weave. They will be held securely in the weave when the chair seat is finished.

When you reach the left side again, wrap the splint up and over the left rail. On this second row across, go under the first two splints, over the second two, and so on.

At the third row across, go over the first splint, under the next two, and over the next two. At the fourth row, go over the first two splints, under the second two, over the third two, and so on.

The fifth row should repeat the pattern of the first row. The sixth row should repeat the pattern of the second row. At the ninth row you will begin with the first row pattern again.

When the seat is filled, the pattern will look like Fig. 9-51. The final splint is connected at the end just as you began. Simply fold the

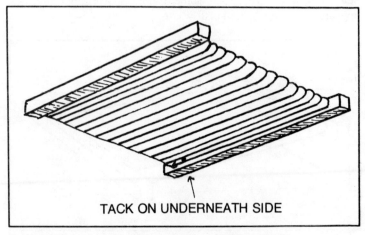

TACK ON UNDERNEATH SIDE

Fig. 9-48. Attach the end of the last splint under the right rail.

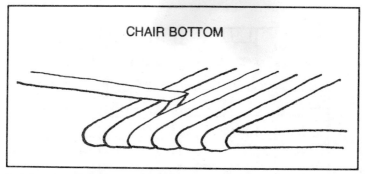

Fig. 9-49. Fold the end of a splint and hook it over another.

end under, and tuck it into the weave by hooking it over a woven strand (Fig. 9-52).

As you take up the slack, each row will become a little more difficult to weave. The weave will naturally tighten, giving you less space to work with. Be patient in this final weaving. You might employ a tool such as a smooth, dull butter knife to help you in sliding the final splints into the weave.

Most chair seats are not square. When the seat is completely woven and the ends are secured, you may need to work in an extra splint on each side to fill the spaces of the splayed design of the seat. It may even be necessary to trim these extra splints a bit with your scissors to make them fit well. Connect these extra, short splints at the end by folding under and hooking this fold over another splint as previously described.

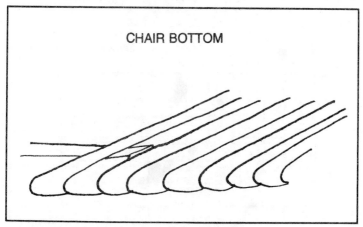

Fig. 9-50. Run the opposite end under the first splint.

Fig. 9-51. Traditional splint seat pattern.

The wood splint chair seat will tighten and dry. When dry, the seat should be finished with any finishing material suited to wood. I suggest tung oil.

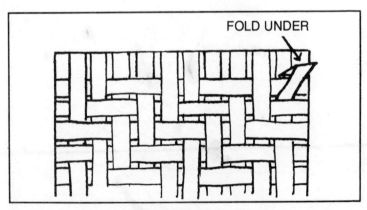

FOLD UNDER

Fig. 9-52. Connect the final end by folding and hooking it.

Automobile Upholstery

Automobiles demand a great deal of attention from the owners. Any phase of automobile maintenance or repair is not only expensive but time-consuming. Although many car or truck owners can learn how to do many kinds of repairs, few have the time to devote to such learning or the inclination to do so. This applies to mechanical work and engine maintenance, but not necessarily to the repair or replacement of upholstery.

There will be times when upholstery work is necessary. It may appear to be difficult, but in most cases the upholstery of a seat or back is quite simple to accomplish with the proper tools and materials.

Automobile seats can be covered in all types of materials, from velvets to natural leather. Since the most familiar upholstery material is *vinyl*, I discuss the techniques of removing a vinyl cover, repairing a broken spring, patching foam padding, and preparing a new seat cover on a conventional pickup truck seat. Methods of repairing bucket seats made almost entirely of foam are considered.

REMOVING THE COVER

The first step is simply removing the bolts that secure the seat to the floor of the automobile. Take the whole seat out, and place it on a table at a comfortable working height.

The seat back is disconnected from the seat proper with the appropriate tool. The upholsterer in Fig. 10-1 is using an adjustable wrench.

Figure 10-2 shows the seat to be reupholstered. The back has been removed. It is obvious in this case why the work is necessary.

Fig. 10-1. Take the seat apart.

A spring has broken on the driver's side and has penetrated the foam padding and torn the cover.

The upholsterer uses a sharp cutting tool to rip the seam between the seat panel and the skirt of the cover (Fig. 10-3). This must be ripped all the way around the seat, and the seat panel is then lifted off (Fig. 10-4). It is possible to remove the whole cover before ripping the seam, but it is much more convenient to rip it while the cover is still in place, holding everything taut.

The skirt is connected to the metal frame of the seat with hog rings. These are quite simple to remove. Just twist them off with pliers (Fig. 10-5).

PATCHING FOAM

In most cases the vinyl cover is sewn to a very thin sheet of soft foam. In Fig. 10-6 the upholsterer uses the sharp ripping tool again to separate the foam from the vinyl. With the first section ripped and folded back (Fig. 10-7), the hole in both the foam and the vinyl is clearly visible.

This seat cover is sewn crosswise in six places, with two seams each. This ribbed look makes an attractive cover; it also helps the vinyl to hold its shape and reduces stretching. The vinyl is sewn through the thin sheet of foam each time. Continue ripping the vinyl from the foam at each seam until they are separated. If you keep your tools sharp, this will only take a few minutes.

Fig. 10-2. Damaged truck seat.

The hole in the foam can be quickly repaired. If it is left unrepaired, you can feel the hole through a new cover. The vinyl cover would probably stretch in that area.

In Fig. 10-8 the upholsterer cuts the rough edges of the hole in the foam, trimming it quickly to a neat little square. He cuts a small piece of new foam of the same thickness and density to fit the hole (Fig. 10-9).

Fig. 10-3. Rip the seat panel from the skirt.

Fig. 10-4. Lift the panel off.

The upholsterer sprays the edges around the hole with spray adhesive, and puts the "plug" in place. Then he cuts a scrap of cambric (the material used for dust covers), sprays adhesive over the area, and spreads the scrap of cambric over the patch, pressing it in place (Fig. 10-10).

The cambric reinforcement covers the lines where the ribbing must be sewn back later. These lines should be clear enough to

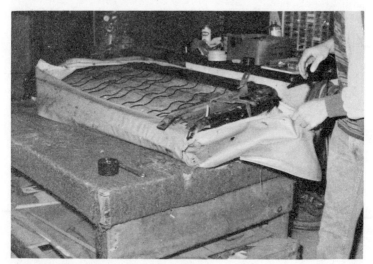

Fig. 10-5. Twist the hog rings off with pliers.

Fig. 10-6. The foam is separated from the vinyl.

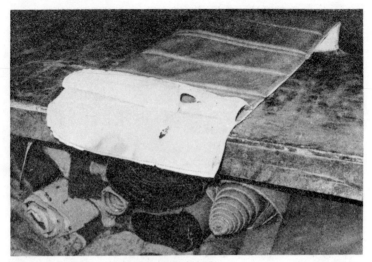

Fig. 10-7. Partially separated foam and vinyl.

follow easily, so in Fig. 10-11 the lines are reestablished with chalk marks.

PREPARING THE COVER

In the sequence of seat reupholstery steps illustrated here, a unique situation exists. The owner wanted as inexpensive a job as

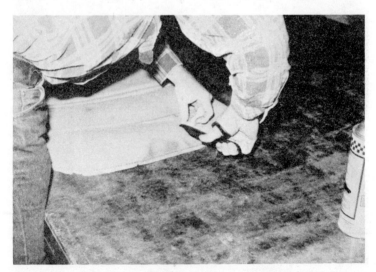

Fig. 10-8. Cut away the ragged edges of foam.

Fig. 10-9. Cut a new foam patch. Fit it in the hole.

possible, but one of good quality. The only damage to the seat cover was in the seat panel. The skirt was still in good shape and could be reused. One way to reduce the cost of the work was to use scraps of vinyl to replace the seat panel. The cover material had to be spliced, since in using scraps there was not enough of a single piece to cover the seat.

Fig. 10-10. Glue the cambric over the patch.

321

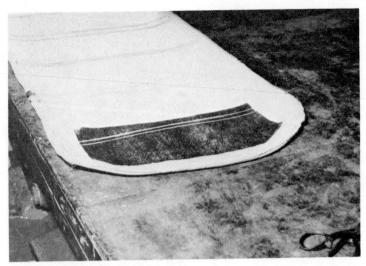

Fig. 10-11. Seam lines on the cambric.

The upholsterer has used the thin foam sheet to cut as big a cover piece as possible. He has used the spray adhesive again to attach the vinyl to the foam. This holds everything neatly in place as the work progresses.

The first splice will be sewn at one of the rib seams. In Fig. 10-12 the upholsterer cuts the excess vinyl off at one of the seam

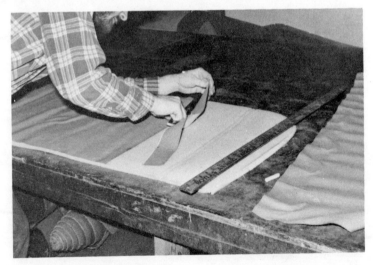

Fig. 10-12. Trim excess vinyl.

322

Fig. 10-13. Measure and cut the first splice.

lines. The first scrap is laid out, measured, and cut (Fig. 10-13). It is not large enough to finish covering the seat; a second splice is necessary.

The first splice is cut. The upholsterer places it, right side together, on the seam line and sews it (Fig. 10-14). This splice is then folded over, checked for a smooth fit, and then secured in place

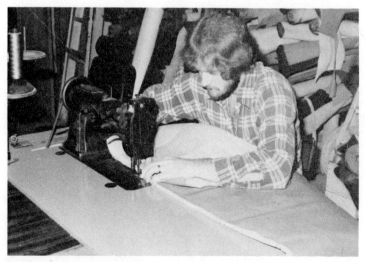

Fig. 10-14. Sew the first splice.

Fig. 10-15. Secure the splice with adhesive.

with the spray adhesive (Fig. 10-15). The excess vinyl is trimmed off to fit (Fig. 10-16).

The second splice is measured, cut, sewn, and secured with glue as the first one was done (Fig. 10-17). The rib seams are sewn from the foam side where the seam lines are clear. Notice in Fig. 10-18 that the upholsterer replaces the rib seams very close to the splicing seams. This does not completely conceal them, but it does

Fig. 10-16. Trim away excess.

Fig. 10-17. Sew the splice at the rib seams.

make the splice less visible. Any seam can rip, but the rib seam next to the splice will almost certainly provide sufficient reinforcement to prevent ripping.

When the seat panel is completed, it must be sewn to the skirt again. The technique known as welting or cording is used here. This welting in vinyl automobile upholstery is actually a molded hollow tube of vinyl with a flange for a seam allowance, instead of a covered

Fig. 10-18. Sew rib seams from the foam side.

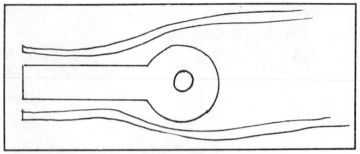

Fig. 10-19. Automobile upholstery vinyl welting.

cord. It is installed as in Fig. 10-19. The skirt on this seat is being reused. It is sewn to the new seat panel (Fig. 10-20).

SPRING REPAIRS

Springs in most automobile seats are very simple. Glance through the illustrations to see how they look. When a spring in an automobile seat breaks, it can be removed and another one put in its place. These replacement springs can be new, or they can be found in salvage yards.

In the project illustrated, the broken spring is one of the support springs at the end of the seat instead of one of the longer ones. Since no identical spring is available for a replacement, a piece of salvage spring is held in a vise (Fig. 10-21) and cut to the

Fig. 10-20. Sew the skirt to the new panel.

Fig. 10-21. Hold the spring in a vise for cutting.

proper size with a hacksaw. In Fig. 10-22 the spring is put back in place with spring clamps and pliers.

With the spring repair completed and the cover ready to replace, the seat is turned upright. The thick foam padding is placed over the springs (Fig. 10-23). Fit the cover back over the foam padding and springs (Fig. 10-24). Hook the new cover to the frame. In Fig. 10-25 the upholsterer is using the hog ringers again to fasten

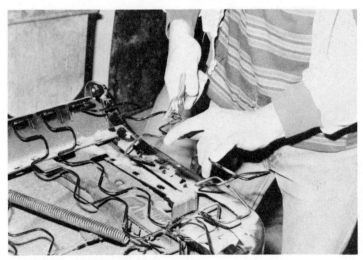

Fig. 10-22. Clamp the replacement spring.

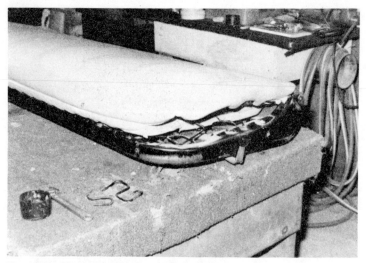

Fig. 10-23. Replace the foam over the springs.

the covers to the frame. This completes the reupholstery project, and the seat is ready to be replaced in the truck.

REBUILDING A BUCKET SEAT

If not for the splicing requirements, all the parts of the old seat cover would be used as a pattern to cut a new one. This process is considered here as it applies to a different kind of automobile seat.

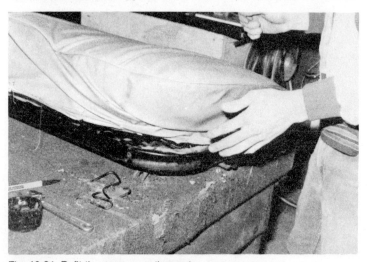

Fig. 10-24. Refit the cover over the seat.

Fig. 10-25. Reconnect the cover to the springs.

The bucket seat to be considered here is a very simple one. It consists of a slab of plywood, foam, and the vinyl cover. The only hardware is a spring or two. The parts of the seat are shown in Fig. 10-26. Notice the shape of the foam. This shape is made with three pieces of foam (Fig. 10-27) secured to one another with adhesive. If

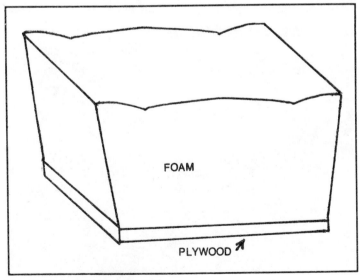

Fig. 10-26. Parts of the foam seat.

329

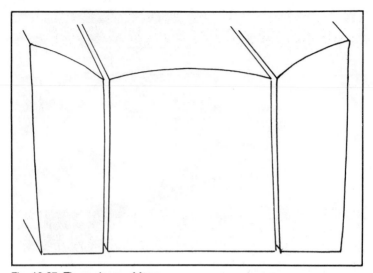

Fig. 10-27. Three pieces of foam.

any part is damaged, a new piece of foam can be cut and glued to the rest.

The old seat cover is removed first. It is only stapled in place. Seams are ripped as in the earlier example, and the pieces are smoothed and placed on a new piece of vinyl. Since the vinyl tends to try to keep the shape it has attained on the seat, it is best to weight it while a pattern is drawn on the new fabric (Fig. 10-28).

Fig. 10-28. Weight the old pattern to mark and cut a new one.

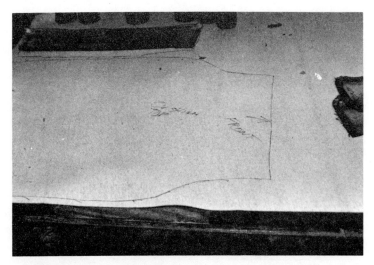

Fig. 10-29. Identify the pattern pieces.

When the cutting lines are drawn on new vinyl, the pieces should be identified with a marking pen (Fig. 10-29). With all the pieces cut, simply sew the skirt to the seat panel (Fig. 10-30), observing seam allowances of the same width as those on the original cover.

In furniture upholstery it is sometimes possible to cover a complete chair or sofa without once using the sewing machine. This

Fig. 10-30. Sew the pieces together.

Fig. 10-31. Sewing completed.

will not be true in automobile upholstery, for these covers will have to be sewn if you are to do a proper job. Depending upon the cover material, you may be able to sew the automobile seat covers on your home sewing machine with appropriate needles and thread. I suggest though, that you cut your new covers, and take them to any upholstery shop with an industrial type sewing machine. Have a shop worker do the sewing for you. Be sure to have accurate

Fig. 10-32. Make a new plywood slab.

Fig. 10-33. Spring between the seat frame and plywood.

measurements or correct seam lines marked. It may be a good idea
to take the old cover along. In Fig. 10-31 all the sewing is completed
for this simple seat cover.

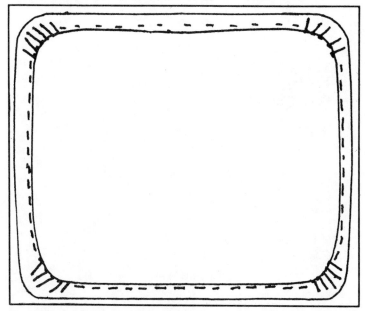

Fig. 10-34. Staple the vinyl to the plywood.

The bottom of the seat is a simple plywood slab. The worker in Fig. 10-32 is preparing to make a new slab. Should you need to do this, simply use the old slab for a pattern, draw around it on a new piece of plywood, and cut it out with a jigsaw.

Any foam seat resting on wood must be provided with vents for the release of air. When you sit on the foam seat, it is compressed. The air must escape. Simply drill a few holes in the slab.

This seat is made more resilient with some coil springs between the automobile floor and the seat. The springs are held in holes in the slab (Fig. 10-33). These holes will also provide for air escape. If there are no such escape holes, the compressed air escapes very slowly through the weakest spot—the seams in the cover. Without escape vents, the seams can split. A vinyl cover will almost certainly lose its shape after a period of too much pressure inside it.

With the slab prepared, the foam pad ready, and the seat cover finished, the assembly is next. Spray the bottom of the foam pad and the top of the plywood slab with adhesive. Put the foam pad in place. Fit the new cover over the foam, pull it around the edge of the plywood, and staple it in place (Fig. 10-34). Pull the cover snug, so the foam is just slightly compressed. When the cover is stapled in place, the seat is ready to be placed in the automobile.

Furniture Construction

As you have read this book, you have become more familiar with furniture construction. Although your primary interest has been in upholstering methods, materials and techniques, you have become acquainted with the components and especially the design of good furniture. You may want to build some furniture pieces.

Chapter 1 was an overview of the more familiar furniture styles. If you glance through the chapter again, you will see that style is the appearance of the piece—whether it is light or heavy, decorated or plain, curved or straight, and so on. The style you select will harmonize with surrounding furniture and features of the room itself. While styles can be mixed within a room, you can only mix style components successfully within a single piece in ways that *do not interrupt harmony*.

The remaining quality to be considered by the beginning furniture builder is *design*. This consists of function, materials, engineering, and workmanship, along with an abstract concept which I call *visual agreement*.

DESIGN

The word design is itself almost an abstract idea. It can be synonymous with purpose, for instance, or intended for a certain function. Design can be thought of as creating a pattern, or even as the execution of a plan. Design is also the conception of an idea in the mind, and the creation of tangible plans which can be used to execute this idea as it is envisioned; this definition is best suited for this book.

Function

The first thing to concern you, once you have decided to build a specific item of furniture, is *function*. While there is immense satisfaction in planning, selecting materials and tools, measuring, sawing, assembling, and finishing a furniture project, that project must be considered a failure if it does not finally fulfill the original purpose as the builder envisioned it. This means, simply, that you must know *why* before you can decide *how*, or that your first step is in careful, detailed consideration of how the finished project will be used.

The process of determining function is a logical, orderly one. Perhaps you need a desk. Where will the desk be placed when it is completed? You cannot put square pegs in round holes, and a 6-foot long desk will not fit in a 4-foot space. Unless you want to work from a high stool, you'd better make the desk a "standard" 29 inches high.

Could there be a case where this wouldn't be true? Certainly. Might there not be a firm reason for departing from standard principles? Yes, and that is the whole point, as well as the beauty of designing and building for yourself. Realize that when you do depart from standard dimensions, you'll either have to do some challenging and innovative shopping or build a chair to fit the desk.

What will you use the desk for? If you prefer to organize your office materials on a wall unit above the desk, you may not need drawer space at all. Perhaps you want a shallow drawer for pencils, stapler, tape, scissors, and other things that tend to clutter. Simply calculate the depth you will need to accommodate these materials and proceed.

You cannot build with real anticipation of pleasure until the question of function has been satisfied. Decide how the item will be used, and then consider materials and engineering-workmanship.

Materials

Visit a building materials supplier. The variety in available materials, from plastics to steel to natural woods, will astound you. This variety makes your choices more difficult. Your natural good taste and common sense won't fail you. If you really don't trust yourself, enlist the help of someone whose taste you do trust.

Taste is another matter. You'll want to choose materials that will be harmonious with the rest of the furnishings and the room. It is probably best to bypass a gleaming plastic desk top if it is to be used in your rustic den. Realize that such things cannot really be dictated, since styles mix well in many cases.

336

Learn about the characteristics of a material. With your skills, will you be able to work successfully with it? How about tools? Sometimes a unique material demands the use of a unique tool, and this can be both annoying and expensive. Finally, consider the material's cost.

Engineering-Workmanship

The craftsman who fails to exercise care, or tries to work too quickly, will often build in a way that prevents functional utility. You can easily build a chair that wobbles when it's sat in, or a drawer that sticks, or a chest with an improperly fitting lid.

Make sure that you have provided for soundness in your design, and don't plan a dining table with very spindly legs or a chair with inadequate stretchers. Such weaknesses occur more often as a result of poor construction than because of improper materials. Always engineer *and execute* the design in a thoughtful manner to insure that the intended function will be satisfied.

Visual Agreement

There are many ways to insure this principle of visual agreement, and as many to violate it. Furniture groupings should be comfortable. If they are not, they will not be visually pleasing. Traditionally, the most comfortable styles are also the most attractive, although this may not be an absolute in every case.

Standard dimensions are often observed in certain pieces. Chairs and sofas, for example, are made to complement each other in height, mass, texture, and other characteristics. While there is no reason why you should always observe these standards, individual items must still be complementary. While you may depart from conventional dimensions, you cannot mix different sizes with much success.

Built-in beds have become quite popular. One reason is that a bed frame may be made a bit smaller or larger than the standard size in order to fit in a particular space. They can also be made higher for drawer space underneath, or lower to create the impression of spaciousness. This is a very convenient approach to bed construction, particularly nowadays when people have become more conscious of space and energy. You shouldn't economize at the expense of tastefulness, and it isn't really necessary. Other furnishings must fit, or the whole room will appear to be out of balance. Sometimes you can walk into a room and immediately feel the lack of visual agreement; yet you are unable to identify the source of your uneasiness.

There is one way that a single piece of furniture can be out of proportion without creating an unharmonious effect. This requires a very sensitive perception on the part of the decorator, but it can be achieved. In such a case, it is necessary to make this item the focal point in the room. The departure from convention will appear as a deliberate exercise in interior decoration. This is a very demanding technique.

The typical home has a kitchen, bedrooms, living room, and perhaps others. As you plan for the creation of the desired visual agreement in your furniture design and construction, decide where you and other members of your family "live" in the house. While every area is probably used, most families have a favorite place for conversation, reading, or other pastimes. Some families favor the kitchen, while others "live" in the family room or living room. If you want to build furniture for the room in which you spend most of your time, keep it as pleasant and harmonious as you can. Perhaps some families could point out a specific reason why they prefer to gather in a certain room, but the main reason surely must be comfort.

Suppose you want to add some kind of wall unit to this room, perhaps floor to ceiling shelves. If the unit is designed well, there is no reason why it should be disturbing in any way. Imagine trying to relax while sitting across from, or worse, beside the wall unit in Fig. 11-1. While this design may be structurally excellent, you get the feeling that it is about to topple over. Figure 11-2 illustrates a much more comfortable unit. It is visually agreeable, and if built of complementary materials, could be an asset to nearly any room.

A table placed somewhere in this room can virtually destroy the aura of relaxation if it is poorly designed. If the table is so large that you have to actually walk around it, it isn't visually agreeable. On the other hand, you will also be distressed by a fragile table, for you cannot feel comfortable placing something on it. You'll feel compelled to walk far around it as well.

The height of the table must be compatible with that of other furniture. From a sitting position, you shouldn't have to stoop to a table, or stretch your neck to see over it. Components of most tables are fairly standard. See that a table with thick legs has a suitable slab, and vice versa, and take care to match materials, colors, textures, and styles within the range of comfort.

The same principles should be applied with other items. As you move forward in designing and building, simply remember how important the visual effect is in insuring comfort and beauty. While it isn't necessarily true that these qualities are more important than techniques of construction, the following *is* true. The project is considered a failure unless it fulfills the function as originally envisioned. It will not do so if the design itself is a failure.

CHARACTERISTICS OF WOOD

Natural wood must surely be the most satisfying building material to work with. The more you handle wood through sawing, gluing, and nailing, the more you learn. When a tree has been sawed into boards, it is dead—yet wood changes. It shrinks and expands, changes colors, and assumes an even more charming character as it ages.

Although there are numerous species of trees used in furniture building, most builders use a relatively limited number of wood species. Each species naturally has its own characteristics, but some characteristics are common to all species.

Wood is incredibly strong and durable when used properly. A ¼-inch dowel in pure tension will support much more than the average man's weight. The phrase "when used properly" is the key to making the most of the strength of wood. Most boards that you buy will have defects. With one notable exception, *shake*, defects in wood do not actually reduce its strength to a serious degree if the builder knows how to use it. I examine the familiar defects, but first you should understand something of how trees grow and are sawed, and the characteristics shared by most species.

Fig. 11-1. Top-heavy wall unit.

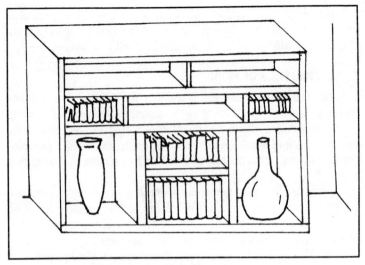

Fig. 11-2. A good balance is pleasing to the eye.

Tree Growth

Wood consists of millions of cellulose fibers per cubic inch. These fibers are bonded by *lignin*, a natural glue. The fibers form long, hollow cells which run lengthwise with the tree, creating the *grain*.

In the center of the tree is a soft material called *pith*. This was originally the sprout.

Surrounding the pith is a material called *duramen*, more commonly known as *heartwood*. The heartwood is physiologically inactive. It is darker in color and more dense and strong than the rest of the tree.

Around the heartwood is the thickest part called *sapwood*. Sapwood is still active in the living tree. It carries sap to the leaves from the tree roots. Sapwood is of a lighter color than heartwood and is less dense.

A thin layer around the sapwood forms new growth cells in the living tree. It is called *cambium*.

The *inner bark* is next. Inner bark carries nourishment to all the physiologically active parts of the tree.

Finally, there is the *outer bark* made of dead cells. The function of the outer bark is basically to protect the living tree from damage.

The *growth rings* appear annually. I suspect every child who has the opportunity to do so attempts at least once to count growth rings and determine the age of a tree.

Trees are categorized as either softwood or hardwood, but this designation doesn't *always* refer to hardness or softness of the wood itself. Softwoods are from evergreen trees; hardwoods are from deciduous (broad leaved) trees. Both types of wood are used in furniture construction. Softwoods are generally less expensive and most readily available, primarily because they grow faster. Beginners in woodworking tend to use softwoods. This is not to suggest that they are less desirable; this depends on the effect you want to create. Most quality furniture is made from hardwoods because these trees have a fine appearance that is often preferred. Hardwoods are also more demanding to work with. Generally, they are harder to cut and nail than softwoods.

Popular, though, is a hardwood that is not difficult to work with; nor does it possess the familiar strengths of most hardwoods. Redwood is a softwood that has more hardwood qualities. You should actually get acquainted with the particular characteristics of any species that you expect to work with. The best way to do this is to use a variety of woods when you have the opportunity.

Grain

The grain pattern and type in any wood depend on different factors, such as the type of wood and the way it has been cut. Hardwoods may be either *open grained* or *closed grained*. Open grained woods, of which oak is the most familiar example, cannot be finished to a gleaming surface without the use of a wood filler, because you can actually feel the grain ridges. Close grained woods are much smoother.

The direction of the grain depends on the way the board is cut from the tree. The wood fibers run lengthwise to the tree. Figures 11-3 through 11-6 indicate the different cutting methods.

The grain may be straight or wavy without appreciable effect upon strength, but wood with a wavy grain is more subject to warping and twisting. As for strength, at least some of the grain lines should run the whole length of the board (Fig. 11-7), or it will have less strength in a position where it must withstand compression or tension forces.

Shake and Pitch Pockets

Shake is a defect that makes a board practically useless. This occurs when the bonding between growth rings is so weak that the wood separates between the rings (Fig. 11-8).

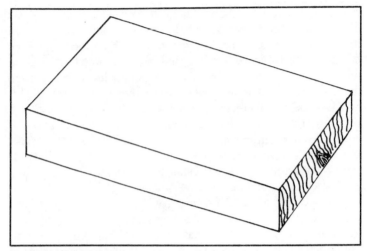

Fig. 11-3. Vertical grain.

Pitch pockets are sometimes found in softwoods, and they are extremely annoying. These are usually gaps in the wood that are filled with or secrete *pitch*, a tarry substance that bleeds through fillers, finishes, and so forth. If you must use a board with these sticky areas, dig them out with a chisel, removing as much as seems practical. If the board is used where it can be seen or might be touched, brush a good sealer like shellac over the area. Then apply the wood filler.

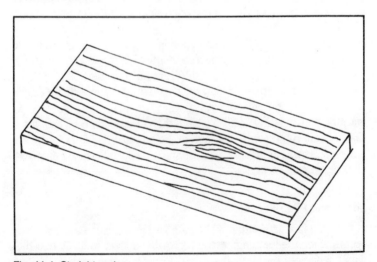

Fig. 11-4. Straight grain.

342

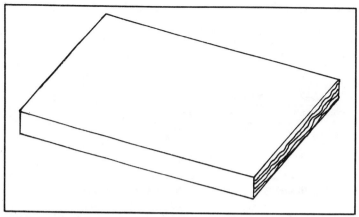

Fig. 11-5. Flat grain.

Knots

You will see more *knots* in wood than any other defect. Knots are usually not too much of a problem unless you do not want them to be in view; in this case you may have to discard some wood. Additionally, knots will have more resin than the rest of the board, so you should apply a sealer before you apply any finish.

In some applications knots will reduce the strength of wood, but this can be minimized with proper use. All wood will be acted upon to different degrees by certain forces. Two forces that will be

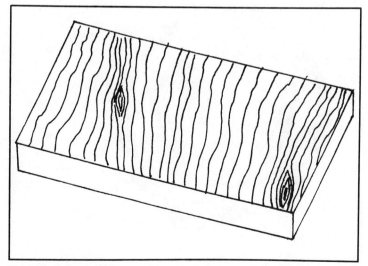

Fig. 11-6. Cross grain.

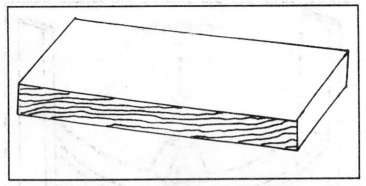

Fig. 11-7. This board will be weak in tension or compression.

important when you use wood with knots are *tension* and *compression*. These forces aren't as effective in furniture construction as in house building, but you should be aware of them. Figure 11-9 illustrates the nature of these two forces.

Suppose you are building a workbench that will support heavy tools, and one of the boards has a large knot in it. Be sure to place the board where the widest side of the knot is in compression (Fig. 11-10). If you place the wide side down, or in tension, the strength of the board is reduced immensely. A knot 2 inches wide on the tension side of a 2 × 4 reduces its strength by half to that of a 2 × 2.

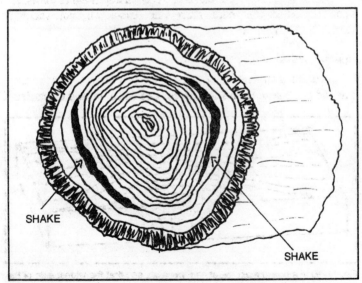

SHAKE

SHAKE

Fig. 11-8. In the defect called shakegrowth rings separate.

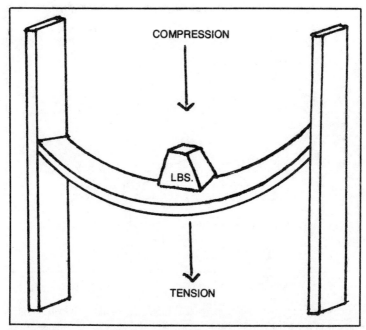

Fig. 11-9. The top of the board is in compression; the bottom of the board is in tension.

Knots are hard to cut and nail. Avoid using them in joints. If a knot falls out of the board, there's no reason why you shouldn't simply glue it back in.

Splits, Checks, and Crooked Boards

A *split* may not be too serious, because it usually occurs only at the end of a board. Such short pieces can be cut off and discarded if

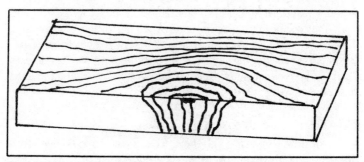

Fig. 11-10. If a board must resist compression, see that the widest side of the knot is on the top side.

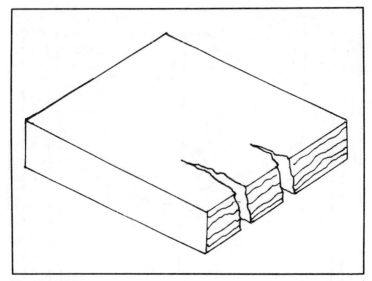

Fig. 11-11. Split.

necessary. Splits cross the growth rings and go all the way through a board (Fig. 11-11).

A *check* also goes across the growth rings, but not all the way through (Fig. 11-12). Both of these defects occur because of uneven drying when the outside of the board dries faster than the inside. As the outer area dries, it contracts. Since the inside remains expanded while it contains moisture, the contracting surface must split.

Boards also *crook, cup, bow,* and *twist.* These are simply different names for boards that are not straight. Such defects are caused primarily by uneven drying and grain direction. If they aren't thoroughly dried when you get them, they may warp or twist afterwards. Store all lumber flat, supported all along its length, and in a dry place. Although such boards are certainly harder to work with, they can nearly always be used by simply forcing or clamping.

Do not hesitate to examine boards before you buy them. There is simply no reason for you to accept boards with serious defects. Look them over carefully. Reject those that will cost you too much in waste or extra work.

PLYWOOD

Not too many years ago there would have been no need for a discussion of plywood. There was a great deal of prejudice where plywood was concerned, and few woodworkers cared to use it.

In recent years, however, people have recognized the many benefits and advantages of using plywood. There are several disadvantages, too. In order to appreciate these, you should know something about the characteristics of plywood.

Plywood is a very strong, flat wood panel made by bonding a number of layers of veneer called *plies.* The two basic types of plywood are *Exterior* and *Interior.* There are *Engineered* and *Appearance* grades, with each grade further classified according to different specifications. The wood species used are divided into five groups according to strength. Each plywood panel is identified as to type, grade, species, etc., by the trademark stamped on the face or edge of the panel.

Plywood has many desirable qualities. The strength and durability of the wood itself is increased by the techniques of manufacture. The most obvious of these is cross-lamination. This consists of placing the grain of alternate plies at right angles to each other. This gives more resistance to the various forces acting upon wood which might weaken it.

Expansion and contraction due to moisture and heat are either much less than that of solid wood, or occur only to an insignificant

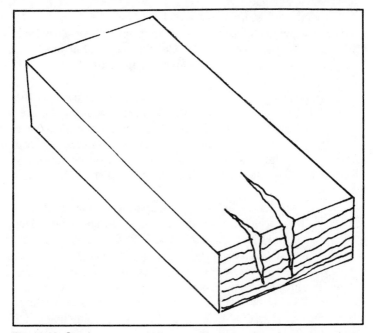

Fig. 11-12. Check.

degree. This, too, is because of the cross-lamination and strong glue bonding. Plywood will warp or twist only when it is not properly cared for during storing and transportation. Warping is caused by unequal moisture content throughout any piece of wood. If plywood is reasonably well protected, it will not warp or twist.

Again because of cross-lamination, plywood has a very high shear strength in any direction. This shear strength and the nail holding capacity of plywood gives it one of the most desirable qualities of all—racking resistance.

Most plywood comes from various hardwood blocks which are cut into 8½-foot lengths. These blocks are literally peeled into continuous thin sheets of veneer. The long sheets are then cut into the desired widths, usually 4 feet, and dried to a low enough moisture content to retain a solid glue bond. Repairs are then made. Defects are cut out and the holes filled. These patches can be seen on the plywood surface as neat oval, circular, or long, narrow strips.

The sheets are covered with glue and then arranged in stacks of correct grading and species. A powerful hydraulic press then compresses the panels. Finally, the panels are trimmed and sanded, except for some grades which are left unsanded, and examined for quality and appearance.

Strength and stiffness of wood are variable according to species. Since plywood might be made from any of 70 or so species, classification of each according to strength would not be practical. The species are classified into five groups closely related in strength.

The *group* does not refer to species used throughout the panel—only to the face and back plies, and to the weakest of these. This does not apply to decorative plywood, because the appearance of the face plies is most important. *Group* in decorative plywood refers only to the face plies. The group, or species rating, is expressed on the panel as G-1, G-2, and on through G-5 for group five.

All the veneer is likewise classified according to certain characteristics, including such defects as splits and knots. The grades are identified by these letters: N, A, B, C, C-plugged, and D. N is the highest quality and is sometimes difficult to obtain at lumberyards, but it can be ordered if it is not available. A is the second best in appearance. It is smooth and can have no more than 18 repairs. It can be painted effectively and may be used as a natural finish material. D is the lowest grade. It can have knotholes and knots up to 2½ inches in width and some splits.

Appearance grades of plywood can be obtained in either Exterior or Interior types. These grades are used where the appearance of the face and/or back is of the most importance. They might be panels that are especially textured for paneling, with very smooth, sanded surfaces or some specific decorative overlays. The grade is shown in the American Plywood Association (APA) trademark as the large lettering that might read A-C. This means that the face is grade A and the back is grade C.

Plywood is inappropriate for carving or turning. There is a limited thickness available. The edges must be covered in some way. There just isn't the same sense of satisfaction for many people in working with plywood as in natural wood.

I think it's a fair assumption that nearly all persons building furniture will use plywood. Its superior strength and large panels make it extremely desirable for many jobs. Probably the most common difficulty in plywood use will be the technique used in concealing edges. It is not always necessary to conceal them. If the finished piece will be painted, simply sand the edges adequately. Fill any gaps that may appear. Paint might cover the edges in a perfectly satisfactory manner.

There are several ways to conceal the edges. If you use joints that will hide them, there is no problem. The most obvious joint to do this is that where the edge is inserted in a slot (Fig. 11-13), called a *dado* joint, or at the end of a piece, known as a *rabbet* joint (Fig. 11-14). Another possibility is the *mitered* joint (Fig. 11-15). Molding can be bought or made to fill corners in plywood more easily than mitering, however, because of the tendency of the face ply to chip or split when you saw it (Fig. 11-16).

Finally, you can use bonding to be applied to the edge with contact cement. You can buy this in rolls from your building materials dealer, or make your own from plywood scraps.

To make your own bonding, first determine the grain direction you will need. Then cut a strip from the side or end as is applicable (Fig. 11-17). Simply peel or slice off the veneer with a sharp chisel, saw, or whatever tool works best (Fig. 11-18). You must first see that the edges to be covered are smooth and flush with any joined members. Then carefully align the bonding with the edge, and apply it. If you make your own bonding, you may find it simpler to make it slightly wider than the edge to be covered. Then sand it to fit after it is attached. If you do this, be very careful while sanding (Fig. 11-19). The face ply will be quite thin. If you get into it at all, you might ruin it.

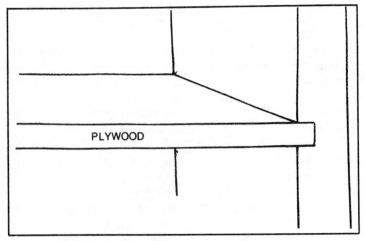

Fig. 11-13. A dado joint hides edges.

TOOLS AND FASTENERS

There are many tools and fasteners used in making furniture. Since some woodworking tools are rather expensive and require a lot of space for their most effective use, you might first consider some alternatives to buying.

One of the alternatives to buying equipment is to have someone else do your cutting for you. This requires that you have very precise measurements. Never depend on one quick measurement for accuracy. Always measure twice. Remember to allow in your

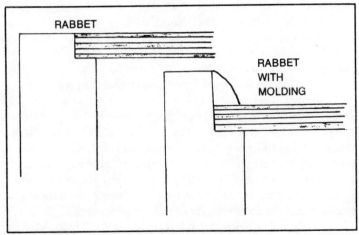

Fig. 11-14. Conceal plywood edges with rabbets.

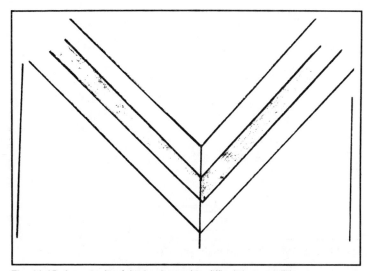

Fig. 11-15. A neat miter joint in plywood is difficult but possible.

measurements for the width of the cut itself. Many lumberyards will do all your cutting, from the more simple cuts to rabbets and dadoes for intricate joints. It is also possible and may be desirable to have someone do lathe work for you, if you plan to use such things as turned legs.

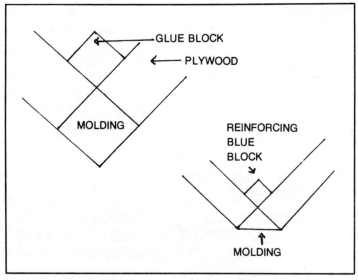

Fig. 11-16. Plywood edges can be concealed with molding.

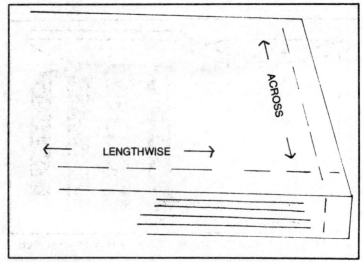

Fig. 11-17. Cut the strip according to the grain direction you need.

You may have a friend or acquaintance who can do this work for you. Arrange to be present when the work is done. This may not be an absolute necessity, but it is wise. By being there, you can permit the use of inferior woods and also see that the work is done carefully.

Cutting Tools

The most basic of all cutting tools in the woodworking shop is the *handsaw* (Fig. 11-20). There are three kinds of handsaws, each for a specific purpose. The *combination saw* is the most familiar one, because it is made for cutting efficiently both with the grain and across the grain. There is a *ripsaw* especially for cutting quickly with the grain, and a *crosscut* saw for cutting across the grain.

Fig. 11-18. Remove the needed ply carefully.

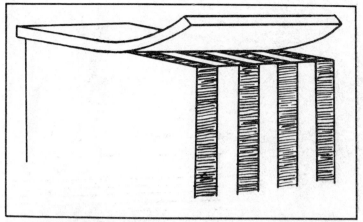

Fig. 11-19. If you make the band too wide, be careful while sanding if flush.

Doing precise cutting with a handsaw is a demanding task, particularly until you have become fairly adept at using this tool. It need not be terribly exhausting to use a handsaw, once you learn to use it properly. The first requirement is that you keep your saw, like any cutting instrument, sharp. It is much more difficult to use a dull tool. The cutting will be much better and more attractive if the saw is sharp. More damage will always be done with a dull cutting tool than with a sharp one.

When using the various handsaws, see that the piece you are cutting is firmly held by a vise or held solidly with the knee. The cutting is done on the downstroke. Do not exert all your energy on this downstroke. Make it a smooth, even stroke with enough pressure to cut, but do not try to force the cutting too quickly. If you do, you will quickly become tired. The underside of the wood you are cutting will splinter and split worse than if you used less force, though perhaps more rapidly.

Fig. 11-20. Handsaw.

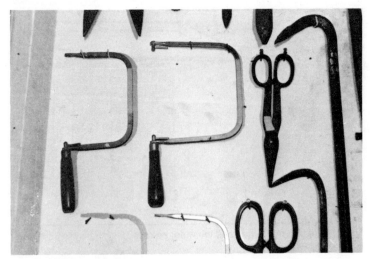

Fig. 11-21. Coping saw.

Regarding this splintering problem on the underside of the wood you are cutting, the most effective way to control it is to put a scrap board beneath the good one. Cutting two boards doesn't require much more energy than cutting one, and the scrap will splinter while the good board won't.

Another kind of inexpensive handsaw used in the woodworking shop is the *coping saw* (Fig. 11-21). The coping saw has a very thin blade which is effective for cutting sharp curves, and also for cutting from the center of a board from a drilled pilot hole.

A second handy tool that is used for cutting less sharp curves and also for cutting from the center of the board is the *keyhole saw* (Fig. 11-22).

The *backsaw* is the third common handsaw. It has a wide and stiff blade, and the teeth are very fine. The backsaw (Fig. 11-23) is especially useful for making small and exact cuts. It is often used

Fig. 11-22. Keyhole saw.

354

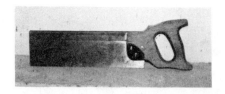

Fig. 11-23. Backsaw.

with a *miter box* (Fig. 11-24) which holds the saw in a position to cut angles such as those for the corners of simple picture frames.

There are several fairly inexpensive power saws that are useful in the home workshop. The most convenient, safe, and useful one is probably the *jigsaw* (Fig. 11-25). You can use many blades for this saw, and an adjustable platform permits you to cut precisely at practically any angle.

The *circular saw* shown in Fig. 11-26 is quite useful in many applications. I cannot recommend the circular saw for the home workshop, though, as I consider it a dangerous tool for anyone not truly skilled in its proper use.

Regarding the more complicated larger saws, I would suggest that you observe them in use and learn about the particular advantages and disadvantages of each. You can then make the choice most suitable for your needs.

The *band saw* (Fig. 11-27) is a versatile tool and is especially fine for cutting curves. It can also be used for straight cuts and for cutting bulky pieces of wood.

You can nearly always see a *table saw* at a house construction site. Table saws are used for quick cutting, such as when ripping panels of plywood.

One of the most versatile of all workshop saws is the *radial arm saw* (Fig. 11-28). This saw can be used with dado attachments

Fig. 11-24. Backsaw with miter box.

Fig. 11-25. Jigsaw.

and is adjustable for miter cuts. The radial arm saw is worth considering for any shop.

Drills

There are several types of drills available. Most woodworkers on a small scale can get by quite effectively with a small electric drill. There are several kinds of bits for use with the electric drill, including a *drill stop* which allows you to drill a hole of a particular depth without going all the way through the material. There are two commonly used hand drills as well. One is the *brace* (Fig. 11-29), and the second is an *eggbeater drill* (Fig. 11-30). Both of these are handy

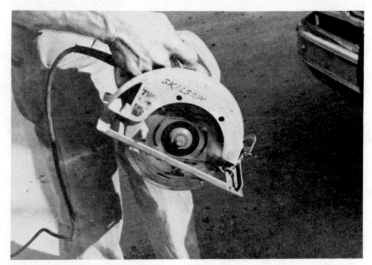

Fig. 11-26. Circular saw.

to have; many woodworkers find them preferable to the electric drill.

A *drill press* (Fig. 11-31) is a marvelous tool to have. It is particularly useful for drilling holes at exact angles.

Hammers

You should select a hammer that feels comfortable when you lift it. The most common weight (of the hammer head) is 16 ounces.

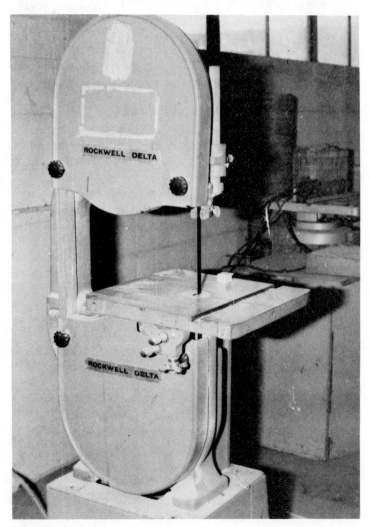

Fig. 11-27. Band saw.

Fig. 11-28. Radial arm saw.

This weight is usually most satisfactory for furniture construction. The face of the hammer can be either flat or convex. The convex face is best, because you can drive nails flush without making dents in the wood. It should be noted, however, that it takes practice to use this hammer effectively.

Handsawing and hammering can make you tired in a hurry if you do not use the tools properly. Using a hammer shouldn't be a terribly exhausting job. The hammer itself is the tool, and its weight drives the nail. Your hand and arm guide the hammer. Don't strike with all your strength. If you are putting up roof decking, it might be permissible to strike the nail with harder blows, but you should never do this in furniture construction. The holding power of the nail is more effective if it is driven with less force.

Nails

Nails are fine for many uses, but their chief strength lies in their resistance to *shear* force. This force is illustrated in Fig. 11-32.

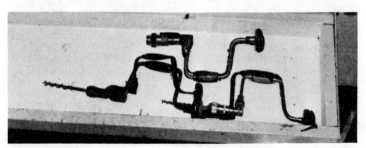

Fig. 11-29. Brace.

Fig. 11-30. Eggbeater drill.

If a withdrawal force is also in effect, a nailed joint is usually inadequate.

Avoid driving two or more nails in a straight line, for this will encourage the wood to split. Always stagger the nails, and arrange them in a triangular shape when possible. Triangulation withstands force equally from all directions (Fig. 11-33).

Fig. 11-31. Drill press.

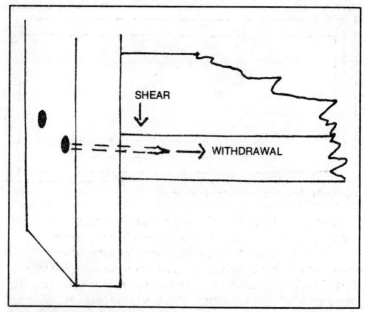

Fig. 11-32. Shear and withdrawal.

Choose nails for both their size and their appearance. Nails come basically in three types (for woodworking): *common* nails, *finishing* nails, and *casing* nails. Casing nails and finishing nails are similar (Fig. 11-34). They are used when the heads need to be hidden. The main difference is that the casing nail is of a heavier gauge.

Common nails are easier to drive because of their flat heads. They shouldn't be used when the heads need to be concealed.

Nails of all three types come in sizes indicated by a number followed by the letter d. The d is an abbreviation for the word penny. A 2d nail is 1 inch long, a 3d nail is 1¼ inches long, an 8d nail is 2½ inches, and so forth. Common nails are available in sizes up to 6 inches in length (60d).

Screws and Bolts

A screw or bolt joint is stronger than the nail joint. The *flathead screw* is the one most commonly used in woodwork, although there are others. Always drill holes for screws; the drilling depth regulator does the job perfectly. It has the same basic shape as the screw (Fig. 11-35) and is thus able to drill the proper hole for all three parts of the screw; the *thread, shank,* and *head.* Always drill

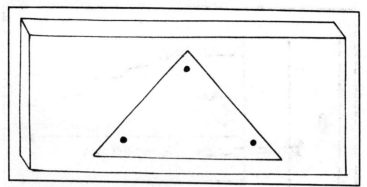

Fig. 11-33. Drive nails in triangular patterns.

the hole for the threads a little shorter than the length of the threads themselves, so the screw will have more holding power.

It is often possible to use bolts when building furniture. Bolts aren't too attractive, but they are superior in strength. The *lag bolt* (Fig. 11-36) is pointed like a screw, but it is not tapered. The *carriage bolt* is to be inserted all the way through the wood and secured with a washer and nut on the other side (Fig. 11-37).

There are too many fasteners to consider in detail here. While some purists in woodworking scorn the use of preformed brackets and braces, I believe you should go to a hardware store and become acquainted with the fascinating things available now. They are convenient, strong, and are designed well.

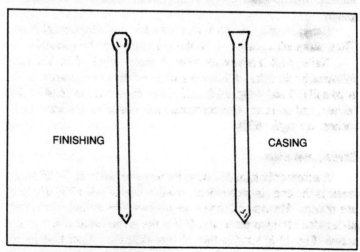

FINISHING   CASING

Fig. 11-34. Finishing and casing nails.

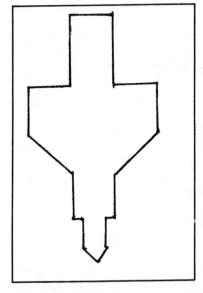

Fig. 11-35. Drilling depth regulator.

FURNITURE CONSTRUCTION CONCEPTS

With a few tools, fasteners, and wood, a great deal of careful planning, and some labor, you can make almost any basic piece of furniture that you desire. Begin with simple designs. Then reach a little further into complexity as you gain familiarity with the tools, materials, and the principles of sound workmanship.

At the risk of oversimplifying, you can begin with this concept. Most furniture consists of a few basic parts, adapted and rearranged for different applications. It is often helpful in developing a new skill to reduce the components and steps to their simplest terms. Therefore, you can say that tables, chairs, cabinets, and beds, in one form or another, encompass most familiar pieces of furniture. These items consist of the following basic parts: *legs* (or posts), *slabs* (tops, sides, backs, doors, shelves), *drawers, braces* (rails, blocks stretchers), *hardware* (hinges, braces, handles), and sometimes *skeleton framing*.

A third simplified concept is that, following design and cutting, furniture construction can be seen as the assembly of parts. Functional and aesthetic assembly is dependent on the best possible joinery techniques you can proceed most effectively with techniques of furniture construction by approaching these three broad concepts in reverse or inductive order: joinery, components, and applications.

362

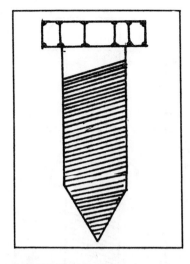

Fig. 11-36. Lag bolt.

JOINERY

I have briefly discussed, nails, screws, and bolts. These can and often will be used in conjunction with the following methods. The same applies to adhesives; while there are occasions when a glued joint is sufficient by itself, more often it is necessary to use glue in combination with other methods.

Glues and Clamps

There are several kinds of glues, but actually you can do almost anything in woodworking with three kinds. The most versatile is *liquid resin* or white glue, and you can buy it in quantities varying from small squeeze bottles to gallon jugs. White glue is a dependable glue that is easy and quick to use. It sets up in a fairly short time. White glue will be sufficient for *most* adhesive tasks, but two others may be needed at times.

If the furniture you build will be exposed to moisture, such as patio furniture, you need a glue that is completely waterproof. *Resorcinol*, which must be mixed, is such a glue.

The only time you need the third kind of glue is when you are using a wood like lemonwood that contains oil. This is *powdered casein glue*. While it is a suitable glue for general furniture building purposes, it is not as convenient as white glue.

There are certain principles that should be practiced when using any kind of adhesive. The first of these is that you should *always* read and follow the directions on the original container.

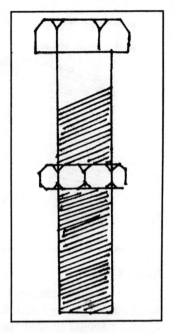

Fig. 11-37. Carriage bolt.

These directions are intended to help you make the most effective use of the material, and they should not be neglected.

Be sure to allow plenty of time for any glue to dry. The directions on the container indicate the length of time required and sometimes suggest methods of speeding the drying process. If your work is planned efficiently, however, you will need to speed drying time. It is better to avoid disturbing the glued parts until they are thoroughly dried, because you can destroy the joints. Then you would not only have to do the job over, but also clean the wood again before you began.

Be sure to clean the surfaces to be glued before you begin. It is pointless to do the rest of the job well, but finish with a weak joint because you have neglected adequate preparation. Also, remember that slick, hard surfaces do not adhere as well as those that are slightly rough. You will sometimes need to sand such a surface across the grain to roughen it before applying the glue.

When you add an adhesive to a dowel or similar joint, be sure to provide a method for excess glue to escape. The dowels may be grooved or spiraled to accomplish this. Also, such a joint should not be made to fit so tightly that the parts have to be forced into place. When you add glue and force two parts together, it is surprisingly easy to cause the wood to split.

There are several kinds of clamps that you can use to hold glued parts together until they are dry. It is best to visit a hardware store and examine the variety of clamps. Ask to see a *web clamp*. Once you examine the web clamp, you can probably fashion one for yourself from materials in your workshop.

Examine the *bar clamps*, *pipe clamps*, *c-clamps*, and *miter clamps* as well as the small spring clamps and press screws. Most of these come in different sizes and with varying characteristics.

When you apply clamps to your glued furniture components, do not put very much force into tightening them. The pressure you can exert with your own hands will likely be sufficient. Tighten the clamps until a little of the glue squeezes out. Don't overdo it, though, for you can squeeze out nearly all the glue. This results in a weak joint.

There are other ways to secure a glued joint until it dries, without using clamps. Sometimes you can use nails, screws, bolts, or corrugated fasteners when appropriate.

Butt Joint

The *butt joint* is probably the simplest joint. Sometimes it is also the least effective, but not necessarily. The butt joint is made simply by butting one member against another and connecting them

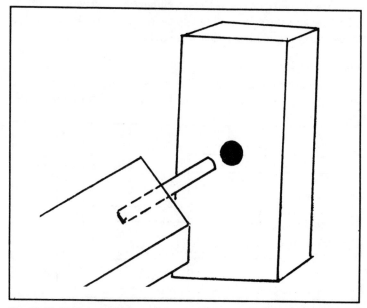

Fig. 11-38. Hidden single dowel joint.

in some manner. The butt joint can be greatly strengthened in several ways. Nails or screws can be used in conjunction with an adhesive to make a strong joint. When practical, a bracket can be used in the corner or a corner block.

Dowel Joint

A *dowel joint* can be one of the strongest possible joints, particularly if more than one dowel is used to give extra security against movement. Dowels can be bought in different sizes and lengths. They can be smooth, spiraled, or ribbed. A dowel joint is almost always strengthened with glue, but this joint should not be made so tight that there is no means of escape for excess glue. There are several different applications for dowel joints. A single dowel might be used to make a hidden joint (Fig. 11-38). More than one dowel gives greater security. It prevents the possibility of turning that exists with a single dowel. Dowels are particularly effective in attaching legs to furniture.

One particularly attractive dowel joint is made when the dowel goes all the way through the member and is rounded at the end (Fig. 11-39). Dowels are often used in conjunction with other types of joints for remarkable strength. Figure 11-40 is a combination of dowel and the mortise and tenon joint.

Dowel joints can also be strengthened by driving a nail or screw through the member and into the dowel itself. One dowel can be used to lock another in place (Fig. 11-41).

Mortise and Tenon Joint

The mortise and tenon joint is shown in Fig. 11-42. This is a strong joint. Like the dowel, it can be reinforced with glue, nails,

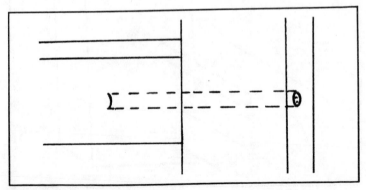

Fig. 11-39. End of the dowel showing.

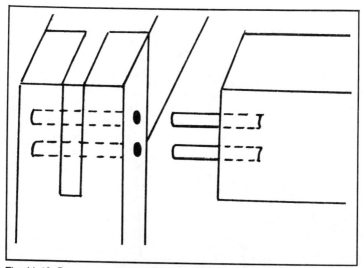

Fig. 11-40. Dowel and mortise and tenon joint.

and screws, or a dowel can be inserted to lock the tenon in place (Fig. 11-43). On some occasions when the tenon goes all the way through the member, it can be made more secure with a wedge driven into a groove in the tenon. After the joint is firmly fixed, it can

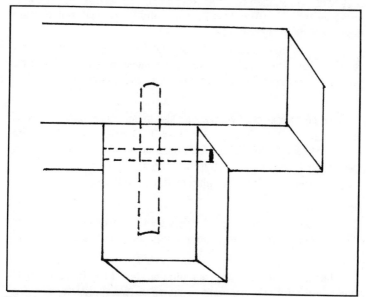

Fig. 11-41. One dowel locks another.

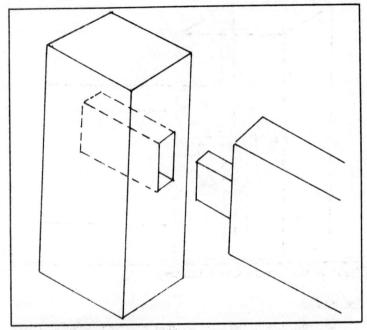

Fig. 11-42. Mortise and tenon.

be sawed and sanded to a nice finish (Fig. 11-44). A side tenon is also a possibility (Fig. 11-45), especially if the material you are working with is quite thin.

If possible, a mortise and tenon joint should be offset slightly (Fig. 11-46). This kind of offset will conceal any crack that may possibly appear as the wood dries more and contracts.

Dado Joint

A *dado* is essentially a *kerf* or a slot in one member, so a second piece can be fitted into it (Fig. 11-47). Dadoes can be cut with ordinary saws if you are careful. Some saws have a special attachment for cutting dadoes. Like the others, dado joints can also be strengthened by the use of glue or finishing nails.

Dovetail Joint

The *dovetail joint* (Fig. 11-48) is another strong one. This joint is often used in drawer construction. It is not as intricate as it looks.

Lap Joint

The *lap joint* is a rather simple one, but it has more strength than a butt joint. The lap joint is shown in two applications in Fig. 11-49.

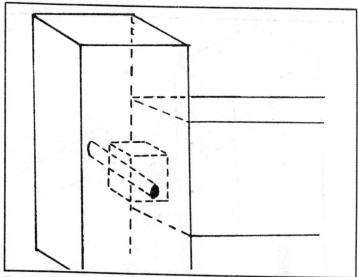

Fig. 11-43. Mortise and tenon with lock dowel.

Rabbet Joint

The *rabbet joint* is another familiar technique in furniture construction. It is effected by fitting the edge of a board into a rabbet in a second board (Fig. 11-50).

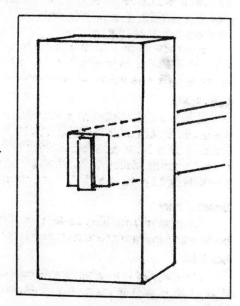

Fig. 11-44. Wedged tenon.

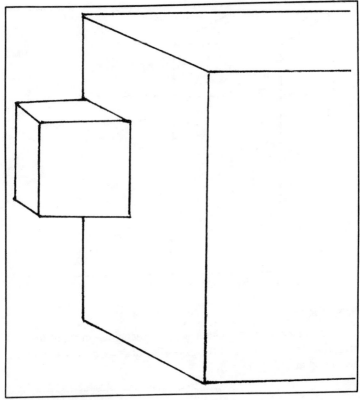

Fig. 11-45. Side tenon.

COMPONENTS

If you are to continue the study of furniture building with the assumption that most furniture consists of a few basic parts, made and applied differently for varied pieces, recognize that any specific piece can be quite simple or very complicated. You should begin with simple designs and progress to the more complex ones. While I discuss the simpler designs in most detail, a few more complex ones are suggested.

Legs

Examine the legs on the various pieces of furniture in your home. Legs can be of many designs and shapes. They may be vertical and squared, vertical but tapered, or shaped and vertical or slanted. Whatever the particular appearance of any leg you might prefer, it must first support the weight imposed upon it. Therefore,

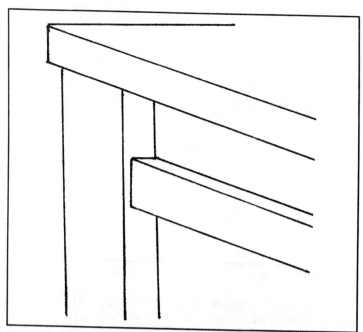

Fig. 11-46. Offset mortise and tenon.

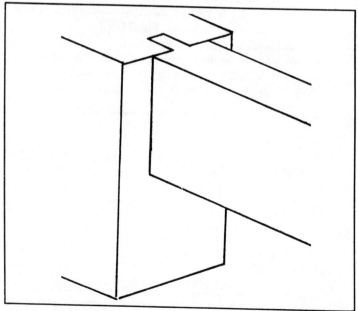

Fig. 11-47. Dado joint.

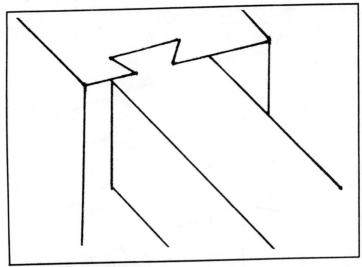

Fig. 11-48. Dovetail joint.

begin with straight legs, for these are not only easier to build but stronger. Nevertheless, a vertical leg can be given the illusion of an angle or slant by tapering (Fig. 11-51).

A very easy kind of vertical leg is the 4 × 4 solid leg as is on the coffee table in Fig. 11-52. Another variation in vertical legs is the post leg, an extension of the frame (Fig. 11-53).

Although I don't discuss lathe work here, many kinds of attractive furniture legs can be made on a lathe by turning cylinders or squares (Fig. 11-54). The really ambitious woodworker might attempt some of the period styles discussed in Chapter 1.

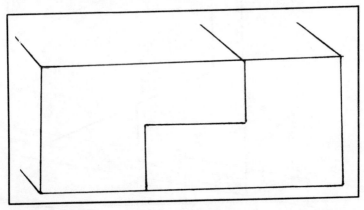

Fig. 11-49. Lap joint.

372

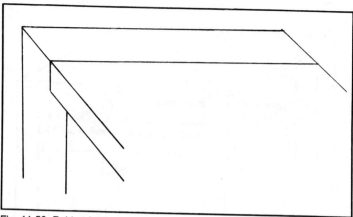

Fig. 11-50. Rabbet joint.

An alternative to doing this complex turning might be worthwhile. It is possible to buy all sorts of ready-made legs in different lengths, styles, and materials. It is certainly possible that ready-made legs will be less expensive in both materials and time consumption than making your own legs would be.

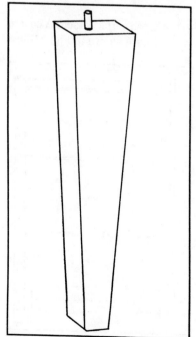

Fig. 11-51. A taper gives the illusion of a slanted leg.

373

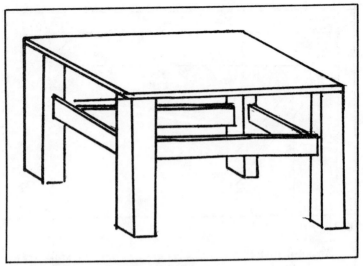

Fig. 11-52. A 4 × 4 inch solid straight leg.

There are many ways to attach legs to furniture. They may be fastened to rails, which are in turn fastened to the top, seat, or frame of the rest of the piece. Figure 11-55 shows two simple methods of attaching legs to rails.

Legs may also be attached to the broad surface itself. A couple of different applications of this approach are shown in Fig. 11-56.

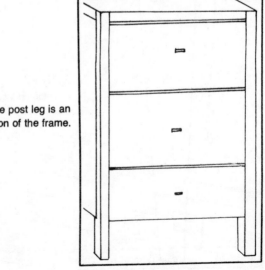

Fig. 11-53. The post leg is an extension of the frame.

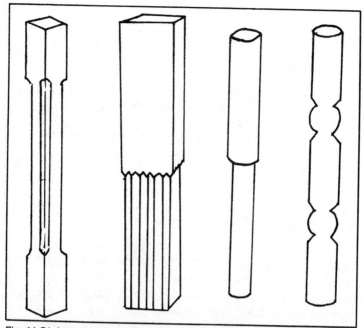

Fig. 11-54. Legs from square or cylindrical blanks.

Legs may be attached with bolts or screws. They may be fastened with simple dowels if little weight is imposed upon the piece, or with dowels reinforced with nails or screws. Legs may be attached with mortise and tenon joints, with rabbet joints (Fig. 11-57), or a combination of these.

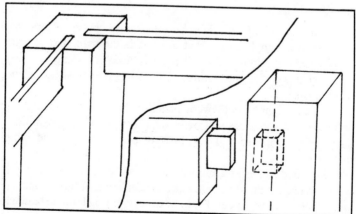

Fig. 11-55. Legs attached to rails.

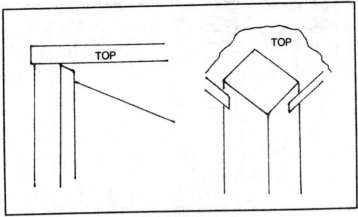

Fig. 11-56. Legs may be attached to the top.

As you plan for making and attaching legs, you should first consider function. See that the leg you choose will support the required weight for the expected life of the rest of the piece. On the other hand, do not ignore appearance, for it is certainly not difficult to make legs that are both attractive and reliable. Do not compromise the strength factor to the degree of building in a weakness, but do try to make the leg attractive.

Finally, when you are ready to attempt legs with a slant, remember that *stretchers* (Fig. 11-58) will add stability to the piece. Always limit the slant even on a very low and lightweight piece of furniture to 15 degrees, and do not use a slant of more than 5 degrees even on a high dining table.

Slabs

Earlier I identified slabs as tops, sides, backs, doors, and shelves. It is simple to see that the slab is the main part of many pieces, and sometimes the whole piece is made of nothing but slabs. Although it is certainly possible to build some pieces without slabs, it is unusual.

A slab might be of plywood paneling, built-up solid boards, or solid wood for small areas. Obviously, there are other possibilities such as a hardboard and a variety of plastic, metal, and other materials.

Plywood panels and similar materials are the easiest to work with, except for disadvantages like concealment of the lamination and thinness of the veneer. Plywood is certainly faster than building up a slab of solid boards.

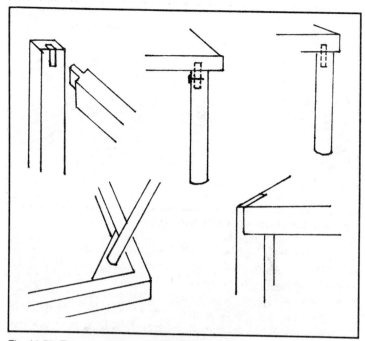

Fig. 11-57. There are many ways to attach legs.

It is often desirable to use a built-up slab. To do this, select the lumber to be used very carefully for appearance. You must think ahead as you are doing this, because any built-up slab should have alternated grain direction in individual boards (Fig. 11-59). If you do not alternate grain direction, any warping that might possibly occur with continued drying will be cumulative in effect.

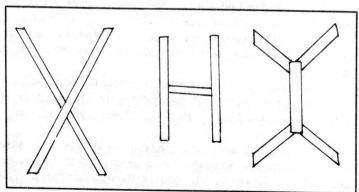

Fig. 11-58. Common stretcher designs.

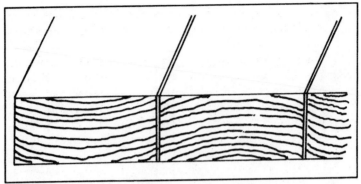

Fig. 11-59. Alternated grain prevents cumulative warping.

You may build up a slab using any of several methods. The simplest method would be either the butt joint or the lap joint (Fig. 11-60). Other possibilities are dowels, tongue and groove, and dovetail joints. Before gluing edges of the boards, see that they are smooth and clean. Apply clamps in a manner that fits the pieces firmly together. Keep the pressure as nearly equal as possible if you use more than one clamp.

Often the slab or broad panel you use is a thin material that is not sufficiently strong alone, but will be applied over a frame. On other occasions a slab might be the back of a chest, an application that does not require very expensive materials or meticulous work.

Finally, when you build a piece of furniture that is mostly or all slabs, match the grain direction where the top member meets the sides, so that a continuous line is apparent. It is rare that you would want contrast here. You must have the direction of cutting in mind when you buy the material, so you will be sure to have enough.

Drawers

Building drawers that are both functional and attractive may be the most demanding of all tasks in furniture building. Yet with careful work, following detailed planning, it need not be too difficult.

A drawer, in an oversimplified way, is a box. A box might be quite simple to build, but in drawer construction you must anticipate the forces that will act upon it. Examples are where the front of the drawer is attached to the side, and when a drawer must hold any weight inside, where the bottom attaches to the sides.

These stresses can be compensated for with some of the same kinds of joints that I have discussed. The most often found joint, particularly in factory-built furniture, is the dovetail, but dowels, screws, or dadoes combined with the reinforcement of glue will be sufficient. I suggest the rabbet joint reinforced with glue and screws (Fig. 11-61).

Aside from the actual construction of the drawer, the whole thing must open and close smoothly. You can remove the drawers from some of your own furniture and see different methods of accomplishing this. The simplest method is shown in Figs. 11-62 and 11-63. Figure 11-62 shows the guide, which is attached to the rails with simple rabbet joints. On the bottom of the drawer itself is a runner that will fit smoothly over the guide. In order for this single guide to make the drawer work well, the sides of the drawer must also touch the rail framing.

When you have made this simplest drawer that works well, you might try the more demanding kinds of guides. They may be stronger and will further develop your skill.

The front of the drawer should harmonize with the rest of the piece. So must the drawer pulls. You will not want a heavy-duty drawer pull on a shallow drawer; nor will you want an inadequate pull on a heavy drawer.

Braces

I am using the word *braces* here in a very general manner to describe the members that are built into furniture to add security and stability. Such braces include rails, stretchers, and corner (or glue) blocks.

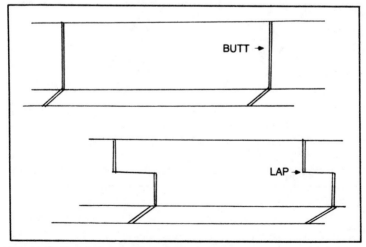

Fig. 11-60. Two ways to build up slabs.

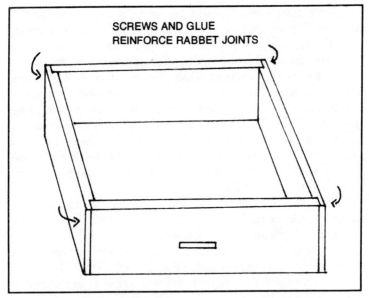

Fig. 11-61. Rabbets, screws, and glue.

If you think about stretchers and rails for a moment, you see that there is really nothing new here. Rails should be attached to legs, top, frame, etc., with strong, secure joints. Again, these might be mortise and tenon joints in heavy material, or simple dowel joints in material of lesser dimension.

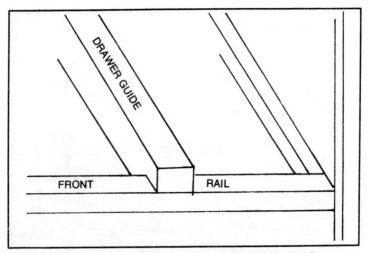

Fig. 11-62. The single drawer guide rests on the front and back rails.

Corner blocks are another form of braces that are often helpful in adding stability. In the small table in (Fig. 11-64) the corner blocks add stability to both the legs and rails, and they also serve as the support for the slab. Chances are that if you have dismantled a factory-made chair or sofa, you have found several of these corner blocks, or glue blocks as they are commonly called, used throughout the piece.

Hardware

You should visit a hardware store and look over the many ready-made braces, brackets, hinges, handles, and drawer pulls. Most of these are simple to use and totally reliable when properly attached.

There are so many kinds of hinges and methods of attachment that I don't discuss them here in detail. I recommend that you use the simplest hinges. Even in those with easy attachments, there are very beautiful and decorative ones available. Be sure to plan ahead for the kind of hinges you will be using, for some require intricate wood cuts.

See that all hardware is complementary to the wood and to the style of the piece. You will not have any difficulty finding suitable hardware; this is one area where there is no shortage in material, style, or design.

TABLES

Table must be sturdily constructed if they are to receive heavy use, and they should be well-built in any instance. I have chosen

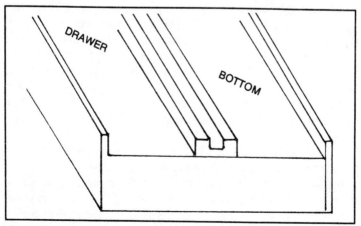

Fig. 11-63. Drawer bottom with runner and long sides.

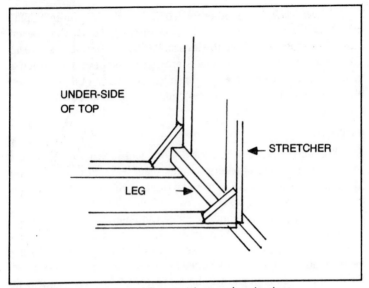

Fig. 11-64. Corner blocks stabilize stretchers and anchor legs.

here to speak of tables with a rather broad definition. Tables include other similarly constructed pieces of furniture such as desks, picnic or patio furniture, and a variety of combinations.

The small table in Fig. 11-65 is one that has been built in similar designs by many beginners. The top could be solid boards, a slab, or glass resting on the rails. This particular design will not support much weight; yet it is simple enough to be built very quickly and inexpensively. It can be an attractive and functional addition to a room. The table would be more sturdy with a slab attached atop the legs, with or without a supporting apron. The rails can be set into the legs with mortise and tenon joints for a strong construction.

The coffee table in Fig. 11-66 has a built-up solid board slab. The tapered and angled legs are attached with screws to corner blocks hidden by a narrow apron. This same table could have vertical legs, straight or tapered, or legs of other styles. The top could also be changed in many ways and still be a rather easy project.

The large table in Fig. 11-67 was built as a dining table by the father of nine children. It is more difficult than others only because of the stretcher design. The man preferred stretchers for extra strength, but H stretchers would have limited the use of the table ends. He used bolts and glue for stretchers and leg joints; screws and glue were used for others.

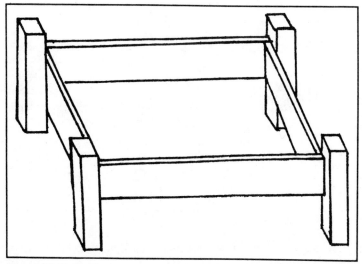

Fig. 11-65. End table.

CHAIRS

Any chair must be sturdy enough to support the weight imposed upon it. A chair should last a long time. The design of the chair should be suitable for the intended use.

Dining chairs are usually *side chairs* (simple vertical and horizontal lines with no armrests). These chairs are not particularly comfortable if you want to relax after a day's work. They are quite comfortable when used while dining or working. Such chairs are deliberately designed to keep the back and legs straight and the seat very nearly horizontal. While this position isn't conducive to an

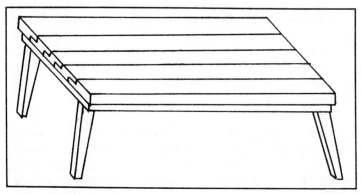

Fig. 11-66. Coffee table.

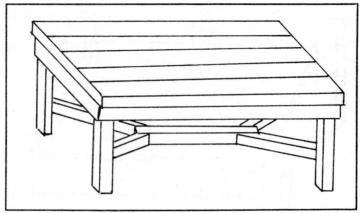

Fig. 11-67. Heavy-duty table.

afternoon nap, it's good for your back and helps you concentrate on the task at hand.

Side chairs, like any style, can be very simple to build. Remember to make the dimensions fitting to the person or accessory furniture; then follow any of several procedures.

The front view of the side chair in Fig. 11-68 shows the basic construction, which can be varied according to individual preference. The back legs can be cut into an illusion of a curve by beginning with a 2 × 6 and cutting as shown in Fig. 11-69. The front legs may be straight and vertical or tapered and vertical. The seat may be solid boards, plywood or hardboard, webbed, caned, or any other variation.

Figure 11-70 is an incomplete illustration of a simple armchair I have made. The seat is covered in plywood. A firm cushion rests on the seat, and a second one is against the back as in Fig. 11-71. The joints are simple ones reinforced with screws and glue, with plugs covering screwheads. The angled back legs are tied to the front with simple stretchers (not shown, for clarity). You can easily build simple chairs like these, or enlarge upon or otherwise modify these designs to suit your own tastes.

CABINETS

Cabinets can be considered to be any kind of shelves, free or in box shapes, and with or without doors or drawers. The cabinet in Fig. 11-72 was chosen here because of its simplicity, usefulness, and attractive appearance. It is made entirely of slabs except for two 1 × 2 nailers affixed below the lowest visible shelf and on top of the

384

floor slab, against which the doors close. Joints can be butt joints with nails or screws strengthened by glue. Nails would usually be sufficient. These can be finishing nails recessed with a nail set and puttied, or even common nails if you choose to paint the cabinet.

It is always exciting to build modular units that can be rearranged to fit different spaces. Dens, bedrooms and living rooms are always suitable areas for modular cabinet units.

BEDS

Dimensions of a bed frame will depend upon where you use it, and whether you plan to use mattresses of standard sizes. When you have made such choices, however, there are many workable techniques.

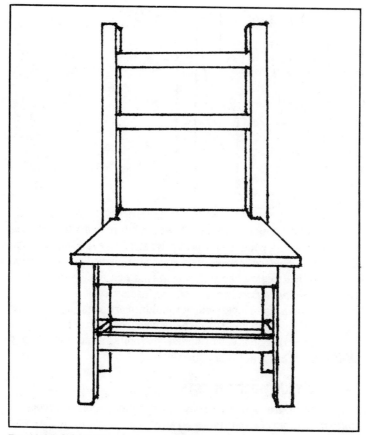

Fig. 11-68. Side chair.

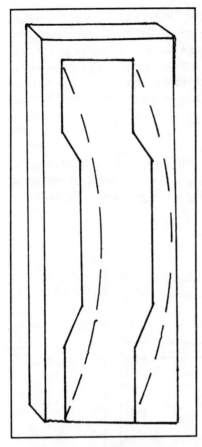

Fig. 11-69. Chair post legs can be cut in several patterns.

The bed frame in Fig. 11-73, with modifications to suit individual tastes, is a good one. It is sturdy, attractive, and can be used with either standard innersprings and mattress or with a plywood slab and a mattress without springs. This bed has no headboard. This makes the bed appear to require less space.

Bunk beds and single beds for children are very practical and reasonably simple to build. These are discussed further in Chapter 8. Remember that beds can be joined with bolts and screws for easy disassembly, but build them sturdy.

FINISHING YOUR WOOD PROJECTS

No furniture building project is complete until the wood is smooth, with its natural colors gleaming through a protective and beautiful finish. Although a proper finishing job requires the application of specific skills, it has been my experience that those most difficult to master are three: patience, knowing when to go slowly, and knowing when to work quickly.

Preparing the Wood

No attractive finish can be achieved without careful preparation. This demands patience. Do not rush. Preparation means, primarily, sanding the wood.

There are three basic rules for sanding which must be observed. First, always sand with the grain. Second, keep any mechanical sander in a level position and in constant motion to avoid digging into the wood. Third never use the sort of disc sander that is available as an attachment to your electric drill. This third rule is actually a second expression of the first, since a disc sander naturally sands across the grain.

If you have used hardwood, it is probably necessary to begin with a coarse grit sandpaper and gradually move through to the finer grits. In softwood, which cuts so much more easily, you will not find it necessary to use as many different grits. When you do use a finer grit, *always* brush the residue of wood dust and sand away before you begin again.

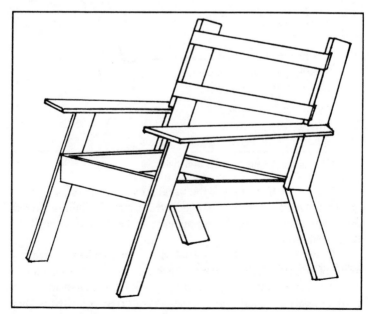

Fig. 11-70. Armchair.

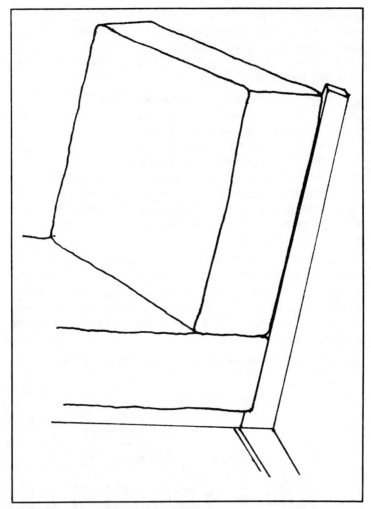

Fig. 11-71. Firm cushions fit in the armchair.

Locate any high areas in the wood. Level these first. When you have achieved a level surface, concentrate upon obtaining a smooth one. When the surface finally appears to be smooth enough, an additional step is required.

If your stain and finish material will be compatible with it, apply a coat of lacquer sanding sealer to the wood. This sanding sealer will raise tiny fibers that must also be sanded off. If you cannot see them, you can easily feel them when the sealer has dried. Sand lightly once more to remove this rough surface. This step is essential, because the fibers will be raised when you apply the stain or finish if you haven't already removed them.

This same step can be done with water. Just dampen the wood lightly with a wet rag, wait for it to dry, and sand. The primary advantage to using sanding sealer is that it dries quicker than water.

When you are completely satisfied with the smoothness of the wood, your patience will have been rewarded. Apply a stain, but first brush the surface again thoroughly.

Staining the Wood

If you want the wood to have a particular color, you must know how the stain you select will really look on the wood. The same stain does not *look* the same on different wood species. Apply the stain to a scrap of the wood you have used, and allow it to dry thoroughly. Only in this way can you be sure of the result in advance. You may find it necessary to use a different stain to get the result you desire.

There are different kinds of stains, as well as different colors. Most advanced woodworkers appear to prefer *oil stains,* feeling that these produce a deeper, richer hue. They are already mixed, so

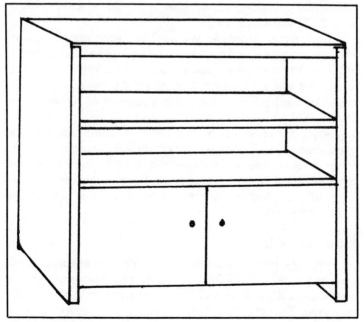

Fig. 11-72. Cabinet.

there is no problem in matching colors. If you use oil stains, be sure to leave a bit in the bottom of each can to insure an even distribution of color pigment. This darker material in the bottom of the can might be added to a fresh can to avoid waste, without adversely affecting the shade.

If you are a beginner in the art of finishing, I suggest you use a water stain, although there is a disadvantage. The advantages, however, are several. The use of water stains will give you a very valuable experience in coloring. The stains are available in a variety of colors and in a packet of dye that must be mixed with water. These dyes can be mixed for some interesting variations. Water stains are also less expensive than others.

The valuable experience in coloring has a built-in sort of disadvantage. If you should fail to mix enough stain in the beginning to complete the project, you might find it difficult to get the same shades in the second mix. This can be overcome with careful, accurate measuring.

There are a few special things to observe during the staining process if a really fine result is to be achieved. The most important of these is to *anticipate each step* before it is begun.

Obviously you know how much area is to be stained. Think through the project before you begin, and decide which area will be done first, second, and so on.

If you do not plan ahead, you won't be able to stop for *anything* without ruining the job. You mustn't overlap an area that has already begun to dry. If you do, it shows clearly when it is all dry. This means that you must often work very rapidly, especially on wide areas. An overlap does no harm if it is done within seconds of the first application.

Apply the stain with a good natural bristle brush, with the grain, and then rub it into the wood with a cloth. You might prefer to apply the stain with a cloth instead of a brush, but brushes are especially convenient for the hard to reach spots. Brushes are also a little faster. Rubbing the stain into the wood produces a much more uniform, rich, and natural appearing effect.

Natural Oil Finish

Once the wood is stained to your liking, some kind of finish must be applied. While I think it is unlikely that you would want to use a *natural oil finish* on your homemade furniture, it must still be mentioned. The natural oil finish is one of the most beautiful ways to finish a wood project, and it has been used for centuries by wood-

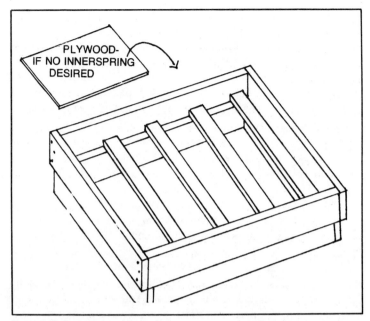

Fig. 11-73. Bed frame.

workers. It consists of an application of oil and *turpentine* which is permitted to soak into the wood. The excess is wiped away after awhile, and the surface is rubbed thoroughly with cloth. The process is repeated many times over an extended period, and the finish assumes more beauty, depth, and durability as time passes.

I have used the natural oil finish on antique furniture. I think it produces the most satisfactory finish where appearance is concerned. It seems to bring more life to the wood without concealing any of the natural beauty.

In some ways, though, natural oil finish is not practical. It requires a great deal of attention and does not cover the wood. While it is most beautiful, I use the *lacquer finish* on furniture that gets continual use.

Lacquer Finish

While the lacquer finish is my own preference, lacquer does not appear to be the choice of most people. Lacquer is a very good choice for several reasons, though. If you want a glossy, shining finish, full strength lacquer will produce one. Thinned lacquer produces a more subdued finish. Lacquer gives a good, hard finish, dries *very* quickly (reducing the chance of spoiling the appearance), and is easy to apply with the proper tools.

Lacquer can be applied with a brush, but this requires some practice. Since lacquer dries so fast, it must be applied quickly. Use a wide, soft natural bristle brush. Instead of brushing, allow the lacquer to flow onto the wood. One brush stroke must be applied next to another immediately, or there will be a noticeable overlap and accumulation where the first application has begun to dry.

The only really practical method of applying lacquer is to use an airbrush with sufficient capacity to handle this heavy material. While there are several kinds of these brushes or guns, I recommend any of the following: the *Wold CF,* the *Wold X8,* or the *Paasche AUTF.*

An airbrush is not terribly expensive, but it does require an air supply, most suitably a compressor. Compressed air tanks can be used, but they are not as convenient, although they are less expensive.

The effective use of lacquer requires an extra expense and mastery of tools. Lacquer is worthwhile for me because of its speedy application and excellent finish. You will probably prefer varnish, the most often used finish.

Varnish

Varnish does not dry quickly. If you choose a varnish with a synthetic rather than a natural resin base, this will not be as much of a handicap.

Varnishes are available in either a glossy or a matte finish. Be sure to select the one you need for the desired appearance.

Varnish must also be applied with a good natural bristle brush. Effect an equal distribution of the material by avoiding accumulations which will not be pleasing when they dry. Any such accumulations can be smoothed by tipping off the work, stroking the tip of the brush over the area just covered. Do this at regular intervals before the material has begun to dry, and do not overlap a partially dried area with fresh varnish.

Allow the first coat plenty of time to dry. Drying time is affected by weather conditions and other factors, so you should not always observe the drying times specified on the container. It never hurts to permit a longer than suggested drying period.

When the first coat is thoroughly dry, sand it lightly over the whole surface, brush, and apply another coat. This procedure can be repeated through several coats if you wish. When a really pleasing appearance has been achieved, your finishing project is complete, unless you wish to wax and buff for an extra measure of protection.

Fillers

Proper use of the foregoing techniques and materials will produce a fine finish to any close grained wood. Open grained woods may have a more pleasing finish with the use of fillers. Fillers are not *essential* even with these woods, but they help to give a really perfect finish.

Helpful Hints

You should always work in a very clean, dry place. See that the lighting is good. Make sure all of the potentially dangerous materials you use are properly and safely stored. Keep your tools in good shape, clean, and in their places. *Never* store flammable materials such as lacquer, etc., near a source of heat. *Always* keep the lids on such items closed tight when they aren't in use.

Keep people out of your workshop when you are working, and when a finished piece is drying. Otherwise, you will do less than your best.

Glossary

apron—The wood member under a window sill; it covers the opening between sill and wall covering.

baste—To sew or tack temporarily in such a manner that tacks or stitches can be removed.

bias—A line diagonal to the grain of fabric.

Bourbon—The name of a French royal family who reigned in various countries from 1589 to 1931.

boxing—A strip of fabric which covers the edge of a cushion around the circumference or perimeter.

buttoning—Not the same as tufting, which also uses buttons. Buttoning creates a low relief only and serves primarily to hold the fabric and padding.

button press—A mechanical device which covers two-piece buttons with fabric.

cambium—Thin layer of wood surrounding the sapwood which forms new growth cells in the living tree.

cambric—Actually a high quality linen fabric, but a cotton resembling it is also called cambric. It is used in upholstery primarily for dust covers.

casing—Any enclosure for a form or stuffing. In upholstery, casings are usually of muslin.

channeling—The technique of padding furniture by stuffing parallel tubes of fabric and covering with upholstery fabric.

check—Because of uneven drying, the board cracks across the growth rings, but doesn't go all the way through the board.

compression—The force which tends to press molecules more closely together.

coverlet—A plain bedspread or quilt that does not reach the floor at the sides or foot. The coverlet barely overlaps the mattress spring level, permitting the dust ruffle to show.

crinoline—A loose-weave cotton fabric, stiffened, and used for interlining.

cushion—An upholstered pad, differing from a pillow in that the cushion has boxed edges while the pillow is sharp edged.

double-hung window—A window that opens by means of one sash sliding vertically in front of the other.

dowel—A round hardwood rod used to connect wood members of a piece of furniture or to lock joints of other types.

draw drapes—Draperies hung from a traverse rod. They overlap at center when closed.

duramen—Heartwood.

dust cover—Usually of cambric, the dust cover is tacked on or stapled on the underside of a sofa or chair to prevent falling particles of stuffing from littering the floor.

dust-ruffle—An attractive ruffled skirt attached to a flat panel that fits between mattress and springs.

edge roll—Tube casings filled with fiber, rolled burlap, or paper. Edge rolls soften edges of springs or furniture, protect cover fabric from excess stains, and add comfort.

Empire—A furniture style popular in early nineteenth century France.

extension—A strip of other than upholstery fabric sewn to the fabric for use when it will not show on the finished piece.

fabric grain—The direction of threads in the weave, either crosswise or lengthwise.

felted cotton—Fiber stuffing materials compressed into sheets of uniform density and thickness.

fiber padding or stuffing—Any kind of stuffing made from fibers, such as cotton or hair.

fluting—Same as channeling.

form—The filler of a cushion or pillow.

gather—To provide fullness or to restrict fullness by folding the fabric edge on a thread.

gimp—Decorative finishing material used to cover tacks and staples and add interest to the chair or sofa.

glue block—A brace which typically fits inside a corner of a chair frame between rails and against the leg. A good reinforcement for seat furniture.

growth rings—Dark rings indicating the amount of a tree's annual growth.

hardwood—Wood from deciduous (leaf shedding) trees.

heartwood—The center or physiologically inactive part of a tree. Heartwood is more dense than the rest of the wood and of a darker color.

hog ringers—Pliers used in furniture spring repairs.

inner bark—Beneath the outer bark, the inner bark carries nourishment to all living parts of the tree.

lignin—The natural glue in wood that binds fibers together.

loose tenon—Same as a dowel, except that loose tenons are squared rather than round.

marquetry—Beautiful wood decoration consisting of pieces of wood, shell, ivory, etc., inlaid in a veneer which is then applied to furniture.

motif—A dominant and recurring theme or idea in any piece of art.

muslin—A plain cotton fabric used in furniture upholstery for casings and undercovers.

panel draperies—Draperies suspended from other than a traverse rod; they meet in the center without overlap when they are closed.

pillow—Upholstered pad differing from a cushion in that a pillow has a sharp rather than a boxed edge.

piping—Same as channeling or fluting, but also sometimes the same as welting.

pitch—The exact center of any wood growth.

pitch pockets—Accumulations of pitch (tar) in some woods.

pleating pins—Metal hooks made to be inserted in narrow channels in pleating tape and hung from curtain rods.

pleating tape—Stiff band of fabric with narrow channels approximately spaced for pleating pins.

plywood—Usually 4 × 8-foot panels made of a varied number of plies glued together in alternating grain direction.

pocket springs—Individual coil springs inserted in cloth pockets. The pockets are then sewn together to form spring units of varying shapes.

pull strip—Same as extension.

quilting—The technique of creating a puffy appearance by equal spacing and patterning of seams through fabric and soft padding.

rail—Structural member in a chair, sofa or other furniture, horizontally connecting or reinforcing the legs.

Regency—Furniture style preferred during the reign of George, Prince of Wales.

Renaissance—A rebirth of interest in classical learning.

Restoration—Preferred furniture of the period of King Charles II.

return—In draperies, the short distance around the curve in the rod; in a dust ruffle, the short distance around the head corners to hold it in place.

sapwood—Surrounds the heartwood and carries sap to leaves from the roots.

selvage—Edge on woven fabric finished to prevent raveling.

shake—When growth rings in a tree separate.

softwood—Wood from evergreen trees.

split—Usually occurring at the end of a board, a split crosses growth rings and goes all the way through the board.

stretcher—In chairs, the horizontal braces between legs.

stretches—In fabric, the same as a pull strip or extension.

tacking strip—Cardboard strips used to keep edges straight.

tension—The force that tends to pull molecules farther apart.

traverse rod—Rods for draw draperies.

tuck-in—Surplus fabric in slipcovers to tuck around the seat in particular, thus absorbing movement when the seat is sat upon.

Victorian—Preferred furniture during the reign of Queen Victoria.

Sources for Upholstery Materials

You can request information about upholstery materials from the following sources.

UPHOLSTERY FABRICS

Adco Auto Upholstery
7081-T Brighton Blvd.
Commerce City, CO

Arnel Plastron, Inc.
3601-T Hempstead Tpk.
Levittown, NY

Auto-Mat Co.
225A Park Ave.
Hicksville, NY

Botany Industries, Inc.
1290 Avenue of the Americas
New York, NY

Burlington Industries, Inc.
3330 W. Friendly Ave., P.O. Box 21207
Greensboro, NC

Cardwood Products Corp.
2715 Webster Ave.
New York, NY

Carolina Mills, Inc.
618 Carolina Ave.
Maiden, NC

Carpet Industries Inc.
Carpet Lane
Kings Mountain, NC
Cheney Bros., Inc.
31 Cooper Hill
Manchester, CT
Conklin Mills, Inc.
Amber and Wishart Sts.
Philadelpha, PA
Continental Felt Co.
26 W. 15th St.
New York, NY
Craftex Mills, Inc. of PA
Kensington Ave. and E. Venango St.
Philadelphia, PA
Crompton Co., Inc.
1071 Avenue of the Americas
New York, NY

Doblin Corp.
P.O. Box 429
Morganton, NC
Duracote Corporation
358 N. Diamond St.
Ravenna, OH
Dutton Andrew, Co.
60 Canal
Boston, MA

Fife Fabrics, Inc.
626 N. Locust St.
Momence, IL
Flexible Foam Div.,
Affiliate of Ohio
Decorative Products Inc.
1103 Wisdom St.
Chatanooga, TN
Ford Motor Co.
Chemical Products Div.,
3001T Miller Rd.
Dearborn, MI

Forster Textile Mills Inc.
17 and Union Aves.
Chicago Heights, IL
Franklin Drapery Co., Inc.
12415 3rd St.
Grandview, MO
Frissell Fabrics, Inc.
Dept. T.R.
P.O. Box 40
Rossville, GA

General Tire and Rubber Co.
Chemical/Plastics Div.
70 General St.
Lawrence, MA
Gibraltar Industries, Inc.
254 36th St. Bldg. 2
Brooklyn, NY
Globe Cotton Mills, Inc.
2170 S. Canalport St.
Chicago, IL

Hand Craft Textile Print Co.
Bishop's Crossing, P.O. Box 165
Plainfield, CT
Harrington, George S., Co., Inc.
5 Dan Rd.
Canton, MA
Hexter, S.M. and Co.
2800 Superior Ave.
Cleveland, OH

Jacquard Fabrics Co., Inc.
Dept. T.
P.O. Box 2172
Paterson, NJ
Joan Fabrics Corp.
122 Western Ave.
Lowell, MA
Joan Mfg. Co.
4-T North St.
Waldwick, NJ

K and R Textiles, Inc.
S. Saginaw and Grant
Grand Blanc, MI
Krabro Fabrics, Inc.
108 W. 39th
New York, NY
LaFrance Industries Div.
Anderson Hwy.
La France, SC
Louisville Textile Weavers, Inc.
1318 McHenry
Louisville, KY

Maharam Fabric Corp.
Rasons Ct.
P.O. Box 300
Hauppauge, NY
Mercer Textile Mills, Inc.
Main St.
Groveville, NJ
Moss Rose Mfg. Co.
Allegheny Ave. and Hancock St.
Philadelphia, PA
Mount Vernon Mills, Inc.
Daniel Bld.
Greenville, SC
MPG Manufacturing Corp.
1275-T, Bloomfield Ave.
Fairfield, NJ

NewCastle Fabrics Corp.
80 Wythe Ave.
Brooklyn, NY
Norton-Blumenthal, Inc.
979 3rd Ave.
New York, NY

Orinoka Mills
475 Park Ave. S
New York, NY

Pervel Industries, Inc.
Plainfield, CT

Plascal Corp.
361 Eastern Parkway
Farmingdale, NY
Portage Draperies Co.
235 5th Ave.
New York, NY

Ramloc Pile Fabric Co.
4517 Wayne Ave.
Philadelphia, PA
Raphael, Edwin, Co., Inc.
Infinity Lane
Holland, MI

Schneider's, Peter, Sons and Co.
160 E. 56th
New York, NY
Schumacher, F., and Co.
939 Third Ave.
New York, NY
Snyder Manufacturing Co. Ltd.
3000 Progress St.
Dover, OH
Standard Tapestry Co.
4434 Penn
Philadelphia, PA
Stroheim and Romann
10 W. 20th St.
New York, NY

Teshon, Joseph
196 21st Avenue
Patterson, NJ
Timme E.F. and Son, Inc.
200 Madison Ave.
New York, NY

U.S. Plush Mills, Inc.
181 Conant
Pawtucket, RI

Valdese Weavers, Inc.
Box 70
Valdese, NC

FOAM PADDING

Accurate Foam Co.
819 Fox St.
La Porte, IN

Conwed Corporation
332 Minnesota St. P.O. Box 43237
St. Paul, MN

Perma Seating Co.
4420 Lee Rd.
Cleveland, OH

Unique Seating, Inc.
711-713 E. Grove St.
Mishawaka, IN
Uniroyal Inc.
P.O. Box 1126, Wall Street Station
New York, NY

Wyandot Seating
1122 E. Warren Ave.
Bucyrus, OH

Index